PENGUIN BOOKS

WHOSE BIBLE IS IT?

Jaroslav Pelikan is Sterling Professor Emeritus of History at Yale University, recent winner of the John W. Kluge Prize for Lifetime Achievement in the Human Sciences, and past president of the American Academy of Arts and Sciences. His many books include the five-volume *The Christian Tradition: A History of the Development of Doctrine, Jesus Through the Centuries,* and *Mary Through the Centuries.* He has received the Thomas Jefferson Medal of the National Endowment for the Humanities and an honorary degree from the Jewish Theological Seminary of America, as well as more than forty other honorary degrees.

Whose Bible Is It?

A SHORT HISTORY
OF THE SCRIPTURES

Jaroslav Pelikan

PENGUIN BOOKS

PENGUIN BOOKS

Published by the Penguin Group
Penguin Group (USA) Inc., 375 Hudson Street, New York, New York 10014, U.S.A.
Penguin Group (Canada), 90 Eglinton Avenue East, Suite 700,
Toronto, Ontario, Canada M4P 2Y3 (a division of Pearson Penguin Canada Inc.)
Penguin Books Ltd, 80 Strand, London WC2R 0RL, England
Penguin Ireland, 25 St Stephen's Green, Dublin 2, Ireland (a division of Penguin Books Ltd)
Penguin Group (Australia), 250 Camberwell Road, Camberwell,
Victoria 3124, Australia (a division of Pearson Australia Group Pty Ltd)
Penguin Books India Pvt Ltd, 11 Community Centre,
Panchsheel Park, New Delhi – 110 017, India
Penguin Group (NZ), cnr Airborne and Rosedale Roads, Albany,
Auckland 1310, New Zealand (a division of Pearson New Zealand Ltd)
Penguin Books (South Africa) (Pty) Ltd, 24 Sturdee Avenue,
Rosebank, Johannesburg 2196, South Africa

Penguin Books Ltd, Registered Offices:
80 Strand, London WC2R 0RL, England

First published in the United States of America by Viking Penguin,
a member of Penguin Group (USA) Inc. 2005
Published in Penguin Books 2006

10 9 8 7 6 5 4 3 2 1

Copyright © Jaroslav Pelikan, 2005
All rights reserved

THE LIBRARY OF CONGRESS HAS CATALOGED THE HARDCOVER EDITION AS FOLLOWS:
Pelikan, Jaroslav.
Whose Bible is it? : a history of the Scriptures through the ages / Jaroslav Pelikan.
p.   cm.
Includes bibliographical references and index.
ISBN 0-670-03385-5 (hc.)
ISBN 0 14 30.3677 7 (pbk.)
1. Bible—History.   I. Title.
BS445.P46   2004
220'.09—dc22   2004058049

Printed in the United States of America
Designed by Nancy Resnick

To all my honorary Christian Alma Maters
—Protestant, Roman Catholic, and Orthodox—

and to The Jewish Theological Seminary of America,
which on 16 May 1991 / 3 Sivan 5751
made me an honorary Doctor of Laws

Contents

Preface

The idea for this book originated in Carnegie Hall at Christmas time 1990, with the annual performance of George Frideric Handel's *Messiah* by Musica Sacra of New York, under the baton of Richard Westenburg.

A longtime friend and colleague, the conductor had invited me to prepare an essay as part of the program notes for *Messiah*. Although I had been listening to *Messiah* all my life, the venue of Carnegie Hall raised a host of new questions about it and sharpened the point of some very old ones. The essay in the program notes, therefore, bore the title "Whose Bible Is It?" which I have now adopted for this entire book. For in Carnegie Hall, at a performance where audience, chorus, and orchestra included not only Christians but Jews and non-believers, the biblical text of *Messiah* (only one-third of whose passages are taken from the New Testament) presupposed—or seemed to presume—something that could not automatically be taken for granted, not in that venue at any rate. *Messiah* seems to be implying, as most Christians in most centuries have maintained, that when the prophet Isaiah in his seventh chapter prophesies (according to the King James Version of the Bible) that "a Virgin shall conceive, and bear a Son, and shall call his name Immanuel," or in his ninth chapter proclaims "For unto us a Child is born, unto us a Son is given," or in his fifty-third chapter describes how "He hath borne our griefs and carried our sorrows," he is speaking not only explicitly but perhaps even exclusively about the virginal birth and the atoning crucifixion of Jesus of Nazareth, "Messiah." Therefore these texts from the Hebrew Bible have been taken not to have a valid meaning in their own

right within the Jewish context but only within the Christian. They had become, as a second-century Christian writer speaking to Jews had called them, "not your Scriptures but ours."

Meanwhile, like many of my contemporaries, I had long been responding—or trying to respond somehow—to the catastrophic events of the 1930s and 1940s. For me that response took the particular form of asking what role, if any, Christian categories and ways of thinking about Judaism and Jews might have played in leading to the Holocaust. As a member of the board of the National Conference of Christians and Jews and in other similar positions, but above all as a historian of Christian doctrine, I found this question—or, rather, this cluster of questions—altogether unavoidable. The reviewers of my five-volume history, *The Christian Tradition: A History of the Development of Doctrine,* which was published between 1971 and 1989, have remarked on two distinctive features in the work as a whole by which it is differentiated from other and previous histories of Christian thought and doctrine: the concentration on identifying the key biblical passages from both Testaments that served the church as the foundation and the proof texts for the various doctrines whose development in various periods was the subject of the book; and the recognition that the relation of Christianity to Judaism was basic not simply to "the emergence of the Catholic tradition" as I treated it in the first volume, but to the entire history of Christian doctrine and to every doctrine and every period in that history, and therefore to each of the five volumes.

The Jewish Theological Seminary of America, on 16 May 1991 / 3 Sivan 5751, recognized both of these dimensions of my work with the signal honor (especially for a Christian scholar of Christian history) to which the dedication of this book is a partial response. The characteristically generous citation for the honorary degree read in part:

> You have taught us all that great religious traditions continuously renew themselves through the ages, generating ever-changing interpretations of the ever-constant sacred

text of Scripture. . . . You have carefully attended to the continuing dialogue between Christians and Jews that informs the church to this day. In awarding you this honorary degree, we recognize and pay tribute to . . . your commitment to the proposition that Jews and Christians are two distinct religious communities with a common commitment to Scripture and its interpretations.

Unbeknownst to the seminary or to me at the time, that citation was a kind of foreword to the present book, which is coming out nearly a decade and a half later.

I said earlier that this book originated in Carnegie Hall at Christmas time 1990, and it did. But I might just as appropriately have given credit for it to my late aunt, Vanda Olga Brazlova, whom my uncle, John M. (Jack) Pelikan, met and married while he was working during the 1920s and 1930s as an electrical engineer in the Soviet Union. After an adventuresome escape that became part of our treasury of family legend, Aunt Vanda came to the United States in the early 1930s from a country where atheism was the official creed and where the reading of the Bible was, at best, "Rated PG 13." But once she arrived in the free world, she voraciously read the Bible—and everything else in sight—with a freshness and a directness that could be, by turns, disarming and devastating, sometimes seemingly naive but actually very sophisticated. One day she asked me rather casually, in what Patrick O'Brian in the fourth of his Aubrey/Maturin novels calls "a fluent though curious English devoid of articles" (a characteristic problem for Slavic speakers with which I, too, for that matter, still have difficulties), an English that remained heavily accented no matter how long she spoke it, "Tall me, vot do you tink of Bible?" It brought me up short, and I can't quite remember my answer, if any. But now finally, after several decades, I am trying to answer dear Aunt Vanda's unforgettable question.

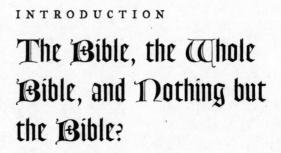

INTRODUCTION

The Bible, the Whole Bible, and Nothing but the Bible?

n a variation on all those old jokes about the rabbi, the priest, and the minister walking together into a bar, three women take advantage of the lunch hour in their downtown office to visit the bookstore across the street. One of them is Jewish, the other two are Christian—one Roman Catholic and the other Protestant. Because it is the season of Passover and Easter (closely related holidays that are nevertheless observed on separate dates), each of them wants to buy a Bible for her daughter.

And yet each of the three needs to buy a different Bible. Therefore, a knowledgeable clerk should ask each of them, "Which Bible do you want?" For not only must any buyer or reader of whatever religious affiliation find the many English translations of the Bible bewildering (King James Version, Revised Standard Version, New Revised Standard Version, Good News Version, Jewish Publication Society Version, New English Bible, Revised English Bible, Jerusalem Bible, New Jerusalem Bible, etc.), but the buyer has the right to expect "the Bible, the whole Bible, and nothing but the Bible." Yet the table of contents—technically called canon, meaning "rule" (see Appendixes)—is fundamentally different in the different Bibles. The difference between the Jewish Bible and all the Christian Bibles is the greatest: there is no New Testament, and the Jewish buyer ought to be able to demand "nothing but the Bible," especially if on her last business trip she examined the Gideon Bible in her hotel room, which includes the New Testament. But the Protestant Bible is also very different from the Roman Catholic Bible: it has no Apocrypha, so the Roman Catholic customer may well ask, "Is this the whole

Bible?" It is sometimes said that these differences are "discernible [only to] ecclesiastical scholars," but five or ten minutes of comparison shopping ought to be enough for anyone to see the contrasts.

Two terms that are often used in connection with the Bible, one from law and one from medicine, will illustrate the importance of "the Bible, the whole Bible, and nothing but the Bible" for anyone who takes the Bible as authoritative: *testament* and *prescription*. We are so accustomed to tossing around the terms "Old Testament" and "New Testament" that we may forget their root meaning, which comes out in the legal title "last will and testament." Such a "will and testament" is a contract between the living and the dead, and both the testator and the heirs are entitled to have the confidence that this document authoritatively represents "the whole testament and nothing but the testament" of the one who has made it and dictated its terms. Similarly, when a physician writes a prescription, it is legitimate for both the doctor and the patient to demand that the pharmacist honor the "authorial intent" in the document and provide "the prescription and nothing but the prescription." Both the testament and the prescription can be matters of life and death, and so can the Bible, which is why we speak of "salvation," which means health, and of "what the Word of God prescribes."

In a sense, *Whose Bible Is It?* may be said to use the "history of the Scriptures through the ages" to tell how all those various Bibles are the same, but also how and why each of them is different—not only initially in what it contains but also in how it has been read and understood, and to explain why that is still important.

The history of Jewish-Christian relations, and then the history of the divisions within Christendom, is at one level the history of biblical interpretation. The parties have faced each other across a sacred page that they held in common but that only served to emphasize their separation. In every Bible, whether Jewish or Christian, God says to Moses: "I will raise up a prophet for them from among their own people, like yourself: I will put My words in his mouth and he will speak to them all that I command him; and if anybody fails to heed the words he speaks in My name, I myself will call him to ac-

count." As quoted in the New Testament, is this a prophecy of the decisive transfer of authority from Moses to Jesus? And in every Christian Bible, Jesus declares: "And I say to you: you are Peter, the Rock; and on this rock I will build my church, and the powers of death shall never conquer it. I will give you the keys of the kingdom of Heaven; what you forbid on earth shall be forbidden in heaven, and what you allow on earth shall be allowed in heaven." Emblazoned around the dome of Saint Peter's Basilica in Rome, is this the charter of the Papacy? It is essential to recognize the importance—but also the limitations—of these issues of doctrine and biblical interpretation in our understanding of how Christians and Jews have viewed each other, and of how Christians have viewed other Christians.

Because of this central concern for the place of the Bible both in Judaism and in Christianity, the nomenclature of the books and portions of the Bible is far more than a matter of names. Christians are accustomed to speak of "the Old Testament" and "the New Testament," the contrast between "the old" and "the new" unavoidably carrying with it connotations such as "the superseded" or at least "the updated." In these pages "New Testament" is retained, because that is what Christians call it. But instead of "Old Testament," or the various recent attempts at politically correct euphemism such as "*First Testament*" or "Hebrew Scripture," it is usually called what it is called within Judaism, *Tanakh,* which is an acronym of the first letters of the Hebrew titles of its three parts: *Torah,* the Five Books of Moses; *Nevi'im,* the Prophets; *Kethuvim,* the Writings. Only as a reference to its place within the Christian Bible is it called here "Old Testament." Following the exalted precedent of Psalm 119, the title of each of the twelve chapters—twelve for the twelve tribes of Israel or for the twelve apostles of Christ—includes the name "Bible" or some synonym for it.

ONE

The God Who Speaks

God Speaks to Moses from the Burning Bush: Synagogue decoration at Dura-Europos, ca. 200 CE: From Carl H. Kraeling, *The Synagogue,* Foreword by Jaroslav Pelikan (New York: Ktav Publishing House, 1979), Plate 76. (Courtesy of Yale University Press)

ll of us could speak before we ever began to read or write. That is true not only of individuals but of entire nations, which, when they have acquired or developed alphabets and scripts, have done so for a tongue that had already been spoken for a long time. And with all due reverence in the presence of an ultimate and unfathomable mystery, it may even be said to be true of the Deity. "In the beginning . . . God *said,* 'Let there be light'"; "In the beginning the [spoken] Word already was." On this, at least, Jews and Christians are in agreement, and so are their Bibles, that there was a Word of God before there was a written Bible of any kind, that the God of the Bible is the God who speaks. "They have mouths, but cannot speak," the Psalm says about idols made with human hands, in utter contrast with the living God who does not have a mouth and yet does speak. Eleven times, the opening chapter of the Torah uses the verb "to say" in reference to God, in addition to the related verbs "to call" and "to bless." But the God who speaks does not write anything in the Torah for eighty chapters, until the giving of the tablets of the Law to Moses at Mount Sinai in the second half of the Second Book. To comprehend the written Bible, moreover, it is essential to understand that most of the words which are now written down in it had been spoken first and, therefore, they had been heard long before they could ever have been read.

Now that we have these words primarily in written form, we need to sound them out, sometimes even aloud, before we can grasp their full meaning. An unexpected example of how a presumed oral original helps to explain the written text is the statement of John the Bap-

tist in the Gospels: "Do not imagine you can say, 'We have Abraham for our father.' I tell you that God can make *children* for Abraham out of these *stones*." Interpreters of this passage were often puzzled about what connection, if any, there is between "children" and "stones" until, in the process of translating (or retranslating) this saying from Greek back into Aramaic (or Hebrew), it became evident: *ben,* as in the title of one of the Apocrypha, "Ben Sirach," means "son" or "child," with the plural *banim;* and *eben,* as in "Eben-Ezer," means "stone," with the plural *ebanim;* so what John the Baptist was saying was that God was able to make *banim* out of *ebanim,* a play on words that is lost not only in the translation from Aramaic to Greek to English, but in the transcription from oral tradition to written text.

THE VOICE OF GOD

Therefore, the Moses who (according to tradition) is the writer of the first five books of the Bible first learns the Name and the Word of God through a voice that calls to him out of "a bush all aflame": "Moses! Moses! I am the God of your father, the God of Abraham, the God of Isaac, and the God of Jacob"—through a voice, not through a book. When Moses asks His name, the voice replies enigmatically, "Ehyeh-Asher-Ehyeh, I Am That I Am." This God-who-is is known by the mysterious name YHWH, the four consonants or "Tetragrammaton." Modern scholars usually explain the Tetragrammaton as having been pronounced "Yahweh," but pious Jews did not—and do not—pronounce it, substituting "the LORD" for it (a practice that Christian translations of the Hebrew follow). Thus, the Being of God remains a transcendent mystery permanently, and it is the Voice and the Word of God that can be known. Therefore, the identification to Moses is: "the God of Abraham, the God of Isaac, and the God of Jacob." To each of these patriarchs God *speaks* in the Genesis account and then acts accordingly. "The LORD said to Abram, 'Go forth from your father's house to the land that I will show you,'" and so the history of the patriarchs and of Israel begins.

Later, "the LORD appeared to Isaac and *said,* 'I will make your heirs as numerous as the stars of heaven.'" Again, and in a dream, "the LORD was standing beside Jacob [whose other name is Israel], and He *said,* 'I am the LORD, the God of your father Abraham and the God of Isaac.'" Speaking and doing are inseparable, for YHWH, the God of Abraham, is the God who speaks.

THE PROPHET

That centrality of speaking is the significance behind the familiar title "prophet," which, despite the presence of seers and sages such as Confucius and Gautama Buddha in many of the world religions, is in this special sense the common heritage and peculiar tradition of Judaism, Christianity, and Islam, the three monotheistic "peoples of the Book." Therefore, the second of the three major sections of the Jewish Tanakh carries the heading Nevi'im, "The Prophets." Likewise, one of the designations for Jesus Christ attributed to popular acclaim in the Gospels is "the prophet Jesus, from Nazareth in Galilee." And in the tradition of the Qur'an, where "Allah, most benevolent, evermerciful" declares, "Never did We send a message before you but through a man, whom We inspired," this is the preeminent way of speaking about Muhammad. Even now Muslims often refer to him simply as "*the* Prophet." The Shahādah, the central creed of Islam, affirms: "There is no God but God, and Muhammad is his prophet."

Despite our speaking about a "weather prophet" who appears on radio or television, or about the more or less reliable "prophecies" of the stock market that come from a broker, the word *prophet* (a compound from the Greek word for "speaker") does not mean in the first instance someone who predicts the future, but one who speaks out on behalf of God—not one who *fore*tells, therefore, but one who tells-*forth* (which often also includes, of course, foretelling the future). The primary and defining characteristic of the biblical prophet, then, is to be sought in the divine vocation and mission of telling and speaking in the name and by the designated authority of Another.

Already in the historical books of the Tanakh, the stock formula employed for a special revelation from God to a prophet is: "The word of the LORD then came to Samuel"; "But that same night the word of the LORD came to Nathan"; "When David rose in the morning, the word of the LORD had come to the prophet Gad, David's seer"; "Then the word of the LORD came to Solomon"; "Before Isaiah had gone out of the middle court, the word of the LORD came to him"; "That same night the word of God came to Nathan"; "The word of the LORD came to Shemaiah, the man of God." Within the texts of the writings of the Prophets, this same formula provides the credentials and the commissioning for the speaking of God to the prophet and therefore through the prophet: "Then the word of the LORD came to Isaiah," who writes the sixty-six chapters of his book. In the prophecies of Ezekiel, it introduces one paragraph after another: "Then the word of the LORD came to me." Jeremiah opens his book: "The words of Jeremiah. . . . The word of the LORD came to him." A majority of the Twelve Minor Prophets invoke it in the very first verse of their prophetic books.

To emphasize the continuity of John the Baptist with the prophets, but then also the change that Christ has brought about, the New Testament also invokes the prophetic formula—but for John and for no one else, not even for the apostles of Christ, because, strictly speaking, the word of God did not come to Jesus, who was himself the Word of God in person and in the flesh: "The word of God came to John son of Zechariah in the wilderness." As the emissaries for the Word of God in person and witnesses to his life, death, and resurrection, the disciples and apostles of Jesus present themselves to their hearers as those to whom this definitive Word of God has come: "It was there from the beginning; we have heard it; we have seen it with our own eyes; we looked upon it, and felt it with our own hands: our theme is the Word which gives life."

Only secondarily, if at all, does the prophet write: "The word which came to Jeremiah from the LORD: Thus *said* the LORD, the God of Israel: *Write down* in a scroll all the words that I have *spoken* to you. . . . And these are the words that the LORD *spoke* concerning

Israel and Judah." In the inaugural vision of the prophet Isaiah, it is the lips of the prophet, not his writing hand, that the seraph touches with a live coal to cleanse it:

> Now that this has touched your lips,
> Your guilt shall depart
> And your sin be purged away.

The twenty-one written books of the major and minor Prophets of Israel that are contained in the Tanakh under the designation "Nevi'im, the Prophets" make no pretense whatever of containing everything that every prophet ever spoke during the long history of prophetism in Israel. Indeed, as one of the Gospels of the New Testament was to say in its concluding chapters, in words that refer specifically to books about Jesus but that are equally applicable to the other, earlier prophets of Israel as well, "There were indeed many other signs that Jesus performed in the presence of his disciples, which are not recorded in this book. . . . If it were all to be recorded in detail, I suppose the world could not hold the books that would be written."

ORAL TRADITION IN THE WORLD LITERATURES

This primacy of the oral word is not confined to the traditions of the Bible, the Tanakh, and the New Testament. One of the most exciting revolutions in the study of Greek literature during the twentieth century was the discovery that the works of Homer (whoever he—or they—may have been, blind or not) were probably composed and for centuries transmitted in oral form before they were ever written down. Proposed as a hypothesis by the brilliant young classicist Milman Parry, this interpretation of the *Iliad* and the *Odyssey* argued that Greek epic verse in its beginnings was the work of illiterate bards, professional musician-poets who sang it to their audiences and taught

it to their pupils by singing it over and over again. The reliance of these singers on the stock formulas and epithets that we still recognize in the Homeric epics and the very complexity of the poetic devices, meter, and language, Parry urged, could be seen as a mnemonic device to protect the poems against the subtle changes and corruptions that might creep in as they were being recited over and over again in the fluid and shifting form that word of mouth necessarily takes on. It is still a favorite party game to pass on a whispered message of some complexity from one person to another, and then to discover how it has been garbled in the transmission after ten or fifteen "repetitions" that prove not to have been verbatim repetitions or even to have preserved the original substance of the message. There were skeptical reactions to Parry's audacious hypothesis from the members of the scholarly establishment, who, then as now, devoted their lives to writing and publishing books and who therefore could not imagine that, in the absence of writing, any work as complex as two entire epic poems consisting of over twenty-seven thousand lines could have been memorized over many generations and preserved relatively unchanged by uneducated and illiterate Greek peasants without ever being put down in permanent form. But Parry found illiterate shepherds in Yugoslavia who had been doing precisely that for centuries. And with some modifications, his theory, or at any rate this aspect of it, now usually labeled "orality" (to be distinguished from "literacy"), has found wide acceptance among students not only of early Greek literature but of other national literatures as well.

Meanwhile, all the way across Europe, the early literatures of Scandinavia and Britain had also been traced to oral sources already in the nineteenth century. The poetic medieval Eddas of Iceland and the Old Norse prose sagas were evidently being recited or sung long before they were written, the latter probably not before the thirteenth century. An eccentric nineteenth-century Danish antiquarian, hymn writer, and bishop, Nikolai F. S. Grundtvig, laid the foundations for the modern study of the Old English epic *Beowulf* with his speculative reconstruction of the earlier oral Scandinavian sources that might underlie that poem in its present written form, which is usually said

to date from the eighth century. Grundtvig also anticipated much of the modern study of the New Testament by similarly positing the existence within the first generation of Christian believers, and tracing back to the teachings of Jesus himself, of a primitive oral confession and proclamation, out of which the Gospels and even in some sense the Epistles of Paul could be said to have emerged. On-site studies by anthropologists of traditional storytelling formulas among various "primitive" and preliterate peoples of quite disparate backgrounds in many parts of the globe have found a surprising level of sophistication, confirming the theory that a culture does not have to possess a developed alphabet and a stabilized written language to be capable of profound "literary" creativity.

The burgeoning study of saga, epic, and oral tradition in the nineteenth and twentieth centuries extended to cultures dating from the region and the period to which we also owe the beginnings of the material that eventually came into our Bible. Such study became possible as a consequence of the development of archaeology into a science in its own right, which led to a refinement of linguistics and the "cracking" of various ancient alphabets; the most celebrated of these was the discovery and deciphering of the Rosetta stone by Jean-François Champollion, which led to the "cracking" of the code of Egyptian hieroglyphics. Prominent among these cultures were those of the ancient Near East, Babylonia, Sumeria, and Mesopotamia, which had given birth to poetic narratives about the creation and the flood that in some respects bore a striking resemblance to the oral narratives that were eventually incorporated into the Hebrew Torah. Written (and presumably recited) in Akkadian, the Gilgamesh Epic contains, among other material, accounts of a primitive man and of a world-destroying deluge that to many Judeo-Christian readers were remarkably (but therefore also sometimes disturbingly) similar to the biblical stories of Adam and Noah. The Babylonian poem known as Enuma Elish, which seems to have been recited once a year or even oftener, contained enough parallels to the first two chapters of the Torah to have become known rather loosely as "the Babylonian Genesis." Both of these ancient epics, together with other tablets and

written sources discovered by archaeological excavation, provided a wealth of information about how such narratives, including the biblical narratives, must have arisen and been transmitted in the ancient world.

Teachers of English literature often need to remind their students that Shakespeare did not write his plays to be studied as texts in seminars but to be performed at the Globe. Not the *page* but the *stage* was—and also is—their proper venue. It sometimes seems that the two Shakespeares, the playing field of the scholars and the shooting script of the actors and directors, have been traveling on separate tracks with very little contact. When there has been such contact, scholars have discovered that the language of the plays has to be heard in order to be read. Unlike most readers in Antiquity who read their books aloud, we have developed the convention of reading silently. This lets us read more widely but often less well, especially when what we are reading—such as the plays of Shakespeare and Holy Scripture—is a body of oral material that has been, almost but not quite accidentally, captured in a book like a fly in amber.

SOCRATES AND JESUS

The most striking examples from Antiquity of a reliance on the oral rather than the written word did not come to light through modern archaeology or recent literary theory at all, however, but had in fact been known in the Western tradition for a very long time. In the words of John Stuart Mill, "Mankind can hardly be too often reminded, that there was once a man named Socrates . . . , acknowledged master of all the eminent thinkers who have since lived." Nevertheless, it does need to be added that mankind can hardly be too often reminded as well that everything we know about Socrates, every piece of wisdom that can be traced to him, is secondhand, having come to us not directly from him but from his disciples and hearers: the philosopher Plato or the historian Xenophon or the dramatic poet Aristophanes. His enormous influence on every generation in all

the centuries between his time and ours—"Saint Socrates, pray for us!" Desiderius Erasmus is reported to have exclaimed—is the result of those intermediary sources, and it has depended on their credibility. For living though he did in the highly literate culture that was Periclean Athens, where books carried a massive weight of authority and influence, Socrates himself did not write a book or even a jotting that has survived. All his ideas remained in oral form, all his words were only spoken. And yet it was for these spoken words and unwritten ideas that he was officially condemned and put to death.

The same is true of Jesus of Nazareth. Practically everything in the preceding paragraph could be applied to Jesus as well as to Socrates. He, too, did not write anything. He was able to read from the scroll of the Prophets, announcing, "Today in your hearing this text has come true," and by that announcement once again giving primacy to hearing over text. But the one mention in the Gospels of his writing, when he "bent down and wrote with his finger on the ground," is of doubtful authenticity in the Greek manuscripts. Even if it is authentic, moreover, it does not report anything about just what it was that he wrote. He criticized his opponents for "studying the scriptures diligently" but not understanding them because they refused to listen to the living words that he, being the Word of God in the flesh, was speaking to them here and now. Otherwise, it is his spoken teachings that we have to go on and exclusively in the form (or forms) in which his pupils wrote them down after the fact. "No one ever *spoke* as this man *speaks*," even his enemies are reported to have acknowledged, if rather grudgingly; for "unlike their *scribes* [people who dealt with the written word] he *taught* [that is, he spoke] with a note of authority."

Apart from the vast differences in content, one difference between Socrates and Jesus is in the interval between their spoken words and the written accounts of their words. A strong argument that some historians have advanced for the inherent credibility of the self-defense of Socrates at his trial before the citizens of Athens, as Plato has written it down in his *Apology of Socrates,* is that the book came so soon after the actual event that any distortion in substance would have caught the attention and aroused the fatal criticism of the many po-

tential readers of the *Apology* who were present and voting when Socrates spoke at his trial. By contrast, the first words of Jesus ever to be written are a few formulaic words of the oral liturgical tradition: "This is my body, which is for you; do this in memory of me" and "This cup is the new covenant sealed by my blood. Whenever you drink it, do this in memory of me." Jesus instituted the Lord's Supper with these words, as they were quoted from that oral liturgical tradition by the apostle Paul writing to the Christian congregation at Corinth twenty years or so after the fact. After that, the first surviving written account of the sayings of Jesus, which most scholars today would identify with the Gospel of Mark, is usually dated just before the year 70 CE (the destruction of Jerusalem by the Roman armies under Titus). The other three Gospels probably came even later, although there is evidence in them that at the same time "many [other] writers have undertaken to draw up an account of the events that have taken place among us, following the traditions handed down to us by the original eyewitnesses and servants of the gospel," traditions that would also appear to have been oral; these "many [other] writers" are not identified more specifically. In any case, there were at least three or four decades during which the deeds of Jesus were being remembered and his words were being recited, but only orally; and the written forms incorporate those oral traditions. As late as the mid-fourth century there was a reluctance to write everything down. Quoting the Christian creed that was used for baptism in the church of Jerusalem, Bishop Cyril of Jerusalem told his hearers: "This summary I wish you both to commit to memory when I recite it, and to rehearse it with all diligence among yourselves, *not writing it out on paper,* but engraving it by the memory upon your heart," for fear that if they were written down, the secrets of the divine mystery would fall into the wrong hands.

There is a valuable tidbit of information in the New Testament about this process, in the farewell discourse of the apostle Paul to the elders of the church in Ephesus, reported in the Acts of the Apostles. It concludes with the admonition that "we should keep in mind the

words of the Lord Jesus, who himself said, 'Happiness lies more in giving than in receiving.'" As it was translated in the King James Version of the English Bible, "It is more blessed to give than to receive," this is among the most frequently quoted—though not at the same time the most faithfully heeded—of the sayings of Jesus. Yet it is not recorded in any of the Gospels, not even in the one written by Luke, the author of Acts who has Paul cite it here. That raises the question of the relation between the written forms of the Bible and the oral traditions that preceded them. It is a question over which the scholarly interpreters of the Gospels have been debating for centuries, but it is also a question that has to be asked about any act of committing an older oral tradition to written text. One of the basic differences between the Pharisees and the Sadducees, the two parties within Judaism that figure the most prominently in the New Testament accounts, was said to be that the Pharisees accepted the authority of traditions alongside the authority of the biblical text, while the Sadducees denied such authority, in principle at any rate. The concept of an "oral Torah" alongside the written Torah underlies the traditions that were then to be collected in the Talmud. Within Christian history the issue became central to the debates of the sixteenth-century Reformation, in which Luther and Calvin rejected the claim that the church's traditional interpretations of the Bible and even its nonbiblical traditions were an authoritative source of divine revelation alongside or in addition to the written Bible. "The Bible only is the religion of Protestants," William Chillingworth insisted. In its response to that elevation of biblical authority, the Roman Catholic church decreed in 1546 that "this truth and rule are contained in written books *and in unwritten traditions* which were received by the apostles from the mouth of Christ himself, or else have come down to us, handed on as it were from the apostles themselves at the inspiration of the Holy Spirit." According to this decree, all of these sources—the Bible, the written traditions, and the unwritten oral traditions—were to be received "with a like feeling of piety and reverence," regardless of the modality in which they had been preserved.

SCRIPTURE AND TRADITION

Even when the written text itself is taken to be the direct product of a special inspiration by God—as both the Tanakh and the New Testament are by their faithful adherents, and as the Qur'an is, supremely and transcendently, by Muslim believers—this question is by no means settled. From the earliest times the Jewish scribes, who were the faithful custodians of the written text of the holy Torah, word by word and even letter by letter, were at the same time passing down from master to pupil and by word of mouth various traditions about both customs and teaching, as well as about the meaning of the written text itself, that were not part of the Torah but of the tradition; the collection of such traditions was the basis of the Talmud. When the Christians accepted the Torah and the rest of the Tanakh but added their New Testament to it to create the Christian Bible, that did not put an end to this process, either. Writing in the fourth century, the Christian theologian Basil of Caesarea insisted that such pious actions as making the sign of the cross or facing the East when praying, neither of them commanded in the Bible, were not simply popular customs which it was possible for believers to obey or to ignore at will but unwritten traditions that had come down from the apostolic beginnings of Christianity and that were therefore of no lesser authority than the written apostolic traditions which were enshrined in the Bible. It was all normative and binding Christian tradition, regardless of the medium, written or unwritten, through which it was conveyed.

The liturgical venue of these traditions as enumerated by Basil is a reminder that behind the written text of the Tanakh as we have received it there also stood not only the sayings of the prophets and sages of Israel but the spoken—or, more often, the sung—traditions of worship. No part of the Scriptures has been more deeply cherished through the ages by Christians no less than by Jews than the Book of Psalms. The first book that was ever produced in America was *The Whole Book of Psalms Faithfully Translated into English Metre,* published

in 1640 *(The Bay Psalm Book).* Although the Book of Psalms, too, has frequently been ransacked by theologians looking for proof texts to quote, the Psalms carry on almost every page of their text the reminder that what was important was not the book as book but the songs of prayer and praise. They had been sung before they were written, and they were primarily intended to be sung over and over again also after they were written: "For the leader; with instrumental music"; "*Shiggaion* of David, which he sang to the LORD"; and so on to the next to the last Psalm, which opens with the admonition "Hallelujah. Sing to the LORD a new song"—a "new song" that, of course, has often turned out in the event to be a very old song indeed. Their written codification, therefore, was not to be seen as an end in itself but as the only possible means of preserving the continuity and guaranteeing that what previous generations once sang could be sung again by later generations. Indeed, they have been for centuries and now for entire millennia, both by Jews and by Christians. The Psalm that is written by the hand of the scribe stands in the service of the Psalm that is sung by the lips of the cantor, choir, or worshiping congregation; and "sung by the lips" has priority both in time and in importance.

But that priority of "the lips" applies no less to the nonpoetic books of the Bible. Not only does the spoken word of the prophet and, ultimately, the word spoken by God to the prophet and through the prophet precede the book that the prophet writes, as we noted from the prophet Jeremiah; but the prophet writes the words in the book precisely for the purpose of their being spoken words again at some future time. The same applies to the New Testament. As Martin Luther once observed, nowhere in the New Testament does Jesus command his disciples to go out into the world and write books, not even the Gospels and the other books of the New Testament. Rather, as the New Testament itself is at pains to attest, "he said to them: 'Go to every part of the world, and *proclaim* the gospel to the whole creation.'" For Luther, therefore, "Scripture" was the name for the Scripture that Jesus had read and quoted, the Tanakh/Old Testament. The best name for the New Testament, according to him, was not

"Scripture" but "proclamation" or "message." In the history of the people of God there have often been entire centuries and entire countries in which the illiterate population of believers outnumbered the literate population. But the message of the prophets and the message of the Gospels did not begin with text, and it does not perpetuate itself only through text: "God *said*, 'Let there be light'"; "In the beginning the [spoken] Word already was."

THE SPOKEN WORD AND THE WRITTEN WORD

This primacy of what "God said" over the written word, even the written word of God, has its grounds in the human psyche and in the very nature of human language. In Plato's *Phaedrus*, Socrates, without writing his criticism on paper, criticizes the excessive reliance of some of his Greek contemporaries on the written word at the expense of "the living word of knowledge which has a soul, and of which the written word is properly no more than an image." Similarly, the most influential letter writer in history, the apostle Paul, when he is compelled to rely on the written word in his letter to the Galatians, expresses his vexation with it: "How I wish I could be with you now, for then I could modify my tone!" Modulating the tone of voice; speaking loudly or whispering; pausing, speeding up, or slowing down; gestures, grimaces, and smiles—all of these are dimensions of oral communication and tools of persuasion that no system of punctuation, capitalization, italics, or boldface type can hope to reproduce. Plato quotes Socrates as saying in the same context in the *Phaedrus,* "Writing has one grave fault in common with painting. . . . You would imagine that [books] had intelligence, but if you require an explanation of something that has been said, they preserve one unvarying meaning. And when they have been once written down they are tumbled about anywhere, all alike, among those who understand them and among strangers, and do not know to whom they should or should not reply: and if they are maltreated or abused, they have no parent to protect them; for the book cannot protect or defend itself."

To give a picture that is perhaps more fair: What is lost when the spoken word (as we often say, perhaps more portentously than we realize) is *reduced to writing* must be balanced against what is preserved in that same process and by means of it. We learn every day that there is nothing more fleeting and evanescent than spoken language. It is, as Keats said of himself (mistakenly) in his epitaph, "writ in water," here one minute and gone the next, resonating for a moment and then disappearing forever. The very spontaneity of the spoken word, which can be its charm and its glory, can also be its fatal weakness. Who of us has not at one time or another said something spontaneously in the intensity or insensitivity of the moment that we wish we could retract or at least revise or, as we sometimes put it, "leave unsaid"? Which is exactly what we can do, at least right after writing it, with a pen or a typewriter or a word processor. Although we remain frustratingly uninformed about the details of the writing habits of the individual biblical writers, we are occasionally afforded some insights: "Because Koheleth was a sage, he listened to and tested the soundness of many maxims. Koheleth sought to discover useful sayings [presumably oral ones] *and recorded* genuinely truthful sayings"; "The scriptures written long ago were all written for our instruction, in order that through the encouragement they give us we may maintain our hope with perseverance." The experience of devout believers, both Jewish and Christian, over the centuries confirms this function of the written word of God in hours of trial and temptation. At such times it has proved to pious readers, as the Christian New Testament says about the Jewish Tanakh, that "all inspired scripture has its use for teaching the truth and refuting error, or for reformation of manners and discipline in right living, so that the man [or woman] of God may be capable and equipped for good work of every kind."

Occasionally, certain devout believers have even pushed this power of the written Word of God and inspired Scripture to the point of attributing their conversion directly to it. Saint Augustine, narrating the account of his own conversion, tells us how, when he was seemingly lost in the depths of self-indulgence and lust, he found himself—and found God—by reading the first words of the Bible that his eyes hap-

pened to catch: "Let us behave with decency as befits the day: no drunken orgies, no debauchery or vice, no quarrels or jealousies!" The British and Foreign Bible Society, the American Bible Society, and the Gideons all came into being at least partly in order to distribute Bibles and tracts that would bring readers everywhere to the faith. It would fly in the face of the historical evidence to suppose that the process has never worked that way. But if we probe the historical evidence, we will often find a human voice hovering somewhere in the vicinity of the written or printed page. When he just happened to read that particular passage from the New Testament, Augustine was responding to the mysterious voice of a child, whether a boy or a girl he did not know, that called out to him: "Pick it up and read it!" And the Bibles and tracts of the Bible societies were often distributed by the hand of a living and speaking human being, not just by mail or in a tract rack. No book of the Tanakh or the New Testament is addressed explicitly to unbelievers, though they are certainly present prominently in both.

Thus for every paragraph in a letter or every chapter in a spiritual autobiography detailing someone's conversion through reading the Book, there are hundreds in which it is the voice of a parent, friend, or stranger—perhaps sometimes even a teacher or preacher—that was the force which did the challenging and summoning and inviting. The message that voice conveyed was, with or without quotation marks, the message of the Book, or at any rate it almost always claimed to be just that. And the bearer of the message had usually read the Book or had even memorized large portions of it. But the agency issuing the invitation and distributing the Book was not a library or a classroom but a community of faith and of worship. Even the Yiddish word for "synagogue," which is *shul* and is derived from the Germanic and originally Latin word for "school," does not mean only a place where learners young and old memorize and recite the Torah (though they certainly do manage to do a great deal of memorizing and reciting there), but one where the human voice reaches out to others in preaching and reaches out to God in prayer. At least in this respect, Paul was speaking as much for Judaism as for Chris-

tianity when he formulated the rule: "So then faith does come from *hearing.*"

The cumulative effect of all this reliance on the spoken word and all this celebration of it was the eventual attribution to "the Word of God" of a status that went beyond grammar or communication to metaphysics and mystery: "In the beginning the [spoken] Word already was. The Word was in God's presence, and what God was, the Word was. He was with God at the beginning, and through him all things came to be; without him no created thing came into being. So the Word became flesh; he made his home among us." These opening words of the first chapter of the Gospel of John declare the common faith that Christianity shares with Judaism, and simultaneously they define the great gap between them. The vocable "word" here translates the Greek noun *logos,* which comes from the verb *legein,* "to say" or "to speak." *Logos* can also mean "reason" or "mind," and in both Jewish and Christian philosophical theology the term took on a life of its own. But whatever other meanings it may or may not be said to have, "In the beginning the Word already was" may be read as a summary and paraphrase of the repetition of the elevenfold "In the beginning God said" from the first chapter of Genesis. Before there was light and order, before there were stars or animals, before there was a human race, "God said"; and therefore "In the beginning the Word already was." That declaration of the common Jewish and Christian faith in the God who speaks then also provides the framework to "define"—which means "to draw the boundary lines"—the distinctive creed of Christianity that the speaking of God had "become flesh" and taken human form in Jesus and had "made his home among us."

TWO

The Truth in Hebrew

Hebrew Fragment of Isaiah 6.7–7.15, Dead Sea Scrolls, ca. 1st or 2nd century BCE.
(© The Dead Sea Scrolls Foundation, Inc./Corbis)

n the beginning God" are the opening words of the Bible. Yet in a real sense it can be said that the story of the Bible does not begin with Adam and Eve but with Abraham and Sarah. For the Bible is not intended to be a universal history of the whole human race, much less a cosmogony that accounts for the structure and laws of the entire physical and biological universe. How could even a minimal cosmogony, one that was based on the sophisticated and well-informed astronomy of the ancient Near East, be content to throw in the phrase "and the stars" as an explanation for what a later chapter of Genesis itself acknowledges to be stars without number, and to leave it at that? Rather, the Bible consistently directs our attention away from cosmogony, be it mythological or scientific, to the special relation between God and the human race:

> When I behold Your heavens, the work of Your fingers,
> the moon and stars that You set in place,
> what is man that You have been mindful of him,
> mortal man that You have taken note of him,
> that You have made him little less than divine,
> and adorned him with glory and majesty.

Therefore the biblical narratives of Adam and Noah, and of the covenant with Noah symbolized by the rainbow, lead up to the covenant of God with the people of God, a covenant that begins with the calling of Abraham and with the promise of God to Abraham and Sarah

that their descendants would always participate in that covenant relation, through which "all the families of the earth shall bless themselves by you." That is what makes Abraham "the father of all who
have faith"—Jews, Christians, and Muslims. In the Genesis account
he is the prototype of the religious pilgrim, responding in faith and
obedience to the divine command, "Go forth from your native land
and from your father's house to the land that I will show you."

The title of this chapter, "The Truth in Hebrew," is the translation
of the Latin *Hebraica veritas,* the title that Jerome, the fourth-century
Christian translator of the Bible into Latin, used for the Tanakh, which
makes up at least three-fourths of the Christian Bible. Traditionally, it
has been divided into three parts: Torah, the Five Books of Moses or
Pentateuch; Nevi'im, the Prophets; and Kethuvim, the Writings or
Hagiographa. The Apocrypha, though a product of Judaism, are not
part of the Jewish canon of the Bible, but they are included in the
Christian canon of the Old Testament for the Roman Catholic and
Orthodox churches. The Torah, the Pentateuch, together with the
Book of Joshua can be seen as the account of how Israel came into
being as a nation and how it possessed the promised land. Nevi'im,
the Prophets, continues the story of Israel in the promised land, describing the establishment and development of the monarchy and
presenting the messages of the prophets to the people. Kethuvim, the
Writings or Hagiographa, include speculation on the place of evil
and death in the scheme of things (Job and Ecclesiastes), the poetical
works (the Psalms above all), and some additional historical books.

The time span covered by the history of the people of Israel in the
main body of the Tanakh is approximately one thousand years. It begins with their exodus from Egypt, which, according to most archaeologists and historians today, must have taken place sometime after
1300 BCE (more precise dating seems impossible). It concludes with
the return of Ezra, "a scribe expert in the Teaching of Moses which
the LORD God of Israel had given," who "came up from Babylon"
to Jerusalem shortly before 400 BCE. Very few chronological data are
available for the accounts preceding the exodus, and those we do have
are exceedingly difficult to synchronize in any satisfactory manner

with other information from ancient history. At the other end of the story of the Tanakh, the Books of the Maccabees provide some additional dates for the period between Ezra and the New Testament. But the history in the Tanakh deals largely with the nine or ten centuries beginning at the exodus from Egypt. Some individual events and persons in that history can be matched up with what is known of ancient history from other sources. Cyrus, Darius, and Nebuchadnezzar, all of whom figure prominently in the biblical narrative, are recognizable historical monarchs whose lives are knowable from ancient historians and other sources, including cuneiform inscriptions and tablets. Even with all of this, however, most assignments of occurrences in the Tanakh to corresponding dates in the Egyptian, Babylonian, Persian, Syrian, and Greek calendars are arbitrary and hypothetical. Many such attempts, indeed, are theologically tendentious and are intended to prove or disprove a point about the inerrancy and authority of the Bible (always a dangerous procedure, because the supposedly assured results of archaeology can be as unstable as the shifting sands where the archaeologists have dug). This leads to a fundamental conclusion about these materials: They are intended not primarily as a chronicle but as a testimony of faith in the One who identified himself to Moses from the burning bush as "the God of Abraham, the God of Isaac, and the God of Jacob," the God of the everlasting covenant. This intention dominates both the form and the content of the Tanakh and is built into the very structure of its several parts. It also dictates the proper method of reading and understanding the Jewish Scriptures (as well as, of course, the Christian Scriptures) in later generations, as the history of such reading through the ages demonstrates.

TORAH, THE PENTATEUCH

In the Torah ("Law," "Instruction") or Pentateuch, the Bible presents the record of the divine action and legislation underlying its entire subsequent account. With the completion of the events related in the

Torah, the people of Israel had finished its captivity in Egypt and its wanderings and was ready to enter the promised land. Thus the Torah in a very real sense is the book of Israel's beginnings.

Genesis, as its title indicates, is a book about beginnings. It deals first with the beginnings of the universe and of the human race, sketched in the dramatic form of divine commands and actions during the six days "when God began to create heaven and earth." There follows the story of how humanity (which is what the name "Adam" means) fell into sin, which is followed in turn by a sequence of events leading up to the deluge. After the deluge comes a second set of beginnings, and it is with these that Genesis is principally concerned. The call of Abraham inaugurates the special covenant of God with him and with his descendants in perpetuity. Although he is historically a shadowy figure, Abraham is seen in the biblical narrative as the founding father of the community of faith. The remainder of the Book of Genesis is devoted to the history of the covenant as it passes from Abraham to Isaac to Jacob and thus to the tribes of Israel. In the narrative about each of the patriarchs, the events of his career are intertwined with reflections that anticipate the later experiences of Israel; they are patriarchs precisely because their history is not only the history of a remarkable series of human individuals seen as individuals but a history of "God in search of man." A noteworthy feature of these narratives is their continuing emphasis on the human frailties of the patriarchs, frailties that also anticipate the history of Israel. Throughout the book the theme is God's promise to Abraham and, through him, to the covenant people. These promises, in turn, form the ground for the commandments and the warnings of later books. In more than a simple chronological way, therefore, Genesis is the "beginning" of the Bible. The outline of the Bible and of its message begins with Genesis; without it the remainder of the biblical narrative, whether the Tanakh or the New Testament, would not make sense. Christian creeds and affirmations of faith, too, have traditionally opened with a statement of belief in God as "Maker of heaven and earth," which is a verbatim quotation from the solemn first verse of the first chapter of the Book of Genesis.

Nevertheless, the foundation of the Tanakh is contained not in Genesis but in Exodus, which recounts the deliverance from Egypt upon which the covenant relationship between God and Israel is based. The drama of the deliverance opens with an account (or accounts) of the call of Moses to lead Israel out of Egyptian bondage, and the self-revelation of God through the voice from the burning bush in the mysterious and inscrutable "name of the Unnameable," Ehyeh-Asher-Ehyeh, I Am That I Am. It continues with the miracles by which God makes known his power and his desire to liberate the people. Repeatedly God gives Pharaoh a chance to save himself by letting the Israelites go free, and repeatedly Pharaoh spurns the offer. Finally, with the institution of the Passover and the death of the first-born in Egypt, the exodus is inaugurated, and the crossing of the Red Sea accomplishes it, as celebrated in the song chanted by "Miriam the prophetess, Aaron's [and Moses'] sister," who "took a timbral in her hand":

Sing to the LORD, for He has triumphed gloriously;
Horse and driver He has hurled into the sea.

At every subsequent celebration of the Passover the question is asked, "Why is this night different from all the nights of the year?" And the answer is that it was on this night that God brought *us* out of the land of Egypt, identifying the observance now with the history then. Next the Book of Exodus makes the transition from the story of the exodus proper to the story of Sinai, which is the second and larger part of the book. The giving of the Law on two tablets of stone at Mount Sinai—which mountain this was on the Sinai Peninsula cannot be answered with any geographical precision—is an occasion for the reminder that God has brought Israel out of Egypt and is now affirming his covenant with the people: "I the LORD am your God who brought you out of the land of Egypt, the house of bondage: [therefore] you shall have no other gods besides Me." Corresponding to the human frailties of the patriarchs is the idolatry of the people in their worship of the golden calf, which they fashioned while Moses was on

the mountain receiving the Law: "This is your god, O Israel, who brought you out of the land of Egypt!" But God graciously pays heed to the intercession of Moses and renews the covenant that they have disrupted. The closing chapters of Exodus describe in some detail the enactment of the prescriptions for worship given at Sinai, the establishment of the Levitical priesthood, and the presentation of the tabernacle.

Further details and prescriptions for worship make up the bulk of the Book of Leviticus, which were in turn to form the basis for much of the analysis and exposition in the Halakhah and the Talmud. They deal with the various types of sacrifice and the appropriate acts accompanying them, with the ceremonial and moral equipment of the Levitical priesthood, with the meaning of ceremonial purity and the many ways it can be jeopardized, and with the main outlines of Israel's liturgical calendar of sacred feasts and fasts and festivals—above all the festival of Passover—by which the remembrance of God's saving actions will remain alive in later generations. Leviticus is thus an extension of the narrative in Exodus, and some sections of it, notably the "laws of holiness," represent an amplification of the legislation in Exodus as well (with occasional inconsistencies that were to keep the scribes and scholars busy for many centuries). When taken together, Exodus and Leviticus summarize the establishment of Israel as God's covenant people and the enactment of the cultic and other laws, including especially the specification of "the creatures that you may eat" from land, sea, and air, and of those countless other species of animals, birds, and reptiles that are forbidden. Later attempts at a rationalistic explanation of these laws on supposed hygienic grounds have usually turned out to be quite lame. This kosher abstemiousness, eventually transplanted to times and climes where many of these creatures were unknown, was to mark the life of Israel as a covenant people.

Numbers and Deuteronomy belong together. The Book of Numbers picks up the narrative at Sinai, adding the account of the divinely mandated "census of the whole Israelite community from the age of twenty years up," from which its English name is derived, and some additional legislation. From Sinai it carries Israel through the forty

years of wandering in the wilderness and describes certain events during those years. Finally, it brings the tribes of Israel to the plains of Moab and prepares the way for the conflict with the various nations and tribes occupying the land of Canaan—"Canaanites, Hittites, Amorites, Perizzites, Hivites, and Jebusites"—which is to be told in the Books of Joshua and Judges. Like Exodus, Numbers repeatedly describes the ingratitude and disobedience of the people, the wrath of God and his forgiveness, and the cycle of sin and repentance that would mark the history of God's dealing with his people throughout the Tanakh and well beyond it.

The setting of the concluding chapters of Numbers on the plains of Moab is also the scene of the discourses of Moses in Deuteronomy. This last book of the Torah is a rehearsal of the events that have brought Israel within sight of the promised land, not so much a narrative as a reminder and a celebration. It reminds the people of the prerogative given them by God in the particular covenant he has made with them through Moses at Sinai: "O happy Israel! Who is like you, a people delivered by the LORD, your protecting Shield, your Sword triumphant!" On the basis of this covenant Moses is represented as repeating and interpreting (and sometimes reinterpreting) the moral, ceremonial, and civil laws summarized in the earlier books of the Torah, with the rewards and punishments attached to them. Deuteronomy closes with Moses' farewell to the people, his final charge to them in the two long poems of Deuteronomy 32 and Deuteronomy 33, and his death (whether revealed to him while he was still alive, or written by God with the hand of another, perhaps Joshua, pious students of the Torah, both Jewish and Christian, have been unable to decide).

Although most modern scholars are agreed that Deuteronomy was not written by the hand of Moses but was composed rather late in Israel's history, they have come to lay increasing stress on it as a summation of the Torah and therefore a link between the Torah and other sections of the Tanakh. The belief underlying the Talmud, that there was an "oral Torah" in addition to and alongside the written Torah, takes some of the edge off the disputed question of "the Mo-

saic authorship of the Pentateuch," the question whose investigation was to be the starting point for so much of the modern critical approach to the Bible. Taken together, the books of the Torah set up the plot for the remainder of the Tanakh. Among Jews, therefore, the Torah has held a unique place within biblical literature, a place that was not changed with the adoption of the other sacred books. It is as "Torah scrolls" that the Sacred Books as a whole are revered.

NEVI'IM, THE PROPHETS

Under this title the Jewish Scriptures include a collection of eight books according to the Jewish reckoning; these eight books are listed separately in Christian Bibles and come to a total of twenty-one. The collection contains the books that have traditionally been ascribed to the prophets and, in addition, several more "historical" books that provide the background and setting for the books of the Prophets.

The historical books among the Nevi'im, called the "former prophets," are Joshua, Judges, 1 Samuel and 2 Samuel, and 1 Kings and 2 Kings. The Book of Joshua in its opening chapter recounts the narrative of how God chose Joshua to be the successor of Moses, promising "As I was with Moses, so I will be with you," and of how under his leadership Israel entered, conquered, and divided up the promised land. Closely related to the Pentateuch as the fulfillment of its promises and the completion of its story, the Book of Joshua repeatedly makes a point of setting this conquest apart from ordinary military and political struggles for territory and hegemony, on the grounds that this was "the promised land," promised by God to Abraham, Isaac, and Jacob and "to their descendants forever"; modern Zionism may be seen as the controversial effort to rehabilitate that divine promise. God had told Moses before he died: "You may view the land from a distance, but you shall not enter it—the land that I am giving to the Israelite people." The "entering" itself was to be the divine vocation of Joshua. The Book of Judges is a frontier story with rough-and-ready frontier heroes like Gideon and, above all, Samson,

the brawler who nevertheless manages to carry out the will of God. Judges forms a transition from the account in Joshua, describing the situation of Israel after it had taken over Palestine but before it had stabilized its political and religious life.

That stabilization came through the establishment of the Jewish monarchy, whose development is portrayed in the Books of Samuel and Kings. The First Book of Samuel begins with the career of Samuel as a prelude to the history of the monarchy. Despite Samuel's warnings that they have been blessed because they were ruled directly by God rather than by a human monarch, the people insist, "We must have a king over us, that we may be like all the other nations," whom they were simultaneously battling and imitating; and Samuel reluctantly anoints Saul as the first king of Israel. The rest of the book is a chronicle of the reign of King Saul over the people of Israel, his successes, and his ultimate downfall. It is especially concerned with the struggle between Saul and the young David, who had been selected as his successor, including the touching account of David's friendship with Jonathan, son of Saul. In 2 Samuel are found the biography and character portrait of David (to be supplemented and revised in 1 Chronicles), one of the most complete and most candid biographies anywhere in the Bible. The book seems to be an official version of his life, but it is by no means an idealized one, as the unexpurgated account of David's adultery with Bathsheba and murder of her husband Uriah graphically proves. The First and Second Books of Kings trace the steady and often disgraceful decline of the monarchy after David. The glory of the reign of David's son Solomon, whom "the LORD endowed with wisdom and discernment in great measure, with understanding as vast as the sands on the seashore," climaxes in the building and dedication of the great Temple of Solomon, which David had not been allowed to build himself because, having been primarily a man of war, he had too much blood on his hands. This high point in the reign of Solomon is followed, however, by his partial apostasy, and after his death the nation is split into the two kingdoms of Judah and Israel. The books conclude with the history of Elijah and Elisha, whose work as "warrior-prophets" is apparently

one of the grounds for classifying these books with the Books of the Prophets, although in the interest of clarity, the term may perhaps be best reserved for the "major" and "minor" prophets, as it tends to be in English usage.

The major prophetic books are Isaiah, Jeremiah, and Ezekiel. Isaiah is probably the most important among them and one of the most influential books in the entire Bible; for example, quotations from the Book of Isaiah (and the Book of Psalms) outnumber all others in the New Testament. Literary study of the book has led most scholars to the conclusion that in its present form Isaiah represents the work of at least two separate prophets. The basis of the entire book is the prophet's inaugural vision of "my Lord seated on a high and lofty throne," whose voice called to him, "Whom shall I send? Who will go for us?" and to whom Isaiah responded, "Here am I; send me." Proceeding from this vision, chapters 1–39 are a commentary on the relation between Judah and other nations, notably Assyria. The prophet interprets the invasions of the Northern Kingdom of Israel by the Assyrian armies in the seventh and eighth centuries BCE as a sign of divine judgment and the "rod of My anger," but he also promises that eventually God will bring salvation to his people and through them to all humankind. In chapters 40–66, Jerusalem has been sacked, and the people have been dispersed in Babylon (597 BCE). These chapters elaborate on the promises of the earlier section, representing the salvation as coming through the faithfulness of God's suffering servant (who is not identified, although the rabbis sometimes saw this as a reference to the people of Israel, and Christians as a description of the suffering Christ, "who makes the many righteous") rather than through the military or political might of the nation.

Similar themes, including an inaugural vision, appear in the prophecies of Jeremiah, whom God calls with the words

> Before I created you in the womb, I selected you;
> Before you were born, I consecrated you;
> I appointed you a prophet concerning the nations.

But the political distress of Judah dominates these prophecies even more than it does Isaiah's. Jeremiah is the voice of doom for the kingdom of Judah. He sees the coming of the Babylonians as an indication that God wanted to wipe Judah off the map as he had Israel. Jeremiah also foresees the coming of "a new covenant with the House of Israel and the House of Judah," which "will not be like the covenant I made with their fathers, when I took them by the hand to lead them out of the land of Egypt," but a new covenant by which "I will put My Teaching into their inmost being and inscribe it upon their hearts," rather than on tablets of stone as he did the covenant and the Law at Mount Sinai. Therefore he summons the people to repent, to acknowledge that their defeat forms part of God's merciful purpose.

Ezekiel, too, interprets Israel's foreign relations in the light of the purposes of God, using visions rather than prophetic discourses as the vehicle for his interpretation. The two most memorable of Ezekiel's visions, which came to be celebrated in the spirituals of African American slaves, are the vision of the wheels "way up in the middle of the air" and the vision of the valley filled with dry bones, to which by divine command Ezekiel announces, "O dry bones, hear the word of the LORD," and the bones come back together into living bodies. In the first half of the book the prophet warns his nation of their impending doom and calls on them to acknowledge their sin, while in the second half he comforts the people in their affliction and promises the new city and new land that God would create for them. Once again judgment and hope are inseparable. For all three of the major prophets, therefore, the purpose of God in permitting the dispersion and captivity of his people is a major theme and a basic problem.

The twelve "minor" prophets are thus designated not because they are less important but because their books are so much smaller. In the Tanakh they stand as a single book, but in the translations they are separated and are usually cited that way also by Jewish scholars. Hosea is a vivid denunciation of Israel's apostasy, seen metaphorically as adultery, illustrated by the infidelity of the prophet's wife, "a wife of whoredom and children of whoredom." Joel uses a plague of

locusts—"spread like soot over the hills, a vast, enormous horde"—
and a drought as the basis of his prophecy that God will punish his
people but eventually deliver them. Amos directs his prophecy against
social and economic injustice, coupled as it was with a smug trust in
the correctness of Israel's worship as a secure guarantee of its future:
"You alone have I singled out of all the families of the earth—*that is
why* I will call you to account for all your iniquities," he booms out in
a denunciation of such smugness wherever and whenever it has appeared. Obadiah is a vindication of the cause of Israel against the
Edomites, who had helped to destroy the kingdom of Judah: "Thus
said my Lord God concerning Edom: 'I will make you least among
nations.'" Jonah contains more narrative than prophecy and is intended to show, through the story of Jonah's being swallowed by "a
huge fish" and then spewed out to continue his prophetic preaching,
that the mercy of God extends not only to the covenant people but
to all nations, even to Nineveh.

Micah echoes the prophecies of Amos against the idle but recur-
ring notion that correct worship "by the book" without social justice
would be able to secure the favor of God:

> He has told you, O man, what is good,
> And what the LORD requires of you:
> *Only* to do justice
> And to love goodness,
> And to walk modestly with your God.

That "only" has rightly been called "the biggest little word in the
Bible." Nahum, like Jonah, deals with the city of Nineveh, capital of
Assyria and seat of its oppression of Israel, but with its ruin rather
than with its repentance. He interprets its fall as God's punishment for
its past sins:

> I will make your grave
> Accord with your worthlessness.

Habakkuk uses the intrusion of marauding bands of Babylonians not to denounce the sins of the people but to consider the providence of God in relation to evil in human history. Zephaniah views the collapse of Israel's enemies as a sign that the terrible day of divine judgment, "the day of the LORD's wrath," is imminent. Haggai is a call to reconstruct the temple in Jerusalem, to "set to work on the House of the LORD of Hosts, their God," after the Babylonian captivity. Zechariah is likewise an appeal for the temple, but it is cast in the form of eight visions of the future, horses and thrones and chariots and flying scrolls. Malachi denounces both the priests and the people for their disobedience to God and for their betrayal of the covenant between God and the nation, but promises, "Behold, I am sending My messenger to clear the way before Me."

Thus the Nevi'im, the books of the Prophets, both major and minor, form a commentary on the history of Judah and of Israel. They interpret this history as a sign of God's judgment and of God's mercy, and they call the nation back to repentance and faithfulness. Their role in the total corpus of the literature of the Tanakh is therefore a very important one, building on the foundational narratives and legislation of the Torah.

KETHUVIM, THE WRITINGS

This division of the Tanakh comprises a miscellaneous collection of sacred writings (often identified by their Greek name "Hagiographa" or "Sacred Writings") that cannot be classified in either the Torah or the Nevi'im.

Psalms, Proverbs, and Job constitute the principal poetic literature of the Tanakh, although there are poetic sections in other books as well, even in some of the more prosaic historical books. In many respects these books may be said to represent the high point of the Tanakh as literature, and it is not an accident that over the centuries readers who have no special interest in the specifically religious mes-

sage of the Bible have frequently turned to these books. In the Psalms are found poems and hymns that date from various periods in the history of Israel, assembled for use at public worship in the Temple of Jerusalem. Tradition maintains that it was David who originally gathered them together into a psalter and that after David, additional psalms were included. The Psalms express the devotion of the individual and of the nation in reflection on the deeds of God. Some of them, such as Psalm 23, "The LORD is my shepherd," and Psalm 90, "O Lord, You have been our refuge in every generation," have embedded themselves through the succeeding ages in the collective memory of "every generation," be it Jewish or Christian or secular.

A different kind of reflection lies behind the Book of Proverbs. Like the Psalms it has a composite origin in the wise sayings of many wise men in Israel and even in the proverbial wisdom of other Near Eastern peoples, many of whom already knew on their own, for example, that "wine is a scoffer, strong drink a roisterer" and did not need divine revelation to learn it. The Book of Proverbs differs from most of the Tanakh in many ways, but the most significant difference is the absence of references to the events of Israel's history during or since the covenant of the exodus, as well as the absence of allusions to the hope of Israel for the future, whether messianic or not. Instead, most of the book is concerned with general maxims about life that would seem to apply even apart from the history and hope of Israel, except perhaps for the voice of personified Wisdom in the eighth chapter about her special relation with God since before the creation of the world, which Jewish and then Christian speculation would eventually make into the foundation for a metaphysical system.

The Book of Job, one of the most difficult and most profound pieces of literature in the entire Bible (or anywhere else), describes the plight of a good man who has become the victim of a series of disasters. From a situation of prosperity and success he descends to utter degradation, losing his wealth, his power, and his family. Through the device of conversations between Job and other people, his friends and his wife, the writer lists most of the explanations that are con-

ventionally put forward, whether by the wisdom of the nations or the wisdom of Israel, to account for such a plight, and in each case the conversation shows that the explanation is wrong or at least greatly oversimplified. Eventually God himself intervenes, not to provide yet another oversimplification but to declare that the ways of God are essentially mysterious and that the only solution is to trust in their hidden purposes:

> Who is this who darkens counsel,
> Speaking without knowledge? . . .
> Where were you when I laid the earth's foundations?

A second group in the Kethuvim are the Megilloth or rolls, consisting of the Song of Songs, Ruth, Lamentations, Ecclesiastes, and Esther. The Song of Songs, attributed to King Solomon, is, in the opinion of many scholars, originally a compilation of poems in praise of human love—

> Eat, lovers, and drink:
> Drink deep of love!

—but by the time it was put into the canon of the Tanakh, it was probably being interpreted as an allegory about the love between God and Israel, and it was as an allegory that it would continue to be interpreted, also by Christians. The Book of Ruth tells the story of a Moabite woman who married an Israelite and became an ancestress of David. Her loyal dedication is expressed in the familiar words, "Wherever you go, I will go; wherever you lodge, I will lodge; your people shall be my people, and your God my God." The Lamentations of Jeremiah is a series of acrostics describing the capture of Jerusalem and mourning its fate; it closes with a petition for divine mercy:

> Take us back, O LORD, to Yourself,
> And let us come back.

With its grim realism bordering on skepticism, as expressed in its opening words, "Utter futility!—said Koheleth," the Book of Ecclesiastes or Koheleth (the Preacher), like the Book of Job, may well be intended to refute the notion that some were drawing from the Proverbs, namely, that the person who obeys the maxims of commonsense morality will prosper on earth. In it the writer describes how he has tried all the conventional roads to happiness—wisdom and pleasure and power—and has found them all inadequate. Reflecting as it does a universal human experience, Ecclesiastes has been the source of many well-known sayings and maxims, such as "Nothing new under the sun." The Book of Esther, which is notable also for not containing a single mention of the name of God, describes the history of King Ahasuerus and Queen Esther as an explanation for the rise of the Jewish festival of Purim. From the Jewish classification of these five books together and from the contents of the books it is evident that the rather "secular" tone of several of them made their status as scripture somewhat problematical.

Also included among the Kethuvim are Daniel, Ezra, Nehemiah, and the First and Second Books of Chronicles. The Book of Daniel describes the career of Daniel and God's interventions on his behalf when he "sent His angel, who shut the mouths of the lions so that they did not injure" him, and its second half is a highly symbolic interpretation of world history as a series of "monarchies" under the direction of divine providence; it would continue to fascinate and puzzle its readers. The other books belong together as apparently the work of one writer, usually called the "chronicler." In the First and Second Books of Chronicles he repeats much of the material from earlier historical books, concentrating on the history of the kingdom of Judah. The First Book of Chronicles is basically a biography of David, which adds further facts to the story as given in the two Books of Samuel. The Second Book of Chronicles begins with Solomon and goes through the division of the kingdom to the reign of Zedekiah; here, too, the chronicler had access to materials that supplemented the account in the First and Second Books of Kings. In the Book of Ezra he describes the return of the Jews from the

Babylonian captivity and the reconstruction of the temple. He includes lists of the families who returned and the texts of the decrees under which they returned. In the Book of Nehemiah, closely related to Ezra, the reconstruction of the city walls of Jerusalem becomes the basis for a meditation on the relation between God and his people. This book, too, contains lists of those who participated in the reconstruction, but much of it concentrates on the description of the prophet Nehemiah and his persistence in performing this assignment.

THE CANON OF THE HEBREW TANAKH

As even this sketchy outline indicates, the books of the Bible were written one at a time and over a long period of time. The title *Biblia* in Greek is originally neuter plural, meaning "little books," and it was construed in Latin as a feminine singular only after the many books had been collected into the one book, which is also why English usage still fluctuates between the singular "Scripture" and the plural "Scriptures." The question as to which books belong in the Tanakh is complicated by its history in Judaism and then in Christianity. Not only is the use of the word *canon* as a designation for an authoritative list of sacred books a rather late phenomenon within the history of the Jewish community, but even the idea of a fixed and final list came about only after a long evolution.

It is not known when and how the earliest collection of sacred writings in Hebrew arose. The report that "the high priest Hilkiah said to the scribe Shaphan, 'I have found a scroll of the Teaching in the House of the Lord'" clearly presupposes the existence of some such collection. But both the incident and the collection are impossible to date, and some critics have even hypothesized that the whole story is actually intended to explain the composition of portions of the Torah, including most or all of the Book of Deuteronomy. Evidently, however, the Pentateuch (or at least its first four books) was in the process of being assembled in Jerusalem before that time.

The division into Torah, Nevi'im, and Kethuvim may reflect stages in the history of canonization. Thus the Law, the Torah (with or without Deuteronomy), may have been the first to be canonized, then the Nevi'im as the written form of the message of the prophets, and then the Kethuvim, which were other writings whose status and scope may in the meanwhile have remained in doubt. On the other hand, some historians of ancient Israel and of the canon of the Tanakh are inclined to question this interpretation. It would be possible to speak with greater authority if the content of the books referred to in Ezra and Nehemiah as "the Law" were known. A late Jewish tradition maintains that a "Great Synagogue" at the time of Ezra and Nehemiah met to establish the canon of the Bible. Although this tradition has enjoyed wide circulation and credence among both Jews and Christians, most historians now are inclined to doubt its reliability, for it is obvious from other and more reliable sources that the extent of the Tanakh continued to be a problem for Jews (and then for Christians) long after the work of Ezra and Nehemiah.

The safest generalization permitted is this: various collections of sacred writings were put together quite early in the history of Israel, as is evident from such terms as "the books," but they did not become a "canon" until much later. The name *canon* may properly be applied to the books that seem to have been adopted by the assembly of rabbis at Jamnia about 90 or 100 CE under the leadership of Rabbi Akiba. Until then, apparently, the status of the Song of Songs and of Koheleth (Ecclesiastes) remained doubtful, but at Jamnia they were definitely included in the canon. Formally, the Jewish canon of the Bible came to include the three divisions of Torah, Nevi'im, and Kethuvim, as we have been employing them here. In this canon, however, the Torah has held, and holds, a special place as a "canon within the canon."

Additional light on the process by which the Jewish canon was formed has come from the discovery of the Dead Sea Scrolls. The books included in them suggest that the Torah and the Nevi'im had been standardized by about the fourth century BCE, together with most of the Kethuvim, but some of the Kethuvim (including appar-

ently Daniel) were still in dispute until the assembly at Jamnia. After the fall of Jerusalem in 70 CE and the rise of the Christian movement, the Jewish community felt obliged, in closing ranks, to fix the limits of its Bible more precisely. So it was that certain books occasionally included were excluded and that others previously challenged were included.

From the sacred narratives of this collection of books and from the faith it set forth came all three of the great monotheistic religions: Judaism, Christianity, and Islam. Thus Abraham became "the father of *all* who have faith": father of the people of Israel through his son Isaac, the child of promise; father of the Christian church through Jesus Christ, who declared "Abraham was overjoyed to see my day; he saw it and was glad"; and father, through his firstborn son, Ishmael, of the people of Islam who were commanded in their Holy Book, the Qur'an, to "remember when Abraham prayed: 'O Lord, make this a city of peace.'" All three professed descent from him and loyalty to him, as his loyalty was to the One True God alone: "And he believed in the LORD, and He counted it to him for righteousness."

THREE

Moses Speaking Greek

Papyrus fragment of Genesis 29.15–27 in the Greek Septuagint, 3rd or 4th century CE: From Frederic G. Kenyon, *The Chester Beatty Biblical Papyri* (London: Emery Walker Limited, 1933), Plate 4. (© The Trustees of the Chester Beatty Library, Dublin)

hat's all Greek to me!" When people say something like that nowadays, they really mean "I simply can't understand a word of it!" But in the Mediterranean world of two thousand years ago, speaking or writing something in Greek was, in fact, simply the best possible way to have it be understood far and wide. Thanks in considerable measure to the fourth-century BCE military conquests and cultural imperialism of Alexander the Great (who was, to be sure, not himself an ethnic Greek at all but a Macedonian), Greek manners and Greek cuisine and Greek wine, and above all Greek language and Greek literature, had acquired the kind of éclat that French culture would enjoy throughout Europe during the eighteenth and nineteenth centuries when Frederick the Great, king of Prussia, wanted only French spoken at his court, and the cream of Russian society in the Moscow of Tsar Alexander I (at least according to Tolstoy's *War and Peace*) were still chattering away in French even while the armies of Napoleon (a latter-day Alexander who also was not an ethnic Frenchman but a Corsican) threatened the capital city in 1812.

Even in proud Rome, the city that gave birth to such immortal Latin classics as the orations of Cicero and the poems of Vergil, it was considered fashionable to use the Greek language, not only among intellectuals, politicians, and merchants but also to some extent even among the common people. A fierce opponent of such trendiness, the Latin satirist Juvenal bitterly referred to the city as "Greek-struck Rome." And so when Paul, the Jewish Pharisee turned Christian

apostle, wrote his most important book and addressed his "Epistle to the Romans" to his fellow believers there in the second half of the first century CE, he wrote to them in Greek even though it was not, or not quite, his native tongue (which seems to have been Aramaic). So did the pagan Roman emperor Marcus Aurelius a hundred years or so later, in the second half of the second century, when he composed his philosophical *Meditations* in his tent while he was on a military campaign against the Germanic tribes somewhere near the present-day territory of the Czech Republic. Greek was the world language, at any rate in what regarded itself—not without a good measure of both ignorance and snobbery when we think of the levels attained in culture and art by China or India at that time—as "*the* civilized world." As even Latin had to yield to Greek, so this applied infinitely more to all the other and more exotic languages that were spoken in Europe, Asia Minor (known simply as "Asia"), and Egypt. Which meant that if a distinctive system of ideas or beliefs or customs was isolated from the rest of "the civilized world" in one of those exotic languages, it would have to be translated, preferably into Greek, or it would run the danger of remaining in obscurity permanently.

THE JEWISH DIASPORA

The outstanding example of such a system of ideas, beliefs, and customs at the time—as it has been, come to think of it, at most other times—was the faith of Israel. The Jewish religion was enshrined, but therefore was also *locked,* in a sacred book, in a code of conduct, and in a liturgical ritual that were purposely being kept hidden from the outside world in one of the most esoteric of all those exotic languages and therefore virtually unavailable, except in bits and pieces, to anyone who did not know Hebrew. But by the third and second centuries BCE, to the regret of many, this category of "anyone who did not know Hebrew" had come to include increasing numbers of people, especially in the younger generation, who by heritage and tradition professed the faith of Israel and who in some measure

wanted to go on practicing it. Painstaking counting by modern scholars has shown that there were Jews dispersed throughout most of the Greco-Roman world, a phenomenon that has acquired the name "the Dispersion" or, in Greek, *Diaspora*. This term is used now for any scattering of a population, for example, the emigration of many Russians to Western Europe, China, and America after the Revolution of 1917, and of the Jews in Germany, Austria, and Eastern Europe who fled from the Nazis in the 1930s, and of Turkish "guest workers" in postwar Germany. The inexorable pattern of assimilation, which has been a source of ferment but also of anguish in every modern émigré population from the Chinese in the Philippines to the Norwegians in Minnesota, has often been expressed, generally by an embattled and despairing older generation, in the slogan, "When you lose the language, you leave the faith!" Often enough this turned out to be true.

This danger has been even greater and even more real for Jews than it has been for other nationalities, because in Judaism the nation and the religion were quite literally coterminous. One symptom of the pattern of cultural assimilation was intermarriage with Gentiles. Reliable data are notoriously unavailable, of course, but there is plenty of anecdotal evidence scattered here and there in the sources of the ancient world. For instance, the New Testament informs us that Timothy, to whom two of the Epistles of Paul are addressed, had a Jewish mother and a Greek father. That New Testament reference to Timothy indicates that he resembled other children of mixed marriages in other times and places also in this respect: that he had not been reared in strict conformity with the Jewish Law but in what was apparently and not uncharacteristically a series of compromises between the Law of Moses and the customs of the Gentiles. He had not been circumcised until Paul himself circumcised him as a Christian. We know nothing about his observance of kosher dietary laws, and there is no indication that he knew any Hebrew. When Paul, writing to him in Greek, commends him for having known the "inspired scriptures" of the Tanakh from his childhood, he apparently would not have been referring to the Hebrew text of those scriptures.

How to keep the faith while living in exile or in the Diaspora? That was the existential question for multitudes of Jewish believers. During an earlier exile, an unknown poet had phrased the question in haunting language:

> By the rivers of Babylon,
> there we sat,
> sat and wept,
> as we thought of Zion.
> There on the poplars
> we hung up our lyres,
> for our captors asked us there for songs,
> our tormentors, for amusement,
> "Sing us one of the songs of Zion."
> *How can we sing a song of the Lord*
> *on alien soil?*

How indeed? Even in the Holy Land, the Hebrew of the Bible had itself become increasingly "alien," having been superseded as a spoken tongue by Aramaic. Just to make things confusing to the modern reader, Aramaic was sometimes called "the Hebrew language," which was how the New Testament referred to it, for example, in quoting the inscription "Jesus of Nazareth, King of the Jews" on the cross. Aramaic was apparently the spoken language of Jesus and of his disciples, including Paul. Hebrew did continue to be the language of liturgy, of law, and of biblical scholarship. But at least Aramaic and Hebrew were linguistic cousins of sorts, written in similar alphabets and closely related enough to be sometimes mistaken for each other, yet at the same time distant enough to be, equally often, mutually unintelligible. The danger of lapsing into a kind of religious amnesia because of such a separation from the Hebrew mother tongue of the faith of Israel was vastly more grave in the Jewish colonies of the Diaspora that girded the Mediterranean Sea, where Greek was the language used also by the non-Greek populations.

By far the most important of these Jewish colonies was in Alexandria, in Egypt. As its name suggests, the city of Alexandria had been founded by Alexander the Great, in 332 BCE. According to tradition it was Alexander himself who encouraged Jews to emigrate and settle there; and according to the Jewish scholar and philosopher Philo, who lived there, the Jewish population of Egypt numbered over a million people. There were other cities bearing this name after Alexander's conquests, but by far the most famous was the Egyptian one. Its strategic geographical location and its almost instant commercial success rapidly made it the most thriving cosmopolitan center of Late Antiquity, a crossroads on the trade routes, by ship and camel, between Europe and the East (or actually the several "Easts") of Arabia and India. The celebrated library of Alexandria was said to hold more than half a million books until its destruction—which took place not primarily in the conquest of the city by the Arabs in 641/642 CE, as legend has it, but in civil conflict some centuries earlier. After that catastrophe the tradition about the library served as a cultural memory of a departed intellectual glory until its attempted reconstruction as part of the new Egypt in our own time.

The city of Alexandria would continue to occupy this prominence even after being conquered several times: by the Romans, who let it have its own senate as a free Greek city; and then by the Christians, who carried on a lively intellectual interchange with Jewish thinkers and with pagan Neoplatonic philosophers there. Alexandria was the capital for a school of theologians who for centuries would be a dominant force, sometimes *the* dominant force, in Christian theology and biblical study; the popularity of the allegorical interpretation of the Bible in the church owes much of its power to the Alexandrian school. But Alexandria was also the scene of one of the darker pages of early church history when, in 415, Hypatia, daughter of the mathematician Theon and the star of Alexandrian Neoplatonic philosophy in her own right as a teacher of mathematics and astronomy, was lynched by a Christian mob. The question "What did the Christian archbishop of Alexandria, Cyril, know about her murder, and when did he know it?" continues to be debated.

THE ORIGIN OF THE SEPTUAGINT

In this cosmopolitan setting the Jewish community had held an honored place for centuries. For not only was Alexandria a commercial and cultural center rivaling Rome itself, though politically Rome remained the capital city, and an intellectual and philosophical center matching Athens or even eventually overshadowing it, but it became in some ways as important for world Judaism as the Holy City of Jerusalem, which it also quite certainly exceeded in size of Jewish population. The inhabitants of Alexandria were divided into three districts: Egyptian, Greek, and Jewish. Within the Jewish quarter (or third), which was increasingly Greek-speaking, the struggle to remain authentically Jewish and to "sing a song of the Lord on alien soil" was combined with the need to explain and defend the faith to Gentile outsiders, who were also Greek-speaking. Those two factors in the situation of Jewish Alexandria—the internal need to guarantee continuity of Jewish worship, teaching, and observance despite the continuing cultural and linguistic change, and the external need to formulate an apologetic for Judaism that would be addressed "to its cultured despisers," as a much later apologetic would define the target audience—were responsible not only for a substantial body of Jewish philosophical theology in Greek, but also for the translation of the Hebrew Bible into Greek, which is usually called "the Septuagint."

According to a legend that was originally published under the pseudonym "Aristeas" and is certainly fictitious but that nevertheless achieved wide circulation as well as considerable embellishment over time, King Ptolemy Philadelphus of Egypt in the third century BCE received from Demetrius of Phalerum, director of the celebrated library at Alexandria, the proposal that the Jewish Law, the Torah, should be translated into Greek to fill a serious gap in the holdings of the library's celebrated collection; librarians, then as now, cannot stand to see a blank space on their shelves. Ptolemy was proud of his

library, and he was also interested in the world religions, having once received an embassy of Buddhist scholars from India. He therefore sent a delegation, of which "Aristeas" claims to have been a member, to Eleazar, the high priest at Jerusalem, with the request that six scholars from each of the twelve tribes of Israel be dispatched to Alexandria to carry out this assignment of translating the Torah. According to one version of the Letter of Aristeas, the Greek translations of the entire Jewish Scriptures from the Hebrew, produced individually by each of these seventy-two scholars, turned out to be identical, which was irrefutable evidence that they were divinely inspired. From the legendary number of the translators, this version acquired the name Septuagint (the Latin word for seventy), which is customarily abbreviated as LXX.

It is almost certain that the original initiative behind the production of the Septuagint was actually Jewish, not Gentile at all. It seems to have been motivated partly by the desire to satisfy the curiosity of Greek-speaking Gentiles concerning what these strange Jews believed and partly by the need to have Scripture available to the new generations of Jews in the Dispersion who could no longer read Hebrew. It is important to note, but not to exaggerate, some of the adaptations of the biblical text to a non-Jewish audience, as when the Hebrew phrase "the hand of God" is translated into Greek as "the power of God," to avoid the impression that the Divine was like a human being, as this impression had been propagated through the anthropomorphism of the mythological Olympian deities. More fundamentally, the enterprise of producing the Septuagint—like any translation of any text, especially of a sacred text, in any period of history—was based on the rather audacious assumption that there really were Greek equivalents for all the original Hebrew words, not only for all those species of animals, birds, and reptiles that were listed in the catalogs of the Book of Leviticus as unclean, but above all for the One True God, "the God of Abraham, the God of Isaac, and the God of Jacob," and for everything that the biblical writers had confessed about the words, actions, and attributes of the One True God. Al-

though it did employ the Greek word *theos*—which had come out of the polytheistic mythology of Mount Olympus and which was generally used by most Greek writers in the plural—to express the primal confession of the monotheistic faith of Israel, the Shema: "Hear, O Israel! The LORD is our God, the LORD alone," it did not try to adapt the names of individual Olympian deities to its monotheistic purposes; such "translations" would have entailed a complicity in the heathen idolatry of the Homeric gods and demigods.

From what we know about the religious life and observance of Alexandrian Jews after the production of the Septuagint, it does seem to have been successful in meeting the changing needs of Jews without Hebrew. For half a millennium, or at least until a large percentage of its members were expelled in the civil disturbances and conflicts with the Christians of 414–415 CE, Alexandrian Judaism appears to have continued to be a thriving community of faith and learning. There seems to be every reason to believe that the knowledge both of the history and of the laws of the Bible, without which it is impossible to affirm the covenant and be an observant Jew, managed to be preserved and transmitted from one generation to the next on the basis of the Greek version of the Scripture. By the nature of the case we are less well informed about the liturgical use of the Bible than we are about its educational use. But there is at least some indication that while the ritual went on being recited in Hebrew, helps were provided for those worshipers who knew only Greek—just as, for that matter, such helps were provided for Palestinian worshipers in Aramaic, perhaps at first orally, in the form of the Targum.

PECULIARITIES OF THE SEPTUAGINT

It is even more certain that the translation was not produced all at once but over a period of a century or two or even more, beginning at first with only the Torah, the Five Books of Moses. Considerably less certain are many of the other questions raised by the translation,

some of them important even today. Because the Greek word for a "messenger" of any kind was *angelos* and the word for "wind" could also mean "spirit," the sentence in the Psalms "He makes the winds His messengers" comes out in the Greek translation as "He makes His angels spirits." It is quoted that way in the New Testament as part of a discussion of the angels, as well as in Christian liturgies to this day, even though that is not what the Hebrew original is saying. Where the Hebrew has "Look, the young woman is with child and about to give birth to a son. Let her name him Immanuel," without specifying the status of the young woman any more precisely, the Septuagint uses the word *parthenos,* "virgin," which the Gospel quotes (in Greek), with the formula "All this happened in order to fulfill what the Lord declared through the prophet," for the virginal conception of Jesus from his mother, Mary. Later in the Book of Isaiah, the Septuagint's "And I saw two mounted horsemen, and a rider on an ass, and a rider on a camel" became an embarrassment to Christian apologists but a welcome support to Muslim disputants, because it seemed to be prophesying not only that Jesus would enter into Jerusalem on Palm Sunday riding on a donkey, as the Christian Gospel described him doing in the New Testament, but that he would be followed (almost exactly six centuries later) by the prophet Muhammad, who was a camel driver.

THE CULTURAL SIGNIFICANCE
OF THE SEPTUAGINT

Whatever the precise details of its composition or its standing within the Jewish community of faith, the creation of the Septuagint brought it about that the Bible became, willy-nilly, part of world literature. Anyone who could read the *Odyssey* could now read the Book of Exodus, even though some of its Greek might seem rather quaint to a pagan Hellenistic reader (which was, of course, true of the archaic Greek of Homer as well). By contrast, the Qur'an would

remain locked in Arabic for many centuries after it had been revealed and committed to writing, and would therefore continue to be inaccessible to friendly outside inquirers, not to mention all its enemies.

It had long been part of the hope of Israel, voiced by the prophets, that peoples "far and remote" would finally come to Mount Zion and learn the Torah, which was intended and revealed by the One True God for all peoples, not only for the people of Israel. Yet without their learning to read Hebrew, that hope was largely beyond realization. But when we read the account of Pentecost in the New Testament, we hear of "devout Jews drawn from every nation under heaven, Parthians, Medes, Elamites; inhabitants of Mesopotamia, of Judaea and Cappadocia, of Pontus and Asia, of Phrygia and Pamphylia, of Egypt and the districts of Lybia around Cyrene; visitors from Rome, both Jews and proselytes, Cretans and Arabs." Many of the "Jews" in this mouth-filling catalog must have been Gentiles by birth but were now converted Jews, "proselytes," by faith and observance. From an obscure sect turned inward, huddled around its Torah and reciting its Shema, Judaism had now become a world religion, a significant force in the civilization of the Mediterranean world, "from the northernmost palm tree to the northernmost olive tree," as the Mediterranean world is defined in Ferdinand Braudel's delightful formula. And nothing had contributed as much to this transformation of the Jewish faith into a world religion as had the Septuagint—whether or not the story was historically true that it had actually been produced through the divine inspiration of those seventy-two bilingual scribes in Alexandria.

THE BIOGRAPHY OF MOSES

The theme of emerging from the shadowy realms of the cave into the bright light of the great world is, of course, not a biblical metaphor but comes from Plato's *Republic*. Nevertheless, it does fit very well as a description of what happened to the Bible as a result of the Septuagint—to the Bible and to its doctrines, and perhaps above all

to the characters and events of biblical history. These golden shekels of the Jewish Bible now became part of a larger, more universal coinage. In similar fashion the words of the final chapter of the first history of the Christian church, the Acts of the Apostles in the New Testament, "And so to Rome," encapsulate the emergence of a self-styled "sect" into the world of the Roman Empire—first as a pilgrim, then as a victim of persecution, then at last as a conqueror, and eventually itself a persecutor.

Now that Moses was speaking Greek and that his words and commandments had become legible to anyone who was "literate"— which meant able to read the Greek language, anyone else being dismissed as a *barbaros*—he could assume his rightful place in the pantheon of world heroes. One of the most effective ways for this to happen was, as it still is, through the medium of a celebratory biography. Thus Plutarch devoted his enormously influential *Parallel Lives* (which has gone on to serve as a continuing source of historical knowledge, as it did for Shakespeare) to exercises in comparative Greek and Roman biography. For example, he looked at the similarities and differences between Alexander the Great and Julius Caesar as conquerors, and between Demosthenes and Cicero as orators, delineating their moral character and seeking to probe the roots of their heroic greatness. He had two Jewish near contemporaries who accorded the same kind of biographical treatment to the moral character of Moses. As a result, Moses was able to join Achilles and Odysseus as an ancient hero, widely known also among Gentile readers throughout the Mediterranean world. Flavius Josephus, who is best known for his history of the Jewish war with Rome and his graphic description of the destruction of Jerusalem in 70 CE, produced near the end of his life a monumental history of the people of Israel, *The Antiquities of the Jews,* written in Greek in twenty books. The latter part of Book Four is a biographical portrait of Moses, paraphrasing the Septuagint of the Books of Exodus and Deuteronomy and employing such concepts of Greek philosophy and psychology as "virtue" and "the passions" to present the personality of Moses as "one that exceeded all men that were in understanding, and made the best use of

what that understanding suggested to him. . . . He had such a full command of his passions, as if he hardly had any such in his soul." That was the very attitude of self-control and objective detachment above the fray that many schools of classical philosophy, most notably but not exclusively the Stoics, sought to inculcate in their disciples. But now, thanks to the appearance of his history in a Greek version, it was a way of describing the moral character of the ancient Jewish lawgiver.

Even more successful in exploiting the Septuagint to make Moses appealing to a Gentile audience, as well as to his fellows among Greek-reading Jews, was Philo of Alexandria. Written in the same city that had initiated the Septuagint and coming a century or two later, Philo's *Life of Moses* was a biographical novella in which Moses became the king and the lawgiver, the prophet and the priest, and as such the model of both the contemplative life and the active life, the two contradictory lifestyles that the Greeks had been trying to harmonize for centuries. Philo saw it as his mission "not only to study the sacred commands of Moses, but also with an ardent love of knowledge to investigate each separate one of them, and to endeavor to reveal and to explain to those who wish to understand them, things concerning them which are not known to the multitude." In that enterprise he was greatly aided by the creative Greek translations of the Septuagint. By the time he had completed his portrait, the pliant vocabulary of the Greek Pentateuch had enabled him to paint Moses as not the exotic prophet of a strange Near Eastern cult but actually the embodiment of all four of the classical virtues that had been expounded by Plato and Aristotle: prudence, temperance, courage, and justice. The wise man of Greek philosophy and the wise man of biblical teaching in the Book of Proverbs and the Wisdom of Solomon, the "justice" of Aristotle's *Nicomachean Ethics* and the "justice" of the major and minor prophets of Israel, came together in Moses.

Nor was the wisdom of Moses expressed only in his moral character and his piety. In many ways the supreme expression of Mosaic wisdom came at the very beginning of the Torah, in the revealed account of divine creation that opened the Book of Genesis, which was

the divine answer to the deepest of all human quests: Where does the world come from? Where do I come from? "It is quite foolish," Philo explained, "to think that the world was created in six days or in a space of time at all." That is not what the creation story in Genesis really meant. Rather, God created the patterns and Ideas from which, in turn, the visible world was produced. Philo had learned to read Genesis this way by reading the other great creation myth in his library, Plato's *Timaeus*. "The Father and Maker of all this universe," *Timaeus* declared in a passage that was constantly being quoted by Hellenistic writers, "is past finding out; and even if we found him, to tell of him to all would be impossible." If the universe was "beautiful and good [*kalon*]," as *Timaeus* and the first chapter of the Septuagint of Genesis were agreed in saying that it was, then the conclusion logically followed that it must have been based on a pattern that was itself *kalon* and therefore eternal; and *kalon* was how the Septuagint had translated the Hebrew word *tōv*, "good," in the repeated declaration of verse after verse of the first chapter of Genesis, "And God saw that this was good." All the profound speculation of *Timaeus* about the nature of the world was thus placed in the service of the interpretation of the Bible, and a speculative-mythological cosmogony was born. This became possible for the first time only with the translation of the Septuagint, as a result of which some reader was said to have exclaimed, upon reading Plato's *Timaeus*, that it was "Moses speaking Attic Greek," and all because Moses had first learned to speak Attic Greek in the Septuagint, which had learned it at least in part from Plato's *Timaeus*.

CHRISTIAN SIGNIFICANCE
OF THE SEPTUAGINT

In many ways the principal legatee of the Jewish Septuagint was not Judaism but Christianity. The tradition of reading the creation story in the Book of Genesis in counterpoint with the creation story in Plato's *Timaeus* found its most sustained continuation in the exegetes

and fathers of the Christian church. The traditional writers of the books of the New Testament, with the exception of Luke, were all Jews; the so-called apostolic fathers and other Christian writers of the second and third centuries were all Gentiles. To the first and second generations of believers, Judaism was their mother, but to the third and subsequent generations she was their mother-in-law. At least some of the writers of the New Testament were in a position to correct the translations of the Septuagint on the basis of their knowledge of the Hebrew Bible. But apart from them, knowledge of the Hebrew original virtually disappeared from the church for a thousand years or more.

The great exceptions to this ignorance of Hebrew (though not quite the only exceptions) were Origen of Alexandria in the East during the third century and, living in both the West and the East at the end of the fourth and the beginning of the fifth century, Jerome, the scholar and translator who produced the Latin version known as the Vulgate. Origen, great master of biblical allegory though he was, cared so much about the original of the Bible and its integrity that he compiled one of the most ambitious textual comparisons of his time or any time, called the *Hexapla*. In six parallel columns—and in many handwritten volumes that have since disappeared except for scraps (even these filling two stout printed volumes)—the *Hexapla* presented the Hebrew text, a Greek transliteration of the Hebrew text, the Septuagint, and three other Greek translations, bearing the names of Aquila, Symmachus, and Theodotion. When it came time to prepare his own meticulous commentaries on the Bible, however, Origen tended to stick to the Septuagint.

And so did the Greek church in his time and ever since. The Septuagint was, according to a Greek Orthodox confession of faith written in the nineteenth century, "a true and perfect version" of the Hebrew text. Whether they are sung in Greek, Slavonic, or Arabic, or now in English, the Psalms, which are the foundation of the Eastern Orthodox liturgy, continue to be based on the Psalter of the Septuagint or on translations from the Septuagint rather than from the Hebrew. In the West, too, even the earliest Latin translations of the books

of the Tanakh (which we have now only in fragments) were based on it, being therefore translations-of-a-translation, in which the human mistakes or idiosyncracies of the seventy (or whoever they were) were compounded rather than corrected, as the words of the Bible made their tortuous way across the several major linguistic boundaries from Hebrew to Greek to Latin.

Not only were Christians the principal beneficiaries of the Septuagint, but its long-range historical significance for Judaism must be recognized as having been in some ways a largely negative one. Some later Jews came to regret the translation of their Scriptures into Greek because of the Christian usage of the Septuagint version of the Book of Isaiah to prove various doctrines such as the virgin birth of Jesus. It is noteworthy that when the lingua franca of the western Mediterranean world shifted back from Greek to Latin, perhaps in the third century or so of the Common Era, the educational and apologetic motivations within Judaism that had been responsible for the creation of the Septuagint did not go on to produce a Latin translation of the Tanakh by Jews; that assignment was left to Christians, climaxing in the masterpiece of Jerome's Vulgate. The Roman destruction of Jerusalem in 70 CE, the gradual entrenchment of the authority of Pharisaism and the Talmud as "normative Judaism," the Christian declaration of independence from Judaism, and the enthronement of Catholic and Orthodox Christianity as the established religion of the Roman Empire under emperors Constantine and Theodosius—all of these forces contributed to a state of mind within the Jewish community that was far less congenial to the idea of translating Torah, Nevi'im, and Kethuvim into the languages of the nations than the Greek-speaking cosmopolitanism of Jewish Alexandria had been.

Above all it was the Greek "New Testament" that became the heir of the Greek "Old Testament." Much of the history of biblical interpretation, especially in the modern period, serves as a cautionary tale to show that the coincidences of the vocabulary of New Testament Greek with the language of Homer or Sophocles (alongside the great differences) must not be permitted to obscure the decisive importance of this massive Greek text, which came between Sophocles and

the New Testament. The Septuagint should not be the only place to look for the meaning of a word in the Gospels or in Saint Paul, but it definitely must be the first place to look. A fine illustration is the New Testament passage with which the preceding chapter closed. "In the beginning the Word [*ho Logos*] already was. The Word was in God's presence, and what God was, the Word was. He was with God at the beginning, and through him all things came to be; without him no created thing came into being"—these famous words with which the Gospel of John opens have sent interpreters and translators scurrying to find the use of *logos* in the Greek philosophers to mean human Word or Reason or Mind or the cosmic Mind. Too often overlooked in that process, however, has been the cluster of related terms in the Greek "Old Testament," which were, interestingly, the primary resource on which the Greek-speaking interpreters of the Gospel of John in the early Christian centuries drew for their understanding of *Logos.* In addition to Word or Reason or Mind, *ho Logos* in John can mean Wisdom (*Sophia*), and this is what *Sophia* says about herself in the Septuagint version of the eighth chapter of the Book of Proverbs: "The Lord made me the beginning of his ways for his works. He established me before time was in the beginning before he made the earth. When he prepared the heaven, I was present with him. I was by him, suiting myself to him, I was that in which he took delight; and daily I rejoiced in his presence continually." This language of the Septuagint gave to the concept of the Logos in the Gospel of John a concreteness and a personal quality, a sense of almost playful "delight," that was hard though perhaps not impossible to supply from the Greek philosophers.

FOUR

Beyond Written Torah: Talmud and Continuing Revelation

מאימתי

קורין את שמע בערבין "משנה שהרבנים נכנסים לאכול בתרומתן עד סוף האשמורה הראשונה דברי ר' אליעזר וחכמים אומרים "עד חצות רבן גמליאל אומר "עד שיעלה עמוד השחר מעשה ובאו בניו מבית המשתה אמרו לו לא קרינו את שמע אמר להם אם לא עלה עמוד השחר חייבין אתם לקרות ולא זו בלבד אמרו אלא "כל מה שאמרו חכמים עד חצות מצותן עד שיעלה השחר "הקטר חלבים ואברים מצותן עד שיעלה עמוד השחר "וכל הנאכלים ליום אחד מצותן עד שיעלה עמוד השחר אם כן למה אמרו חכמים עד חצות כדי להרחיק אדם מן העבירה: גמ' תנא היכא קאי דקתני מאימתי ותו מאי שנא דתני בערבית ברישא לתני דשחרית תנא אקרא קאי "דכתיב בשכבך ובקומך והכי קתני זמן קריאת שמע דשכיבה אימת משהכהנים נכנסין לאכול בתרומתן ואי בעית אימא יליף מברייתו של עולם דכתיב "ויהי ערב ויהי בקר יום אחד אי הכי סיפא דקתני "בשחר מברך שתים לפניה ואחת לאחריה בערב מברך שתים לפניה ושתים לאחריה לתני דערבית ברישא תנא פתח בערבית והדר תני בשחרית עד דקאי בשחרית פריש מילי דשחרית והדר פריש מילי דערבית: אמר מר משעה שהכהנים נכנסין לאכול בתרומתן מכדי כהנים אימת קא אכלי תרומה משעת צאת הכוכבים לתני משעת צאת הכוכבים מלתא אגב אורחיה קמשמע לן "כהנים אימת קא אכלי בתרומה משעת צאת הכוכבים וה"ק זמן קריאת שמע דערבית משעת צאת הכוכבים והא קמ"ל דכפרה לא מעכבא "כדתניא "ובא השמש וטהר ביאת שמשו מעכבתו מלאכול בתרומה ואין כפרתו מעכבתו מלאכול בתרומה "וממאי דהאי ובא השמש ביאת השמש והאי וטהר טהר יומא דילמא ביאת אורו הוא וטהר טהר גברא

[Right marginal glosses — מסורת הש"ס and cross-references, partially legible]

[Left column — Rashi commentary in Rashi script]

מאימתי קורין וכו'. פי' רש"י וא"ת והיכי קרינן מבעוד יום וכו' עד מצוה: על כן פי' רש"י שקרית שמע שעל המטה עיקר ולאחר צאת הכוכבים. והכי איתא בירושלמי אם קרא קודם לכן לא יצא...

[bottom wide commentary band — Tosafot etc.]

ומסתמא גם היה קול קרית שמע. ומכל אותן הראיות ומשמע שקרית שמע של ערבית קודם הכוכבים...

לתני דשחרית ברישא. כדמשמע בתמיד דבקר זבח של בקר תחלה. אלא... אקרייתא שמע וכו'

אי הכי דקתני שחרית ברישא. כדמשמע דקאמר לעיל דבשלמא דקחני דבערבא...

מברך ג' לפניה וכו'. [בירושלמי וכו'] שתקנו רבנן כד' להזמין חבורים...

והא קמ"ל דכפרה לא מעכבא.

s the authority of the Bible actually functions in the ongoing life and practice of the community of faith, it is in Judaism no less than in Christianity the authority of a Bible that has constantly been in the process of being normatively interpreted and then reinterpreted, ever since its various component parts, as the community of faith affirms, were first written down by the writers and prophets under the inspiration of the Spirit of God. The relation of the authority of that ongoing normative interpretation of Holy Scripture to the authority of the original text of Holy Scripture is an issue with which both the Jewish and the Christian traditions have had to struggle, each in its own special way. There was an oral tradition preceding and underlying the New Testament, and by no means all of that tradition is contained in the New Testament or exhausted by it; the ongoing presence and guidance of the Holy Spirit in the church, moreover, can carry with it the authority of continuing revelation. Therefore, the relation between tradition and Scripture—their origin, their content, their authority—has often become controversial throughout the history of the Christian interpretation of the Bible.

For Judaism, similarly, this interpretation of the Bible after the Bible, of Torah beyond Torah, took several—characteristically Judaic—forms, which were closely interrelated and which overlapped chronologically as well as substantively. Except for Apocrypha (which is a Greek word), these are generally designated by their Hebrew names, including (listing them for now in alphabetical order according to the English alphabet): Gemara, Haggadah, Halakhah, Kabbalah, Midrash,

Mishnah, Talmud, Targum, and Tosefta. Most of these methods of biblical interpretation and literary genres came together in the massive—
and, to the uninitiated outsider, downright labyrinthine as well as
intimidating—encyclopedic structure of the Talmud, which in a
modern English translation comprises thirty-five volumes of closely
written, highly allusive, and consistently intertextual analysis. The Talmud also became, for teaching purposes, the identification of the
so-called talmudic academies, or *yeshivot,* that have transmitted the
instruction in the traditional Jewish interpretation of the Bible.

Many encyclopedias, dictionaries, and other standard reference
books contain helpful definitions and discussions of these and other
technical terms from the rabbinical tradition of postbiblical Judaism.
Rather than simply providing yet another glossary of these titles,
however, and in the interest of clarity and as part of the larger history
of the interpretation of the Bible through the ages, this chapter will
group them by themes and classes, defining or describing each of
them in the course of that more ample exposition.

APOCRYPHA

In a category of their own among what might be called the "post-
Scriptural scriptures" of Judaism are the so-called Apocrypha, which
are not part of the Jewish canon of the Tanakh in Hebrew. The name
"Apocrypha" is the plural of the Greek word for "hidden," *apo-
kryphon,* and is the usual term among Protestants when referring to the
ambiguous position of these books. In opposition, Roman Catholicism and Eastern Orthodoxy, which also speak of "Apocrypha,"
have sometimes called them "deuterocanonical," to concede that
their position in the canon has been subject to question but to declare
that they nevertheless belong to canonical Scripture. They are in a
special category because they are included together with and in several
instances—namely, the additions to Jeremiah, Esther, and Daniel—are
integral parts of the "canonical" books of the Tanakh in the Septuagint
translation into Greek. Their inclusion in the Greek version without

authorization in the Hebrew is not easy to explain. Does it mean that there were at one and the same time two distinct and alternative canons of the Tanakh within Judaism, a narrower one that had been preserved in Hebrew by the Jews in the Holy Land and a broader one that was translated into Greek by the Jews in the Diaspora? Or is it a historical anachronism to speak of a "Jewish canon" at all in these centuries before the Common Era, as though it was something closed and set, so that the act of binding all of these writings together into a single volume and translating them into Greek did not really imply that they were all being endowed with the same measure of authority?

As part of the Septuagint "canon," the Apocrypha became and still are part of the Christian Bible in both the Eastern Orthodox and the Western Roman Catholic churches. They continued to hold this position, though without definitive and formal church legislation according it to them, until the Reformation churches assigned them (at best) second-class status, on the grounds that they were books which "the church doth read for example of life and instruction of manners, but yet doth it not apply them to establish any doctrine." For most of Christendom during most of Christian history, however, they were and still are simply part of the Bible. Although all the books of the Apocrypha are Jewish in origin, they have in fact played a far more important role in Christian history than in Jewish history.

The Apocrypha include additions to the Books of Esther, Jeremiah, and Daniel, but they are made up chiefly of Tobit, Judith, the Wisdom of Solomon, Ecclesiasticus (the Wisdom of Jesus, Son of Sirach), Baruch, and the two (or three) Books of the Maccabees. The Book of Tobit tells the separate stories of Tobit and Sarah, each of whom turned to God in prayer after enduring great anguish. With the help of the angel Raphael, Tobit's son Tobias and his bride, Sarah, are brought together and are married; the book closes with a description of their blessed estate before God. The Book of Judith is a story of how the beautiful Jewish widow Judith tricked the Assyrian general Holofernes and enabled Israel to resist and defeat its enemy. Like the Book of Proverbs, the Book of Wisdom, which seems from its

language and style to have been originally composed in Greek rather than Hebrew, contains advice for both rulers and subjects; and like Proverbs, it also establishes the origin of wisdom in God and places it within a total cosmic context. Ecclesiasticus, too, belongs to the wisdom literature and is sometimes called "the Wisdom of Jesus Ben [the Son of] Sirach" or simply "Sirach." ("Jesus" is the Greek form of the Hebrew name "Joshua," also in the Septuagint, and was fairly common in Jewish families.) Baruch is apparently a blending of several elements: confessions of sins, a praise of divine wisdom, and a series of poems.

The Books of the Maccabees—two books in the Roman Catholic canon, but three in the Eastern Orthodox canon—are probably the most important and most widely read (even by Protestants) in this entire group, supplying much of the narrative of Jewish history in what Christians call "the intertestamental period" between Tanakh and New Testament. They relate the struggles of the Jews, under the leadership of the seven Maccabee brothers, to defend the monotheistic worship of the God of Israel against the encroachments and atrocities of pagans like King Antiochus Epiphanes. Taken together they are a major source of information about the history of the Jews until a century or so before the Common Era and were the inspiration for George Frideric Handel's popular oratorio of 1746, *Judas Maccabaeus.*

"NOT SPAKE BUT SPEAKETH": THE PERSISTENCE OF THE ORAL TORAH

When the young Ralph Waldo Emerson in 1838 dramatically declared his independence from the orthodoxy of all the churches— even from what must be called, by something of a historical and theological oxymoron, the "orthodoxy" of his own New England Unitarian church—he coined the phrase "not spake but speaketh" to express his deepening conviction that divine revelation was not to be confined to any sacred book or inspired individual but continues into

the present. Even today, therefore, one could aspire to become, as he urged his young hearers at the Harvard Divinity School, "yourself a newborn bard of the Holy Ghost, cast behind you all conformity, and acquaint men at first hand with Deity." In point of fact that is not quite the way it has worked either in the history of Judaism or in the history of Christianity. For "not spake but speaketh" aptly describes the ongoing revelation of the word of God that has come over and over again and that still continues to come now, not in some kind of high-flying independence from but, to the contrary, in a devout and persevering engagement with the pages of the Sacred Book.

According to Jewish tradition such textual engagement and commentary has been coexisting side by side with the Sacred Scriptures of the Tanakh from the very beginning in the form of what came to be called "the oral Torah." Moses himself—or, to be utterly precise and faithful to the tradition, God speaking to and through his servant Moses to the people of Israel—was the source of this oral tradition as well as of the written Torah. Part of what Moses heard from God he wrote down in the Torah as we have it, but part he kept unwritten, handing it on in oral form. Through such handing on—our English word *tradition* comes from the Latin verb *tradere,* "to hand down"— both the written Torah and the oral Torah have been kept inviolate within the community of faith from generation to generation. Thus, because the sacred text was not and is not automatically clear in and of itself but requires interpretation, there immediately began the oral commentary on the written text, drawing on the resources of this oral Torah. Reflecting at least in part the bitter experience of the Jewish community with the Christian appropriation of the originally Jewish Septuagint, some of the later Jewish sages suggested that the reason for not writing down this oral tradition was to keep it from being translated into Greek and thereby, like the Septuagint, falling into the wrong hands. The foundation of the Talmud is the Mishnah, which even in its eventual written form goes on being identified by the rabbis as "*oral* tradition"; it is earlier than the written commentary on the Mishnah, the Gemara, and is deemed to be superior in authority to it.

The most momentous body of oral tradition to be directly con-
nected with the text of the Tanakh consisted in the supplying of the
vowels that made it possible to pronounce the Hebrew words, which
in the original texts did not possess either vowels or punctuation or,
so it seems, word divisions, only a continuing line of consonants.
Even someone who has never tried it should be able to imagine that
reading a Hebrew text (or an English or a French text) made up solely
of unseparated consonants can be a daunting assignment indeed:
THLRDSMSHPHRDLCKNTHNGHMKSMLDWNNGRNPST
RSHLDSMTWTRNPLCSFRPS—this is how the first two verses of
Psalm 23 would look in the English of the Jewish Publication Society
Version, which reads:

> The LORD is my shepherd;
> I lack nothing.
> He makes me lie down in green pastures;
> He leads me to water in places of repose.

It is still an illuminating experience to visit a class in which mere boys
are learning how to read unpointed Hebrew text, often by methods
of teaching and learning that seem to be almost as old as the oral
tradition itself.

But it would be ridiculous to suppose that because it was only the
consonants that had been written down in the received text of the
Tanakh, only they were transmitted. The Hebrew words did have to
be pronounced, and for that they needed vowels. And so there has existed from the very beginning an oral tradition, handed down from
teacher to pupil through countless generations, of precisely which
vowels went with the consonants that appeared on the page. The only
difference was that these vowels had to be committed to memory instead of being part of the transmitted written text. When the scholars known to history as the Massoretes—the name seems to come
from a Hebrew word for "tradition"—working between the sixth
and tenth centuries of the Common Era (therefore, it must be remembered, as much as a millennium or more after the original com-

for-letter transliteration. As the preface to Sirach (or Ecclesiasticus), one of the books of the Apocrypha, acknowledged in a statement that accurately reflects the linguistic and the religious state of affairs obtaining in postbiblical Judaism, "What is said in Hebrew does not have the same force when translated into another tongue. . . . Even the law itself, as well as the prophets and the other writings, are not a little different when spoken in the original." Therefore it often required paraphrase or circumlocution to say in Aramaic what the original Hebrew had said, which unavoidably made the Targum into a biblical commentary of sorts. Likewise, explanation often required expansion. To the biblical text, "The descendants of Japheth: Gomer, Magog, Javan, Tubal, Meshech, and Tiras," the Targum adds the explanation and expansion: "And the names of their provinces were: Phrygia, Germania, Media, Macedonia, Bithynia, Asia, and Thrace." The sheer mass and complexity of the resulting material eventually made it necessary to put the Targum in writing—and, surprisingly soon after the invention of printing in the latter half of the fifteenth century CE, to put it also into print. Perhaps the most important of the Targums was Targum Onkelos (Onqelos) on the Torah, which was printed in Aramaic as early as 1480 and then was included as part of the six-volume Complutensian Polyglot Bible published at Alcalá de Henares in Spain between 1514 and 1517, with a Latin translation for use by Christian biblical scholars, thereby giving them access to the standard Jewish understanding of the many verses in the Pentateuch that Christian exegesis had long since been claiming as its own. These explanations and comments in the Targum format are an essential component of the accumulating tradition of Jewish biblical exegesis.

Among glosses and paraphrases there was some effort by the rabbis to distinguish between Targum as translation-*cum*-explanation and Midrash as comment-*cum*-addition. A central feature of Midrash was the application of the biblical text to circumstances and needs that differed in some way from the original context of a passage. This often called for an explanatory gloss or addition to the original text. It

position of the Torah and the rest of the Tanakh), supplied the vowels, which are written as "vowel points" under the consonantal text, they were repeating, with a deep and reverential sense of fidelity to the past, what this tradition had passed on to them through generation after generation of rote memorization and constant recitation. But if, as Jewish doctrine and then, on the basis of Jewish doctrine, Christian doctrine also maintained, the Tanakh was "inspired scripture," did that imply that not only the consonants of the original writing but also the vowels, first memorized and then written down much later, were the product of a special act of God as the Inspirer of Scripture? And so, because the transmission of the vowels had come down through the generations by means of an oral tradition, did that make this tradition "inspired," too, and in the same sense as the written text?

Because the translation of the Tanakh into Greek had come nearly a millennium before the Massoretes did their work, it follows that "any Hebrew text retroverted from the Greek Bible will in fact predate by several hundred years the complete manuscript on which our Hebrew Bible is based." If we "retrovert" this way and seek to reconstruct the Hebrew original that seems to be underlying the Greek, it becomes clear that in a number of passages the Jewish translators of the Septuagint were reading the consonants with vowels other than the ones that were eventually supplied by the Massoretes for the text and that we read now in printed editions of the Hebrew Bible (and use for the interpretation and translation of the Hebrew text). In one of the Psalms, where the Massoretes (and all our translations into modern languages) have "*Your people* come forward," the Greek of the Septuagint version has "*With you*," the difference depending on which subscript vowel is added to the identical set of Hebrew consonants.

Other differences are considerably less trivial. In the "cry of dereliction" that, according to the Gospels, Jesus recited—but, it should be noted, in Aramaic—on the cross, "My God, my God, why have You abandoned me?" the Hebrew text of a later verse as transmitted by the Massoretes reads, "*Like lions* [they maul] my hands and feet."

But the Septuagint has "*They have pierced* my hands and feet," the differences being in the tiniest letter of the Hebrew alphabet, the yōd (ʼ), which, if elongated just a little by the scribe's pen or brush, becomes a wāw (ו). In the constant arguments between Jews and Christians, during the Middle Ages and well beyond, over whether this "cry of dereliction" expressed the despair of the Psalmist or the redemptive voice of Jesus the Messiah, that elongation of one letter amounted to much more than a technicality and made much more than the proverbial "iota of diffference."

The tradition that had been handed down orally through the generations to the Massoretes and then was committed to writing by them did not consist solely of the vowels for the text but included other lists and explanations to help make sense of the consonantal text and to preserve it free from error and contamination. These, too, belonged to the total tradition of the centuries, of which the Massoretes regarded themselves as the authorized bearers. Explanations and lists of this kind necessarily turned out to be a kind of commentary in themselves, dealing in the first place with such problems as correct spelling and the inconsistencies between one and another appearance of the same Hebrew word but going on from simple proofreading and copyediting to more substantive questions about the sacred text.

GLOSSES AND PARAPHRASES
OF THE SACRED TEXT

Within postbiblical Judaism the oral transmission and then the codification of such explanations of individual Hebrew words were necessary even for those who had retained a fluency in Hebrew. But their importance increased as such fluency declined among Jews, both in Palestine and in the Diaspora. Aramaic gradually displaced Hebrew as the spoken tongue of Palestinian and other Jews. Later on, Aramaic (which today is still a spoken language for a small enclave) was to be succeeded as a Jewish vernacular in different areas and periods by Ara-

bic (also in medieval Spain), by Yiddish (among the Ashkenazi Jews of Central and Eastern Europe into the twentieth century), and by Ladino (among the Sephardic Jews of the Mediterranean region), but Hebrew was revived as a spoken language for Jews only in modern times. Already a few verses of the Tanakh, in the books of Ezra, Daniel, and Jeremiah, are written in Aramaic rather than Hebrew; and at one place we even find this request, which is symptomatic of the linguistic transition that had been going on: "Please, speak to your servants in Aramaic, for we understand it; do not speak to us in Judean [Hebrew]." The dozen or so references to the "Hebrew" language that occur in the New Testament really mean "Aramaic."

With the sacred text of the Tanakh in a language that was increasingly unintelligible to the worshiping congregation, Jewish liturgical practice had to resort to the use of Aramaic paraphrase and translation, known as Targum (meaning "translation"), which also became part of the normative tradition. After the reading of the text in the original Hebrew from the scroll of the Tanakh, another person would recite (not read) the Aramaic Targum of the prescribed reading. Then he or another officiant at the synagogue service would expound the text, as Jesus did in his hometown of Nazareth; or if there was a visitor with the necessary credentials, the officers might call upon him to do so, as they called on the apostle Paul in Antioch. The exposition was also in Aramaic, based on the Targum. A revealing passage from the Book of Nehemiah is thought to be a description of this process as it was going on within the worshiping community of Judaism already in the time of Ezra the scribe, which was in the fifth or fourth century BCE: "They read [in Hebrew] from the scroll of the Teaching [*Torah*] of God, translating it and giving the sense [in the Aramaic Targum]; so they understood the reading."

These Targums, too, were originally oral. Pupils received them from their masters, and apprentices from their mentors, and often sons from their fathers, as part of their training for the rabbinical office. In spite of the linguistic affinity and similarity between Hebrew and Aramaic—or, rather, precisely because of this similarity and affinity—such a "translation" had to be far more than a simple letter-

is amusing to note that the early Christian exegetes, while often objecting to rabbinic methods of interpretation as artificial and arbitrary, actually created their own Targum and Midrash, as when they quoted the words "The LORD reigns" with their addition, "from the tree"—that is, from the tree of the cross, which is not in the Hebrew or even in the Septuagint. And then they accused the Jewish interpreters of having distorted the biblical text by deleting this addition from the Psalms because it was such an obvious prophecy about the crucifixion of Christ.

APPLICATIONS AND AMPLIFICATIONS OF THE LAW

Also in Christian Bibles, the Book of Leviticus contains hundreds, even thousands, of minute hygienic, dietary, and ritual prescriptions that are laid down as binding law, enforceable on the faithful Jew sometimes to the point of death. It may be hard for someone to believe after having even looked at these, but no recipe book of conduct and observance, regardless of how meticulously detailed it might be or even how divinely inspired it was believed to be, could hope to cover all the contingencies and questions, both real and hypothetical, that might arise in the course of time for anyone who religiously strove to be able to say with the Psalmist,

> I have hurried and not delayed
> to keep Your commandments

—every single one of them. Many of these passages of the written Torah, moreover, presupposed social and political conditions that did not obtain at a later date, especially in the exile of Israel "by the rivers of Babylon" and later on (and to the present) in the Diaspora over all the globe. Even within the biblical period itself, divine commandments that had originally pertained to a nomadic people without a

fixed home were often difficult to apply to the urban society of the later Jewish monarchy. But at least the Judaism of that later biblical period was able to count on the living voice of the prophets as a guide to conduct in accordance with the Law. Now it had to rely on the tradition of Halakhah, which means "the right way to walk."

Halakhah, then, is the body of interpretations of the Law. To cite an important example: The law of the Sabbath, expanding on the earlier version of the Ten Commandments, specifically required:

> On six days work may be done, but on the seventh day you shall have a sabbath of complete rest, holy to the LORD; whoever does any work on it shall be put to death. *You shall kindle no fire throughout your settlements on the sabbath day.*

There therefore had to be detailed interpretations of what these prohibitory phrases "any work" and "no fire" covered and, consequently, what had to be done before sunset on Friday in preparation for the Sabbath. The specific reference to "fire" meant that the ceremonial candles had to be lit before the Sabbath evening began; in a modern industrial society, for example, electrical wires, as conductors of "fire" because it is at least potentially present, should not be carried on the Sabbath day. Some of the bitterest theological and political controversies in the State of Israel since 1948 have pertained to the applicability of the rabbinic Halakhah to the total life of a modern nation, with the religious parties lined up for strict construction and stringent enforcement against seemingly minor accommodations also in the law of the Sabbath. In the modern Diaspora, especially in the United States, Reform Judaism and Orthodox Judaism have diverged over these issues of the interpretation of the biblical laws and over the legitimacy of adjustments of traditional observance, such as kosher diet, to a predominantly Gentile culture.

Even more fundamentally, Halakhah as a body of biblical interpretation was made necessary by seeming inconsistencies or contradictions to be found within the text of the written Torah itself. On so

central a part of divine revelation as the celebration of Passover, the infinite details of which occupy almost half of the Halakhah, being observant required obedience to the strict command of the Fifth Book of Moses: "You are not permitted to slaughter the passover sacrifice in any of the settlements that the LORD your God is giving you; but at the place where the LORD your God will choose to establish His name, there alone . . . you shall cook and eat it," namely, at the Temple. But an earlier passage from the Second Book of Moses in the Torah identifies not the Temple in Jerusalem but the individual Jewish household as the place where the observant shall keep the Passover. "In joining the two conceptions," Jacob Neusner has explained, "with its rules for the household wherever it is located, the Halakhah has made a statement of its own out of the disharmonious facts received from Scripture. . . . The Israelite abode is treated as comparable to the Temple not merely in the aspect of cultic cleanness, but in the aspect of cultic activity."

Closely related to this problem is a similar contradiction between those same two portions of the Torah as they lay down other rules for the observance of the Passover. The original rule in the Second Book of Moses, which is part of what already before the exodus "the LORD said to Moses and Aaron in the land of Egypt," specifies concerning the Passover lamb: "Do not eat any of it raw, *or cooked in any way with water,* but roasted." But after the exodus, in the Fifth Book of Moses, in close connection with the command quoted earlier, the rule expressly states: "You shall cook and eat it." Already within the text of the Tanakh itself, and on almost its final page as the order of the books is arranged in the Hebrew canon, there is a resolution of this contradiction through combination or compromise: "They roasted the passover sacrifice in fire, as prescribed, while the sacred offerings they cooked in pots, cauldrons, and pans, and conveyed them with dispatch to all the people." With that as a scriptural model, the Halakhah in the Talmud was able to cope with similar contradictions and anomalies as these appeared throughout the text of the written Torah.

LEGENDS OF THE JEWS AND
"SAYINGS OF THE FATHERS"

Halakhah, as containing interpretations of the biblical Law, is generally distinguished from Haggadah, "narrative" or "biblical interpretation." Therefore, the materials of the Haggadah often have a direct appeal also to readers who do not stand in the Jewish tradition, including Christians, in a way that Halakhah, concerned so much with those aspects of the Pentateuch and its legislation that are not shared by other traditions, does not. The Tosefta is an especially rich source of Haggadic texts and, like most of the other materials being discussed in this chapter, has recently become available in English translation.

Under the title *Legends of the Jews,* published in English translation from 1909 to 1938, Louis Ginzberg assembled in seven volumes a selection of some of the most charming and most profound anecdotes usually identified as Haggadah. The title "The Sayings of the Fathers," *Pirqe Aboth,* a heading for one of the sections of the Mishnah, may also be used more broadly to identify a literary genre whose development can be traced from the canonical books of Proverbs and Ecclesiastes-Koheleth (both traditionally attributed to King Solomon) to the Apocryphal Book of Wisdom (likewise attributed to Solomon) and the Wisdom of Jesus Son of Sirach (Ecclesiasticus). There are many echoes (in one direction or the other) between the *Pirqe Aboth* and Sirach, and they may have come from a common source, perhaps originally from an oral source, like most of the material we have been describing here.

In a class by themselves among these interpretations of the sacred text of the Torah are the speculative mystical systems identified with the Kabbalah, which became a force also in Christian thought during the Renaissance and which continue to arouse interest among non-Jews. At their center is the contemplation and reflection on the Divine

Name as revealed to Moses at the burning bush, "Ehyeh-Asher-Ehyeh," which has been left untranslated in the body of the text of the Jewish Publication Society Version of the Tanakh, but is rendered in a footnote as "I Am That I Am." From its four consonants, YHWH, it came to be called the Tetragrammaton. For the Kabbalah and its practitioners, the Tetragrammaton is the key to the mystery of all Being, divine or created, but also the key to the meaning of the Bible.

THE UNIVERSALITY OF THE TORAH?

One of the persistent issues in the Talmud as continuing revelation is the universality of the Torah. The "one LORD" celebrated in the daily recitation of the Shema, "Hear, O Israel! The LORD is our God, the LORD alone" (Deuteronomy 6.4), was the God of Israel, but not in the same ethnocentric way that the idols were the gods of the Canaanites and other Gentiles:

> To Me, O Israelites, you are
> Just like the Ethiopians
>   —declares the LORD.
> True, I brought Israel up
> From the land of Egypt,
> But also the Philistines from Caphtor
> And the Arameans from Kir.

The God of Israel was not a tribal deity but the God of all the nations, the One and Only True God, which implied that there was a will of God for all the nations, not only for the people of Israel. Was that will identical with the Law of the Torah—with *all* the laws of the Torah and of the Halakhah? Or was it possible to identify, within that vast body of material, some commands and prohibitions that specifically could be said to apply to all the nations?

The Talmud finds the answer to those questions in the distinction between the Law as it was given in the Torah, written and oral, to Moses, and the Law as it had already been given to Noah, who was, because of the flood, the second Adam and the ancestor of the entire human race through his three sons, Shem, Ham, and Japheth; "and from these," the Torah explains, "the nations branched out over the earth after the Flood" to replenish the population of the earth and to become the new human race. To identify the pre-Mosaic Law as it came to Noah, the Talmud singles out seven violations of the will of God: worship of idols, profaning the name of God, murder, unlawful sex, theft, eating the meat of a living animal, and failure to enforce laws. In this identification the Talmud was setting forth the content of what would come to be known in later philosophy and theology as "natural law," that part of the content of the Law that did not depend either for its knowledge or for its force on the authority of a unique historical revelation from God, whether through Moses or through Jesus Christ, but that was knowable (and had historically been known) also to the Gentiles. This was a Christian as well as a Jewish concept and extended well beyond the orthodox boundaries of either of these communities, as the reference to "the laws of Nature and of Nature's God" in the American Declaration of Independence shows.

If this natural law did not depend on revelation, it had to have come through a universal tradition and/or through the use of human reason. In its more extreme form, such an appeal to the power of reason in relation to the Torah was an anticipation of the Jewish Enlightenment, the Haskalah. But already in the Talmud, and then in the commentators on the Talmud, there was much attention to the capacity of the human mind to discern the divine will on the basis of the structure of the universe and the cumulative experience of the human race. The very processes of reasoning that were at work in the questions and responses of the Talmudic sages, as well as the methods of analysis that were at work in the Jewish exegesis of the Tanakh (and in the Christian exegesis of Scripture), implied that the divine revelation of the Law, though written on tablets of stone for Moses,

was intended to be received through the more sensitive, though less durable, instrumentality of human speech and human thought.

Combined with the consistent emphasis of the Talmud on the oneness of God and the universality of the will of God for all humanity, this recognition prepared the students of the Talmud for an emphasis on the transcendent Law that was present within the written Torah and the oral Torah, but also beyond them. During the march for civil rights in twentieth-century America, therefore, it was not only Christian clergy such as the Reverend Martin Luther King, Jr., exegete of the Sermon on the Mount and disciple of Mahatma Gandhi, but scions of the Talmud such as Rabbi Abraham Joshua Heschel, exegete of the Hebrew Prophets and disciple of Rabbi Akiba, who spoke the truth to those in power, regardless of where (if anywhere) those in power were saying their prayers.

All of this tradition presupposes that commentary on a sacred text can be a supreme form both of obedience to God and of intellectual activity. As Leon Wieseltier has wisely observed:

> Anyone who knows the history of commentary knows that it was for many centuries, and in some ways still is— at least in the books that will really matter—one of the great intellectual opportunities for originality, indeed radicalism, of thought. Certainly the great works of Jewish philosophy are almost all of them works of scriptural commentary, from Philo through the medieval tradition, most notably through Maimonides and his *The Guide of the Perplexed* (which is the greatest single book ever written by a Jew).

And the same is true of the great works of Christian philosophy. Commentary and liturgy were two ways, greatly different and yet ultimately complementary, of making the sacred text contemporary.

Implicit throughout this chapter and strikingly evident repeatedly throughout this commentary material is the parallelism between these

ultra-Jewish methods of dealing with the message of the Bible and the styles of exegesis that have been developed by Christians in isolation from, and in hostility to, Judaism with all its works and all its ways. The more we understand that parallelism, the more profound are the affinities and the more tragic the mutual ignorance and misunderstanding. There is, therefore, some more than superficial sense in which the Talmud and the New Testament, together with the traditions of speculation, exegesis, and casuistry coming out of both, may be seen as alternative directions, so near to each other and yet so far from each other, in which the later interpretations of Torah and Tanakh could move, with Abraham as the father of both and Moses as the lawgiver of both—and, lest anyone forget, the One God of Israel, who is the Father of Jesus Christ, as the Lord (and the Judge) of both.

FIVE

The Law and the Prophets Fulfilled

"Starting from Moses and all the prophets, [the risen Christ] explained to them in the whole of scripture the things that referred to himself" (Luke 24.27): William Blake, *Christ Appearing to the Apostles after the Resurrection,* ca. 1795. (Courtesy of Yale Center for British Art, Yale Art Collection, Purchased 1929)

ccording to Judaism, the written Torah is made complete and fulfilled in the oral Torah, so that the Talmud is in many ways the Jewish counterpart to the New Testament—and not merely the Jewish counterpart to the canon law of the church. For "Christianity enters the world," as Reinhold Niebuhr once put it, "with the stupendous claim that in Christ (that is in both the character of Christ and the epic of his life) the expectations of the ages have been fulfilled. The specific form of this claim was the belief that the Kingdom of God had come, or in the words of Jesus, 'This day is this scripture fulfilled in your ears.'" Jesus spoke those words in his first public appearance, after he had read the book of the prophet Isaiah to the assembled congregation in the synagogue of his home city of Nazareth:

> The spirit of the Lord GOD is upon me,
> Because the LORD has anointed me;
> He has sent me as a herald of joy to the humble,
> To bind up the wounded of heart,
> To proclaim release to the captives,
> Liberation to the imprisoned;
> To proclaim a year of the LORD's favor.

What he was saying here, at the very inauguration of his public ministry, was that the prophetic words "upon *me*," "has anointed *me*," and "has sent *me*" had now at last been uniquely "fulfilled" in the person of Jesus of Nazareth. "*This day* is this scripture fulfilled in your

ears" meant that it had not been fulfilled before and that now it was being fulfilled in him "once and for all."

That "stupendous claim" that the Law and the Prophets had now been uniquely fulfilled by his coming is the theme of the early Christian tradition about Jesus from beginning to end. His miraculous conception and birth "happened in order to fulfill what the Lord declared through the prophet," meaning the Septuagint of Isaiah: "Therefore the Lord himself shall give you a sign: Behold, a virgin shall conceive, and bear a son, and shall call his name Immanuel." His escape to Egypt as an infant to avoid being murdered by King Herod "was to fulfill what the Lord had declared through the prophet: 'Out of Egypt I have called my son.'" Here the prophecy was one that in the original had clearly been intended to refer to the exodus of Israel from Egypt: "When Israel was a child, then I loved him, and called my son out of Egypt." Now it was being appropriated to have been "fulfilled" not in the history of the exodus, but in the history of the baby Jesus.

Also at the conclusion of his earthly ministry, Jesus was seen by early tradition as the "fulfillment" of the Law and the Prophets. In one of the earliest traditions about his resurrection, he says to his still unbelieving disciples, "How dull you are! Was not the Messiah bound to suffer in this way before entering upon his glory?" And "then," the tradition continues, "starting from Moses and all the prophets, he explained to them in the whole of scripture the things that referred to himself." A little later in another encounter, continuing the Bible class, the risen Christ "said to them, 'This is what I meant by saying, while I was still with you, that everything written about me in the law of Moses and in the prophets and psalms was bound to be fulfilled.' Then he opened their minds to understand the scriptures. 'So you see,' he said, 'that scripture foretells the sufferings of the Messiah and his rising from the dead on the third day.'" "The Messiah was *bound* to suffer" and "Everything was *bound* to be fulfilled" would seem to mean that it absolutely could not have been any other way, that those who did not comprehend this were simply "dull" and "slow to believe all that the prophets said." What they needed was to

have "their minds opened" and "the whole of scripture," the Law and the Prophets, "explained" to them in the light of the new reality of Jesus as Christ the Messiah, the fulfillment of the Law and the Prophets, so that "their minds would be opened to understand the scripture."

Such "explaining" and such "understanding" are the burden of the poignant encounter between one of the earliest Christian missionaries, the apostle Philip, and "a high official" from the court of the queen (or "kandake") of Ethiopia. Sitting in his chariot, the Ethiopian had been reading, presumably out loud and from the Greek Septuagint, another chapter from the prophet Isaiah:

> Like a sheep being led to slaughter,
> Like a ewe, dumb before those who shear her,
> He did not open his mouth.
> By oppressive judgment he was taken away,
> Who could describe his abode?
> For he was cut off from the land of the living.

Having heard him read this passage, Philip asked, "Do you understand what you are reading?" To which the Ethiopian replied, "How can I without someone to guide me? Please tell me, who is it that the prophet is speaking about here: himself or someone else?" Philip's answer was that Isaiah was not speaking about himself or about one of his contemporaries, but only about the person of Jesus Christ. The outcome of this encounter was that the Ethiopian official requested Christian baptism, confessing (according to one version): "I believe that Jesus Christ is the Son of God." The Ethiopian's question, "Who is it that the prophet is speaking about here?" and his plaintive petition, "How can I [understand] without someone to guide me?" are answered in the primal Christian tradition of prophecy fulfilled.

A principal bearer of that tradition was the apostle Paul. He began his life as Saul of Tarsus, one who accepted the Law and the Prophets without the fulfillment, as he writes in his miniature autobiography: "You have heard what my manner of life was when I was still a prac-

tising Jew: how savagely I persecuted the church of God and tried to destroy it; and how in the practice of our national religion I out-stripped most of my Jewish contemporaries by my boundless devo-tion to the traditions of my ancestors." A "heavenly vision" of Christ appeared to Saul as he journeyed to Damascus to carry on his savage persecution, and Saul of Tarsus was transformed into Paul, the "cho-sen instrument" of Jesus Christ. But the transformation did not mean that he gave up "our national religion." Quite the opposite. In his first public appearance after his conversion, he did just what Jesus had done at his first public appearance: "He proclaimed Jesus publicly in the synagogues, declaring him to be the Son of God" who had been promised in the Law and the Prophets. His missionary journeys even-tually took him to Athens and then to Rome. But in Athens, before arguing with "Epicurean and Stoic philosophers," he first "argued in the synagogue." And in Rome "he called together the local Jewish leaders, and when they were assembled, he said to them, 'My broth-ers, I never did anything against our people or against the customs of our forefathers. It is for loyalty to the hope of Israel that I am in these chains.' From dawn to dusk he put his case to them; he spoke urgently of the kingdom of God and sought to convince them about Jesus by appealing to the law of Moses and the prophets."

BAPTIZING THE TANAKH AS
THE CHRISTIAN BIBLE

In the earliest recorded Jewish-Christian dialogue, which was written around the middle of the second century CE (whether the dialogue ever actually took place or not), the Christian interlocutor, quoting proof texts from the Psalms and the Prophets, asks the Jewish inter-locutor: "Are you acquainted with them? They are contained in your Scriptures, or rather not yours, but ours. For we believe them; but you, though you read them, do not catch the spirit that is in them." This argumentation strikingly expresses the Christian belief, which is

at work already throughout the New Testament and through most of subsequent Christian history, that by the authority of prophecy and fulfillment the Jewish Scripture was now Christian Scripture and had been meant to be this all along because, as Eusebius, the first Christian historian, said, it was not a stretch to call Abraham a "Christian." The Christians expressed that belief by calling themselves not only "the new Israel" but "the true Israel," and eventually by calling the Tanakh "Old Testament," which is therefore being used for it in this book only when it is being referred to not as Jewish Scripture but as the first and longer part of the Christian Bible.

This claim that this Scripture was "ours" did not go unchallenged within the Christian movement itself. Speaking for what must have been a sizeable number of Christians in the second century and therefore gaining many adherents and even founding churches, the heretical Marcion of Pontus was devoted to celebrating the novelty and uniqueness of the message of the gospel. According to him, the God whom Jesus proclaimed as Father was a God of love but not of law, the Redeemer but not the Creator, revealed in the Epistles of Paul and the Gospel of Luke but not in the Jewish scriptures. Although it was an exaggeration when some historical scholars in the nineteenth century, on the basis of Marcion's idea of a New Testament that would replace the Old Testament, attributed to him the actual invention of a Christian canon of Scripture as distinct from the Jewish canon, he did help to make such a development necessary and to provoke it. His radical disjunction between the Creator God and the Savior threatened the monotheistic faith that was shared by Jews and Christians, and his resistance to the full implications of the church's insistence that Jesus was fully human, "tested in every way as we are, only without sinning," set him apart from the orthodox mainstream. But underlying these aberrant views, for which he was also condemned, was his extreme hostility to the Old Testament and to the standard Christian method of interpreting it. The church's rejection of Marcion's teaching on these several doctrinal issues also served to confirm the growing concept of the one Bible that consisted of the two Testaments.

The Jewish translation of Jewish Scripture into Greek, the Septuagint, became the Christian Bible. Its standing within the Jewish community, even in Alexandria where it had originated, gradually declined, at least partly, it would seem, because of the way Christians were using it to prove their distinctive interpretations. Conversely, the Septuagint acquired a special, indeed an inspired, status in the Christian church. There were several ways that the first generations of Christians interpreted the Septuagint Tanakh to apply it as Christian Scripture.

The simplest of these was the Christians' use of the Tanakh as a repository of maxims and general principles and as a source of examples and warnings. Christians remembered that when Satan the tempter addressed to Jesus the three questions in which, as Dostoevsky said, "the whole subsequent history of mankind is, as it were, brought together into one whole, and foretold, and in them are united all the unsolved historical contradictions of human nature," he responded by quoting the Book of Deuteronomy. To the tempter's challenge, "If you are the Son of God, tell these stones to become bread," he replied: "Scripture says, 'Man is not to live on bread alone, but on every word that comes from the mouth of God.'" Proving that he, too, could quote Scripture, the devil took him to a high place and put his second question, based on the Book of Psalms: "If you are the Son of God, throw yourself down; for scripture says, 'He will put his angels in charge of you, and they will support you in their arms, for fear you should strike your foot against a stone.'" To which the answer of Jesus was: "Scripture also says, 'You are not to put the Lord your God to the test.'" And when "the devil took him next to a very high mountain, and showed him all the kingdoms of the world in their glory," promising, "All these I will give you, if you will only fall down and do me homage," once again Jesus countered with the words of Deuteronomy: "Scripture says, 'You shall do homage to the Lord your God and worship him alone.'" Three temptations, but the same weapon against each: "Scripture says" (meaning the Torah). Those who wanted to be his followers were to use the same weapon against all temptations.

Indeed, the entire Tanakh: "The scriptures written long ago were *all* written for *our* instruction, in order that through the encouragement they give us we may maintain our hope with perseverance." The Book of Psalms, when baptized as Christian Scripture, provided not only hymns for corporate Christian worship but consolation to individual believers in sorrow and temptation. The sayings in the Book of Proverbs or Ecclesiastes or the Wisdom of Solomon were a source of wisdom for the aged and of guidance for the young. Above all, the Ten Commandments given to Moses would become, in later catechisms, the basis for the Christian instruction of children and adults about their moral duties. This necessitated a distinction between those elements of Old Testament law that continued to carry force also after the coming of Christ and those that had been "no more than a shadow," which referred either to the ceremonial rules applying to the Jewish liturgy or to the civil legislation pertaining to Israel as a political commonwealth.

Similarly, when Ecclesiastes warned that "there is not one good man on earth who does what is best and doesn't err," Christians could quote this universal warning as evidence "that all, Jews and Greeks alike, are under the power of sin." When Christians urged one another to "stand firm" in difficult times, the Tanakh provided them with the basis for saying, "You have heard how Job stood firm, and you have seen how the Lord treated him in the end, for the Lord is merciful and compassionate." But the Torah also contained examples aplenty of those who had not stood firm, and these could serve as universally applicable cautionary tales: "Do not be idolaters, like some of them; as scripture says, 'The people sat down to feast and rose up to revel.' Let us not commit fornication; some of them did, and twenty-three thousand died in one day. Let us not put the Lord to the test as some of them did; they were destroyed by the snakes. Do not grumble as some of them did; they were destroyed by the Destroyer."

Yet even in citing these stories from the Books of Exodus and Numbers "as warnings to us not to set our desires on evil things as they did," the Christians had begun to treat "all these things that happened to *them*" in previous ages as "symbolic," intended chiefly "as a

warning for *us,* upon whom the end of the ages has come." Beyond
the universally applicable words and examples, therefore, some parts
of the Law and the Prophets were seen as "types" and "foreshadowings," which had been real in and of themselves but were now finding their fuller meaning in Christ. Christ was the Second Adam,
undoing by his obedience the mortal damage that the First Adam had
done by his disobedience. (Very early this "typology" was extended
to Mary as the Second Eve, who said in her obedience what Eve in
her disobedience had failed to say: "Be it unto me according to thy
word.")

Many of these "foreshadowings," however, soon came to be seen
as having lost their original validity now that the foreshadowed reality had arrived. The observances prescribed in the Torah, as they were
to be systematized and elaborated in the Talmud—"what you eat or
drink, the observance of festival, new moon, or sabbath"—were all to
be dismissed now as "no more than a shadow of what was to come;
the reality is Christ's." The early identification of Jesus as, in the
words of the Psalm, "a priest for ever" and as "the Lamb of God,
who takes away the sin of the world"—therefore simultaneously and
uniquely both the sacrificial victim and the sacrificing priest—
became part of an elaborate scheme of interpretation by which the
liturgy prescribed in the Torah, especially Exodus and Leviticus, was
seen as having become obsolete now that the One it pictured had finally come into human history in the person of Jesus Christ. What
had been "*fore*shadowed" in the Torah had now been "*over*shadowed"
in him as the fulfillment.

Thus the fundamental category for the Christian interpretation of
the Old Testament was prophecy and fulfillment, as applied above all
to the life, death, and resurrection of Jesus Christ. Therefore, when
"Christ died for our sins," this was said to have occurred "in accordance with the scriptures"; and when "he was raised to life on the
third day," this, too, was regarded as having been "in accordance with
the Scriptures." Christians seized upon the mention of "wood" or
"tree" in an Old Testament passage to make it a prophecy of the crucifixion. Such prophecies as the oracle of Isaiah—

For a child has been born to us,
A son has been given us.
And authority has settled on his shoulders.
He has been named
"The Mighty God is planning grace;
The Eternal Father, a peaceable ruler"—
In token of abundant authority
And of peace without limit
Upon David's throne and kingdom,
That it may be firmly established
In justice and in equity
Now and evermore.
The zeal of the LORD of Hosts
Shall bring this to pass.

—which is so familiar from its appearance in Handel's *Messiah*, were taken up into the grand historical scheme, according to which the promises of the Old Testament had been meaningless before but now found their completion in the events of the New through the coming of Jesus Christ.

That historical scheme was greatly enhanced and facilitated by the Christian use of allegorical interpretation. Allegory had already been a standard part of the interpretation of ancient texts in both the Jewish and Greek traditions (where Homer's *Odyssey* had been an especially important resource), but Christians developed it beyond those modest beginnings. The precedent and authorization for their doing this came from the apostle Paul, who had argued on the basis of the Book of Genesis:

It is written that Abraham had two sons, the one by a slave, the other by a free-born woman. The slave's son was born in the ordinary course of nature, but the free woman's through God's promise. *This is an allegory:* the two women stand for two covenants. The one covenant comes from Mount Sinai; that is Hagar, and her children are born into slavery. Sinai is a

mountain in Arabia and represents the Jerusalem of today, for she and her children are in slavery. But the heavenly Jerusalem is the free woman; she is our mother.

The history and the imagery in the Old Testament became a fertile field for such allegorization from the early days of the church, and it would blossom in later centuries.

These several ways of seeing the Law and the Prophets as fulfilled in Jesus came together in the identification of him as "Messiah," the Anointed One, a Hebrew title that in Greek, already in the Septuagint, became "Christ." Christians who are so accustomed to this identification that they sometimes think of "Christ" as a personal name rather than a title are often surprised to find that it is in fact much less prominent than they might suppose it to be in the Tanakh, where "the term 'anointed' is never used of a future savior/redeemer, and in later Jewish writings of the period between 200 B.C. and A.D. 100 the term is used only infrequently in connection with agents of divine deliverance expected in the future." Nevertheless, as early as we have any knowledge of it, the Christian tradition was applying this title to Jesus; moreover, it was also, in unprecedented fashion, equating it with the title of "Suffering Servant" from Isaiah. Jesus the crucified and risen was "Messiah" *and* "King of glory" *and* "despised, shunned by men, a man of suffering"—all at the same time.

This baptism of the Tanakh and identification of the church with ancient Israel enabled the exponents and defenders of Christianity to claim a long and distinguished lineage, going back through the prophets to Abraham, Isaac, and Jacob, thus making the apparent novelty of the Christian gospel, beginning in the first century of the Common Era during the reign of the Roman emperor Augustus, actually the first and most ancient of all religions. Yet at some point this "stupendous claim" of prophecy and fulfillment could no longer function with the combination of written Tanakh and oral tradition as its composite authority, but had to develop its own written authority, which would embody the oral tradition but not exhaust it. That written authority was what we now call "the New Testament."

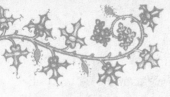

SIX

Formation of a
Second Testament

Papyrus fragment of Philippians 4.14–Colossians 1.2, early 3rd century CE: From
Frederic G. Kenyon, *The Chester Beatty Biblical Papyri* (London: Emery Walker
Limited, 1933), Plate 2. (© The Trustees of the Chester Beatty Library, Dublin)

lthough the usage of various languages, both ancient and modern, fluctuates between the singular term *Scripture* and the plural term *Scriptures,* as we have also been doing in the pages of this book, the plural predominates in the New Testament and is the more accurate designation because the Book is in fact made up of many books. But the Christian Bible is unlike the Jewish Tanakh in being permanently and unavoidably plural, consisting as it does of two quite separate though interlocking Testaments:

> The New is in the Old concealed,
> The Old is in the New revealed,

as the familiar Latin couplet said. The emergence of this novel concept of the one Bible that contains two Testaments has been correctly called the most momentous event in the history of early Christianity, even more far-reaching in its consequences than the conversion of the emperor Constantine. But it is an event that has also been no less momentous for the history of "the Bible through the ages" and for the history of the relations between Judaism and Christianity. The one Bible of the two Testaments was a Greek Bible (as can be seen in some of the greatest manuscripts such as the celebrated *Codex Sinaiticus*) and eventually a Latin Bible. But the idea of a Hebrew Tanakh and a Greek New Testament standing side by side on the bookshelf, which became a commonplace after the "return to the sources" in the Renaissance and the Reformation and still is in thousands of

studies and libraries (including the one in which this book is being written), was largely unknown. Thus it was both the canonization of a second, exclusively Christian Testament and the adoption of a version of the First Testament in a language other than the original that added to the separation of Jews and Christians even when they claimed to be obeying the same Law and reading the same Prophets and chanting the same Psalms, and quoting all of these in different languages at—or, rather, against—each other.

THE "NEW" TESTAMENT

The New Testament is by far the shorter portion of the Christian Bible, occupying less total space than the Psalms plus the major Prophets. Through its association with the spread of Christianity, however, the New Testament has wielded an influence far out of proportion to its modest size. Christians—and, for that matter, most general readers—are usually more familiar with the content of the New Testament, and more has been written about it, both by scholars or theologians and popular writers.

The New Testament is not a book but an entire library that includes a variety of early Christian literature in several quite distinct genres. The four canonical Gospels, survivors of a winnowing process whose scope we are only now beginning to recognize, deal with the life, the person, and the teachings of Jesus as he was remembered by the Christian community. The Book of the Acts of the Apostles, written by the author of the Gospel of Luke, carries the story of Christianity from the resurrection of Jesus to near the end of the career of Paul. The Epistles are letters by various leaders of the early church, chief among them the apostle Paul, applying the message of the church to the sundry needs and problems of the early Christian congregations. The Book of Revelation (the Apocalypse) is the only canonical representative of a large genre of apocalyptic literature that appeared in the Christian movement (and well beyond it). Common

to all these types of Christian literature is their setting within the communal life of early Christianity. Christian believers gathered together in homes, in Jewish houses of worship, and in public places. Knowing themselves to be part of a universal tradition that extended backward to the beginnings of time and forward to the glorious second coming of Christ, they nevertheless formed particular and local communities. Here they served those in need, studied the Law and the Prophets together, and shared in the sacraments. It was here, too, that they squabbled, often quite fiercely, as the Epistles to the Corinthians and Galatians amply document. That communal life is presupposed throughout, even in those New Testament passages that do not seem to reflect it. Its worship, its teaching, its use of the Old Testament, and its hope for the future are at work in the language and content of all the books in the New Testament, despite the diversity among them.

The setting of the New Testament within the Christian community is one factor that makes a "biography of Jesus" or a history of the first-century church so difficult or even impossible. As the tradition of the church had always maintained and as the modern study of the New Testament has confirmed, the twenty-seven books of the New Testament were composed not in order to satisfy historical curiosity about the events they recount but to bear witness to a faith in the action of God that took place through those events. A history of the New Testament is made difficult also by the relatively short time span covered by its books when compared with the millennium or so of history described by the Old Testament. There is less historical information in the New Testament than in the Old, and many historical facts about the church in the first century must be arrived at by inference from a statement in one of the Gospels or Epistles, with only occasional cross-references to the "secular" history of Rome, primarily in the Gospel of Luke and the Book of Acts. (This chapter discusses the books of the New Testament in the order in which they stand in Christian Bibles, which is neither simply chronological nor based only on their relative importance.)

THE GOSPELS

What the Torah is to the Tanakh, the Gospels are to the New Testament: the testimony of faith to the basic redemptive events and actions of God by which the believing community has been constituted. For the Torah these are the events surrounding the exodus from Egypt; for the Gospels they are the events surrounding Jesus Christ. The Gospels also share with the Torah the distinction of being that portion of the Scriptures to which the modern historical-critical study of the Bible since the eighteenth century has devoted the most detailed attention. Though they seem to be, and are, dependent for much of their material on one another (as well as on earlier traditional material, at least some of it oral), the first three Gospels are distinct books, each with its own purpose and structure; and the Fourth Gospel, whatever its origin, is more individual than any of the others. Seen as a composite, however, these four portraits form the basis for the rest of the New Testament. Other parts are earlier, and some may seem to our tastes more beautiful as literature or theologically more profound. But the Gospels occupy a special place in the outline of the Christian Bible as the presupposition for all subsequent history and instruction.

The Gospel of Matthew begins with the genealogy of Jesus, followed by an account of his birth and infancy. Its narrative of Jesus' public career opens with the story of his baptism, which is the public inauguration of his ministry, and with his temptation in the wilderness. The next major section of the Gospel presents the collection of sayings known as the Sermon on the Mount in the most complete version extant. It opens with the Beatitudes, "Blessed are the poor in spirit," and includes the Lord's Prayer. This summary of the teachings of Jesus has occupied a special place in the history of Christian reflection and proclamation, with commentaries on it by such theologians as John Chrysostom for the Greek tradition, Augustine for the Latin tradition, and Martin Luther for the Reformation tradi-

tion. The Sermon on the Mount is followed by a series of healing miracles and by the sending of the twelve disciples. The clash between Jesus and his adversaries, a series of parables, and the story of his repudiation at Nazareth, his home town, prompting the observation, "A prophet never lacks honor, except in his home town and in his own family," prepare the way for the second half of the Gospel. In this Jesus is represented as resolutely going up to Jerusalem with his disciples and preparing them for the events of his suffering by his warnings and examples (which go largely unheeded). His controversies with his Jewish opponents become more intense, and thus the Gospel sets the stage for the account of his suffering and death. This account now follows, containing some details that are not reported in the other Gospels. Matthew's Gospel concludes with a brief account of some of Jesus' appearances after the resurrection and with his "great commission" to extend the ranks of his disciples to all nations, which becomes the basis for the missionary expansion of Christianity through twenty centuries. Throughout the Gospel of Matthew there are many references to the Old Testament and quotations from it, leading many scholars to the conclusion that it was intended for Jews who had become Christian and for Jews who might consider doing so. On the basis of a few early reports it has sometimes even been supposed that Matthew originally wrote it in Aramaic, and alleged copies of this Aramaic original have periodically surfaced in Near Eastern bazaars; but the search for it has proved to be in vain.

The Gospel of Mark is the shortest and (in the opinion of most New Testament scholars) the earliest of the four Gospels. It has no data about Jesus' beginnings at all but plunges *in medias res* with his ministry of miracles and teaching, inaugurated by his baptism at the hands of John the Baptist. The early chapters contain miracles of feeding, healing, and power over natural forces, as well as a number of parables. Like Matthew, Mark devotes the middle chapters to preparation for the story of the crucifixion. Jesus is seen as warning his disciples of the impending events, as entering Jesusalem and cleansing its temple, and as predicting the end of the city and the world. The last chapters of the Gospel contain a narrative of the last days of Jesus on

earth, of his capture and execution, and of his appearances after the resurrection. In the middle of telling about these appearances, the text of the Gospel breaks off rather abruptly with the words: "They said nothing to anyone, for they were afraid." At least two attempts, the so-called long endings of Mark, were made in the early church to fill out the story, and modern editions in English usually present them together, sometimes as an appendix or a footnote, for the reader to make the choice. If the emphasis of Matthew is on Jesus as the fulfillment of Old Testament prophecy, the emphasis of Mark is less on this fulfillment than on Jesus as the worker of mighty deeds.

The Gospel of Luke contains much material that is in neither Matthew nor Mark. It opens with stories about the birth and the early life of Jesus that are unique to it, and to these it adds its own genealogy. The baptism and the temptation of Jesus form the prelude to his ministry. This ministry is described first in its Galilean phase, which includes many miracles of healing as well as some instruction, part of which is Luke's shorter version of the Sermon on the Mount (the Sermon on the Plain), which, for example, simply has "Blessed are you who are in need" instead of Matthew's "Blessed are the poor *in spirit*." There follows the largest single section of the Gospel, recounting the travels of Jesus through Samaria, Judaea, and Perea. Some of the material in this section appears elsewhere, but much of it is peculiar to Luke—for example, the parable of the prodigal son, who went away from home to "waste his substance in riotous living" and then returned and was accepted by his forgiving father. Like Matthew and Mark, Luke prefaces his version of the passion story with an account of Jesus' activities in Jerusalem in the last days, as "he set his face resolutely towards Jerusalem." His account of the passion contains some facts that are absent from the other Gospels, and his reports of the appearances of Jesus after the resurrection are particularly detailed, especially the encounter at the village of Emmaus, during which, "starting from Moses and all the prophets, he explained to them in the whole of scripture the things that referred to himself." The Gospel of Luke seems to have been written for Christians of non-Jewish origin, of whom the otherwise unknown Theophilus ad-

dressed in the salutation both of the Gospel and of the Book of Acts was a representative. One of its purposes seems to have been to show that neither Jesus Christ nor his followers could justly be accused of sedition against Rome.

The Gospel of John has very little in common with any of the other Gospels. After its famous prologue, dealing with the incarnation of the Word of God, the Gospel narrates the adult life of Jesus around the framework of several Jewish festivals. Thus it is from this Gospel that the supposition of three years, more or less, as the duration of Jesus' public ministry is derived. From the first three Gospels it would be easy to conclude, as early Christian theologians such as Irenaeus of Lyons did in the second century, that it lasted for only one year or so. Into the first year this Gospel seems to put the early miracles of Jesus, the cleansing of the temple (assigned to the last days of Jesus by the other Gospels), and activity in both Judaea and Galilee. As this Gospel seems to reckon the chronology, the second year contains much of the Galilean ministry recounted by the other Gospels. Most of the Gospel of John is concerned with the third year, into which it seems to put the majority of its discourses. In addition to details of the passion that appear elsewhere, the Fourth Gospel presents the closing words of Jesus to his disciples in the upper room, such as "Peace is my parting gift to you, my own peace, such as the world cannot give," and his last "high-priestly" prayer to the Father before his suffering. In the usage of the Christian church and in the spiritual life of individual believers, these have been among the most precious of the mementos of the life and teaching of Jesus. "Let not your hearts be troubled: ye believe in God, believe also in me. In my Father's house are many mansions," together with "The Lord is my shepherd: I shall not want," are words that have been recited, often from memory, at many a deathbed. Most of the material in the resurrection accounts of John is also unique to this Gospel. Interpreters are not in agreement about whether the Gospel intends its framework to be chronological or symbolic, but they are agreed in assigning it a distinctive place among the four portraits of Jesus.

From the reference at the beginning of the Gospel of Luke to the "many" who already had undertaken to write accounts of what Jesus

was and did, and then from the occasional citations (usually disparaging) in ancient Christian writers of the second and third centuries, it has been known all along that these four Gospels included within the covers of the canonized New Testament were by no means the only ones written. But only in the twentieth century have several others surfaced, including the Gospel of Thomas and the Gospel of Philip (both of them found in Coptic versions at Nag Hammadi in Egypt in 1945–46), evoking various reactions from both the scholarly community and the general public. The intense scholarly debate over these extracanonical Gospels since their discovery has concentrated on their relation to the canonical Gospels. Many of the sayings of Jesus in the Gospels of Thomas and of Philip are parallel to what we have in the New Testament; some of them may well have been part of the oral tradition on which all Gospels drew; and, in the judgment of some interpreters, other sayings reflect the origin and use of these books in communities that stood outside the "normative" Christian movement as this developed during the first two or three centuries. The most striking difference of the Gospel of Thomas is that it does not contain the sort of detailed accounts of the suffering and death of Jesus that dominate Matthew, Mark, Luke, and John. Whether or not it was for these reasons, these books were not included even in the earliest known collections that became our New Testament. In spite of this—or, in some instances, precisely because of this—they have appealed to those readers who have found the canonical version of the life of Jesus unbelievable or unacceptable or both, while to more orthodox Christians of various denominations these very qualities of novelty have been seen as a vindication of the process of selection through which the early church sorted out its canon.

THE ACTS OF THE APOSTLES

Written as a continuation of the Gospel of Luke and by the same unidentified author, the Acts of the Apostles is also a link between

the Gospels and the Epistles, especially because of its information about the apostle Paul. The ascension of Christ and the coming of the Holy Spirit introduce the story of the growth of Christianity. In the early chapters of the book, the dominant figure is Peter, who is the spokesman for the church and the leader of the twelve apostles. In this Peter was carrying out the special position that Jesus assigns to him in the Gospels when he says, "You are Peter, the Rock; and on this rock I will build my church," which would be of such importance during the following centuries in the development of authority that led to the supremacy of the Papacy. The preaching and the martyrdom of Stephen close this description of the congregation at Jerusalem and provide a transition to the main section of the Acts, the ministry of Paul to the Gentiles. A heavenly vision is instrumental in converting Paul, and another convinces Peter that the gospel is intended for Gentiles as well as Jews.

Most of the remaining chapters describe the missionary journeys of Paul. Beginning as Saul of Tarsus, a Pharisee who fiercely persecutes Christians, Paul is converted by Christ appearing on the road to Damascus and becomes a fervent apostle for Jesus Christ and the Christian message. After that his life is one of unceasing activity as he and his associates cover much of Asia Minor and parts of Europe, including Athens, preaching to Jews and to Gentiles. The missionary practice on those journeys raises once more the question of applying the Levitical regulations to Gentile converts, and a council at Jerusalem has to settle the question dealing with the very questions—and some of the same solutions—that are raised in the Talmud about the universality of the Torah. On a subsequent visit to Jerusalem, Paul is involved in a riot and appeals to his Roman citizenship. As a result he appears before various Roman officials; after delays, including a shipwreck, the frenetic narrative reaches its historic climax in the words: "And so to Rome!" Here the book leaves him, and the denouement of the story—a legendary journey to Spain and the much more reliable account that he was martyred in Rome under the emperor Nero—must be supplied from the Pauline Epistles and from subse-

quent tradition. Neglected though it has sometimes been, having been the subject of many fewer commentaries than the Gospel of John or the Epistle to the Romans, the Book of Acts performs for the New Testament something of the same function that is performed for the Tanakh by its historical books. Without it, readers of the Epistles would frequently lose their orientation.

THE EPISTLES

By far the largest number of writings in the New Testament are the Epistles, twenty-one in all. Most of them were composed in response to a specific need in one of the first-century Christian congregations, but one or more of them seem to have been circular letters intended for several congregations, perhaps even with the name of the addressee inserted and then changed. More than half of them are ascribed to Paul, although critics have questioned this ascription in some cases.

The Epistle to the Romans has the most complete statement of Paul's teaching contained in any one letter. Throughout Christian history, reform movements, and not just the one we usually call "the Reformation" in the sixteenth century, have been provoked by a fresh reading of this Epistle. From the demonstration of the universality of human guilt it moves to the doctrine of justification, exhibited in the faith of Abraham. Next the apostle discusses the new life that comes in justification together with his own struggles of faith. Consideration of this leads him to ponder the mystery of how "the whole of Israel will be saved" and of divine election—a discussion that for some reason has had far more influence on various Christian doctrines of predestination than it has had on Christian views of Judaism. The second part of the Epistle lists some of the concrete personal and social situations in which the new life is to find expression. First Corinthians describes some of the problems that were afflicting early Christian communities: schism and an overemphasis on the eloquence of certain preachers, sexual immorality, eating meat offered to

idols, discrimination and other disorders at the Lord's Supper, confusion because of the gift of tongues, and denial of the resurrection. In contrast to all of these, it celebrates the supreme greatness of love in chapter 13, which, as "the hymn to love," has been memorized and quoted even by those who do not claim to stand in the continuity of the faith of the church. Second Corinthians, too, considers the problems of the congregation, but not in such detail. It consists largely of a vindication of Paul's apostolic ministry against his detractors and a commendation of the generosity of the Corinthian congregation.

Vindication of Paul's apostolic ministry is likewise a major theme of the Epistle to the Galatians, which distinguishes between the Christian gospel and the Jewish law even more sharply than does the Epistle to the Romans. It is thus a defense of Christian liberty and an exhortation to hold on to it. The Epistle to the Ephesians also seems to have been occasioned by the problem of Jewish-Christian relations, but here the theme is the unity of Jew and Gentile as "fellow-citizens with God's people" in the one church of which Christ is the head. The Epistle then applies that unity to the ethical life of Christians, especially to marriage and the family. The Epistle to the Colossians has much in common with Ephesians, and the literary relationship between them has been a puzzle to New Testament scholars. Like Ephesians, Colossians concentrates its attention on the nature of the church as "the body of Christ"; but it seems to have been evoked by a denial of the church's view of Christ, and therefore the close connection of Christ and the church receives a new emphasis, as does the larger context of that connection, in a vision of the cosmic Christ in whom all things hold together. The Epistle to the Philippians is one of the more personal of Paul's letters. After describing his personal feelings for the church at Philippi in Macedonia, he holds up the humility of Christ as an exemplar for its members and recounts his own faith and experience. On the basis of this he urges them to fulfill their Christian vocation.

The First Epistle to the Thessalonians, like Philippians, has a strongly personal tone. It describes the history of Paul's relation with the congregation at Thessalonica and then sets forth the second com-

ing of Christ as a comfort to those who were mourning the death of their fellow Christians. Second Thessalonians seems to have been intended chiefly as a corrective for the impression created by 1 Thessalonians. Expectation of the second coming of Christ had unsettled the congregation, and therefore the writer (who uses the name Paul, although many critics doubt that Paul was the author) describes some of the events that had to precede the advent of Christ, especially the rise of the Antichrist; he concludes with an admonition to steadiness and industry.

The so-called Pastoral Epistles are written in the form of advice from the apostle Paul to two young associates, Timothy and Titus. Since the beginning of the nineteenth century their authorship by Paul has been widely questioned by biblical scholars. The First Epistle to Timothy urges Timothy to "keep safe what has been entrusted to you," the deposit of the faith, against false teachers and to conduct his ministry according to the instruction and the example of Paul. Second Timothy also counsels him to be steadfast in the conflict with false teachers, and it adds some personal notes about Paul as he faces "the hour for my departure" and martyrdom. In the Epistle to Philemon, Paul pleads the cause of a runaway slave, Onesimus, and asks that he be treated kindly by his master; but it bears mentioning, in relation to the later history of emancipation, that he does not demand that Onesimus be set free.

The Epistle to the Hebrews has sometimes been attributed to Paul, but the vast majority of scholars would not maintain that Paul wrote it, nor was it the consensus of early tradition that he did; neither does it carry his name. With many echoes of the way of reading the Tanakh that was characteristic of Alexandrian Judaism, it is an elaborate argument for Christianity as the successor of Judaism. To support this argument it describes the superiority of Christ to the angelic and human mediators of the old covenant. It is especially concerned with showing that he is superior to the priests of the Old Testament and that his sacrifice is permanent while theirs was temporary. The Epistle concludes with an exhortation to follow the example of the heroes of faith, past and present, in what has often been

called "the roll call of the saints," which includes, interestingly, not only lives of saints from the canonical books of the Tanakh but some incidents from the Apocrypha (and other sources).

The seven remaining letters in the New Testament are often grouped as the "Catholic [general or universal] Epistles." The Epistle of James seeks to combat the notion that the free grace of God makes good works unnecessary, and it contrasts a false religion of outward Christian profession with the true religion of Christian service; harmonizing it with the Epistle to the Romans therefore proved to be a major task for the Protestant Reformers of the sixteenth century. The First Epistle of Peter encourages Christians in the midst of suffering by describing their prerogatives as recipients of God's inheritance, and it urges them to live so blamelessly that if they do suffer, it will be for their loyalty to Christ and not for any failure in morals. Second Peter is much different in character and purpose. It warns its readers against false teachers who have come into the church, describing both their heresies and the horrible fate that awaits them. The Epistle of Jude contains the same warning and seems to be echoed in 2 Peter. First John also directs itself against the false teachers, but it places this warning in the context of a discussion about love. Reflection of God's love in human life and a proper confession of Jesus as the Christ are, taken together, the marks of the true Christian. Second John is another admonition to beware of false teachers and to practice Christian charity. Third John is a brief letter of recommendation for one Demetrius, addressed to one Gaius.

THE BOOK OF REVELATION

The last book of the New Testament and of the Bible, the Revelation to John, or Apocalypse, consists of a series of visions granted to the writer and now communicated by him to several Christian congregations in Asia Minor. In these visions, whose details have always caused consternation to students of the Bible, the seer glimpses the eventual victory of the church over its enemies through the power of

Christ, the Lamb of God, but only after a bitter conflict. The victory is to lead to "a new heaven and a new earth" and to the destruction of the enemies of the church. Written to churches that faced the twin perils of persecution and indifference, these visions were intended to strengthen their hope and their resolution. Some of the most vivid chapters in the history of biblical interpretation have risen from the Book of Revelation. Above all, the prediction of a binding of Satan and a reign of Christ that would last a thousand years has inspired graphic expectations of the end in both art and spirituality, including William Blake's haunting *Vision of the Last Judgment* and countless eruptions of false expectations, making this in many ways the most controversial book of the Bible.

THE CHRISTIAN BIBLE IN
THE CHRISTIAN CHURCH

Several factors seem to have been responsible for the formation of a second "testament" in the church alongside the Old Testament. One factor certainly was the sheer passage of time, as the church needed to discover whatever resources it could to bind it to its past and to guarantee its continuance in the tradition of the faith. Together with the codification of the tradition in creeds and liturgies, as well as the growth of the office of bishop into a monarchical episcopate, the "memoirs of the apostles" were such a resource for continuity. Also responsible for the establishment of the canon was the circulation of writings that bore the names of apostles but did not contain apostolic teaching (as that apostolic teaching was being defined by the church in its creed and enforced by its bishops); as has been noted, some of these rejected writings, notably the Gospel of Thomas and the Gospel of Philip, went underground and have surfaced only in very recent times. The task of sifting through the writings purporting to come from the apostolic generation occupied Christians well into the fourth century. In the early fourth century the church historian Eusebius of Caesarea suggested the following division of these writings:

some that were acknowledged almost universally as part of the New Testament; others that were disputed but finally accepted; still others that were considered in one or another part of the church with greater or lesser seriousness but were eventually rejected.

ACKNOWLEDGED BOOKS AND DISPUTED BOOKS

The earliest pieces of Christian literature to be collected seem to have been the letters of Paul. From the liturgical use of the church at Rome it would appear that the Gospels were the first Christian books to be added to the Old Testament as supplementary Scripture, and that this had happened by the middle of the second century. Also from Rome, and also apparently from the second century, comes the oldest extant list of New Testament writings, the Muratorian fragment, so named because it was first published by Ludovico Muratori in 1740 from an early medieval Latin manuscript that was based on earlier documents. It contains the names of the books that were being read in the church at Rome in about 200 CE. By about that time, as the writings of early Christian authors from Lyons, Carthage, and Alexandria also suggest, the Gospels, the Epistles of Paul, and some other Epistles were being used as Scripture. From these sources we may gather a list of books on which they all seem to have been agreed. That list would include the following, given in the order now employed in the New Testament: Matthew, Mark, Luke, John, Acts, Romans, 1 Corinthians, 2 Corinthians, Galatians, Ephesians, Philippians, Colossians, 1 Thessalonians, 2 Thessalonians, 1 Timothy, 2 Timothy, Titus, Philemon, and 1 John.

From these same sources we may also assemble a list of those books that were disputed but that eventually were included in the canon of the New Testament. The Epistle to the Hebrews belongs in this category. It seems to have been accepted in the Eastern section of the church but disputed in the West, for it does not appear in the Muratorian canon and is also questioned by other writers. The Epistle of James was in doubt among even more writers. Although 1 Peter is al-

most universally acknowledged, it is not listed in the preceding paragraph because of its absence from the Muratorian catalog. Second Peter, on the other hand, was questioned by many early Christian writers who accepted 1 Peter. The Epistle of Jude appears in the Muratorian canon but was rejected elsewhere. Second John and 3 John sometimes were included with 1 John as one book, but they did not receive the universal support that it did. The Book of Revelation probably was the object of more antagonism than any other of the books eventually canonized, partly because apocalypticism acquired a bad name through its association with heretical and schismatic movements very early in Christian history and partly because some did not believe that the same man who had written the Gospel of John was also the author of Revelation. In general, the books that came to be acknowledged as "canonical" were associated in one way or another with the name of an apostle; this helps to explain the inclusion of the Epistle of Jude. On the other hand, the Epistle to the Hebrews does not carry the name of any apostle (the attribution of it to Paul being later, as we have noted); but its sheer power seems to have provided persuasive evidence that if there was to be a normative collection of Christian writings from the generation of the apostles, this book had to be part of it regardless of who composed it.

FORMATION OF THE NEW TESTAMENT CANON

The writings of Eusebius and of his contemporary, Athanasius of Alexandria, make it evident that agreement on the disputed books was approaching by the middle of the fourth century and that the canon of the New Testament which now appears in Christian Bibles was gaining general, if not quite universal, acceptance. That canon appears for the first time in a letter of Athanasius issued in 367 CE.

After that letter other traditions held their own for a time. Thus the scholars and theologians of Antioch in general accepted only three Catholic Epistles—James, 1 Peter, and 1 John—while one of its most illustrious representatives, Theodore of Mopsuestia, rejected the

whole of this section of the canon. The West followed the lead of Athanasius. In 382 a synod was held at Rome under Pope Damasus, at which the influence of Jerome secured the adoption of a list of books answering to that of Athanasius. This was ratified by Pope Gelasius at the end of the fifth century. The same list was confirmed independently for the province of Africa at Hippo Regius in 393 and at Carthage in 397 and 419 under the leadership of Augustine of Hippo. The second canon of the Second Trullan Council of 692, known to canon lawyers as the Quinisext, may be taken to have formally closed the process of the formation of the New Testament canon for East and West. This stands in sharp contrast to the status of the Old Testament canon within the church, which was not acted upon by an "ecumenical" church council until the Council of Trent in 1546 and then in a way that has gone on being disputed because of the status of the Apocrypha.

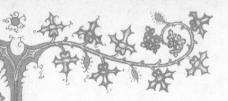

SEVEN

The Peoples of the Book

Portrait of Saint Jerome from a 13th-century Parisian manuscript of the Vulgate. (From the collection of the Bridwell Library, Perkins School of Theology, Southern Methodist University)

e have really everything in common with America nowadays," the British wit and man of letters Oscar Wilde once commented; but then he added, with a characteristic twist: "except, of course, language." For it has often been observed that the British and the Americans are kept apart by a common language, which both of them nevertheless call "English." But according to that eminent authority on language, Professor Higgins in *My Fair Lady*, "The Americans haven't spoken it for years." Yet such one-liners should not be permitted to obscure the paradox that sharing a common language really can be a surprisingly divisive force.

The divisive power of a mutual *ignorance* of languages is familiar enough to everyone, from tourists shopping for souvenirs to diplomats trying to craft a treaty or even a simple memorandum of understanding. It can be humorous, as when an American visitor in Paris looking for a bookstore is puzzled to find only *librairies*. It can also be tragic, as when foreign service staff who were posted to countries where they did not speak the language have gratuitously insulted their hosts by misunderstanding a word or mispronouncing the name of their host and turning it into an obscenity.

SEPARATED BY A COMMON LANGUAGE

When we have finished tittering over such blunders, some of us will usually launch into a tirade about the dangers of neglecting the study

of foreign languages and about the precipitous decline in such study that has marked recent decades. How much better the nations of the world would understand one another, we regularly urge, if only they all knew what those "others" are saying, unfiltered through a translation. True enough. But the historical situation is considerably more complicated, as just one example from recent headlines will suffice to show. Serbian and Croatian, the two principal languages of the former Yugoslavia, are essentially one language, with relatively minor historical and local variations. But Serbian is written in the Cyrillic alphabet while Croatian is written in the Latin alphabet, because in the cultural and religious turmoil following the Christianization of the Slavs, which began in the ninth century, the Croats sided with Rome, defended the authority of the pope over all the churches, and worshiped with the Latin Mass (and therefore are denominated "Roman Catholic"), whereas the Serbs supported Constantinople, asserted the autonomy of each national church, and prayed the Liturgy in Church Slavonic (and hence are "Eastern Orthodox"). They speak basically the same language—which means they can understand each other very well when they call each other some of those obscene and quite untranslatable names, and they are kept apart by a common language. Sometimes it almost seems as though the peoples of the Balkans might get along better if only they could *not* understand each other's languages so well.

So also during the "Middle Ages," both in Western Europe and in the Eastern Roman so-called Byzantine Empire, rabbinical scholars and Christian scholars were kept apart by a common text, whether they called it *Tanakh* in Hebrew or *Graphē* in Greek or *Biblia Sacra* in Latin. Of course, names such as Moses and David and Jeremiah were the same in all three, or at least similar enough to be recognizable, and words such as "Amen" and "Hallelujah" (with slight variations in how they were pronounced) were common liturgical property in all three forms of worship. As this suggests, one of the reasons the Bible kept them apart was that the rabbis were reading it in Hebrew, the Byzantines in Greek (including the Old Testament in the Greek Sep-

tuagint rather than in Hebrew), and the Western monks in Latin (rather than in Hebrew or in Greek). It takes a lifetime of trying to make sense of these three ancient languages—not to say, of trying to make English of them—to appreciate fully the vastly different thought worlds (which sometimes seem to be entire universes) that they represent. For example, the system of "tenses" in Hebrew does not really correspond to the ones familiar to us in any of the Indo-European languages, including English. Therefore the same Hebrew verb in the Psalms was translated with the perfect tense in Latin, "I have lifted up my eyes to the hills" (and the Psalm was therefore called *Levavi*), but in the English of the Jewish Publication Society Version it is translated with the present, "I turn my eye to the mountains," and in the King James Version as "I will lift up mine eyes unto the hills."

After various early attempts at a Latin translation of the Bible, in whole or in part (which are conventionally and imprecisely lumped together under the title "Old Latin," *Vetus Latina*), the assignment of bridging the chasm between Latin and the biblical languages in a definitive version fell to Jerome—or, to give him his full proper name, Eusebius Hieronymus—at the end of the fourth and the beginning of the fifth century. Fortunately—or even providentially—Jerome was quite simply the greatest scholar of his time in the West. Almost uniquely among his contemporaries and successors, he was a "three-language man," as Augustine once called him with an unmistakable envy for his command of Latin, Greek, and Hebrew. Augustine himself—of whom it has been said that "whether Augustine be the greatest Latin writer or not, he is the greatest man who ever wrote Latin"—had only a fragmentary knowledge of Greek and a second-hand acquaintance with Hebrew (plus just a smattering of some North African "Punic" dialects).

Originally, Jerome continued the practice of his anonymous predecessors in basing his revision of the Latin translation of the Tanakh on the Greek text of the Septuagint, which he knew to possess a high and authoritative standing (as it still does today) among the Greek-speaking theologians and scholars in the Eastern parts of what was

then still the undivided church. But deeper study, which had also been stimulated (or, rather, had been provoked) by the challenges of rabbis to the accuracy of the Septuagint and therefore to the correctness of Christian interpretations that were based on the Septuagint, led Jerome to a recognition of what he called the *Hebraica veritas,* "the truth in Hebrew." At the urging of Pope Damasus he carried out the task of a new translation of the Tanakh into Latin that would be based on the original Hebrew. For his revision of the New Testament, Jerome of course used the Greek text, completing the text of the Gospels in 384 but probably not being able to finish all of the remaining books. Jerome's regard for "the truth in Hebrew" also led him to regard the Apocrypha as secondary in value and authority to the Jewish canon, but that opinion remained a decided minority throughout the Middle Ages, which preferred Augustine's distinction between "the Jewish canon" and "the church's canon"; and Jerome did translate the Apocrypha as part of the Latin Bible.

THE VULGATE

At some point in its subsequent history Jerome's Latin translation of the Bible acquired the name "Vulgate" (which, of course, does not mean "vulgar" at all but something closer to our term "vernacular," Latin being the vernacular language of international communication across medieval Europe in commerce and law, scholarship and worship). This nomenclature does have its own whimsical side because the campaign for the use of the vernacular in the Bible and in the liturgy, both during the Protestant Reformation of the sixteenth century and during the debates surrounding the Second Vatican Council of the Roman Catholic Church in the twentieth century, has usually pitted "vernacular" against "Vulgate" even though originally they were almost synonymous terms. Although it became fashionable in the period of the Renaissance and Reformation to ridicule the shortcomings of Jerome's translation and to challenge the official theolog-

ical interpretations that were grounded (without a knowledge of the original) in its idiosyncracies, this must not be permitted to obscure its monumental influence or its enormous literary and religious power. To anyone who approaches it from a background in Vergil and Cicero—Jerome once had a dream in which God reproved him for being more of a "Ciceronian" than a "Christian"—its historical narratives are paced and vivid, its poetry is lyrical and moving, and its prophetic passages are thunderous and rhetorical.

The Vulgate was *the* Bible of Europe for over a thousand years, and it was the mother lode of the Latin Mass. Those who, from the perspective of the Protestant Reformation with its doctrine of "the Bible only," criticize the Middle Ages for having neglected the study of the Bible should examine the text of the Latin Mass with a concordance to the Vulgate in hand. Phrase by phrase, sometimes single word by single word, it is a daisy chain of biblical quotations; and the Ave Maria, often attacked for its "Mariolatry," strings together the Vulgate of verses from the Gospel of Luke.

But when Cyril and Methodius came from Constantinople in the ninth century as "the apostles to the Slavs," they did not teach their converts Greek but translated the Gospel and the liturgy into Slavonic, inventing an alphabet for that purpose. In the West, by contrast, when the Franks or the Lombards or the Celts became Catholic Christians, they had to learn Latin—at least enough Latin to pray the Pater Noster and to sing the Creed. As a cultural by-product, the Latin of the Vulgate provided to those who learned it well at least some access to all Latin, to the Roman classics and the legal tradition; and it thus became a way to inherit the tradition of Western civilization. At the same time, and more important for its patrons in the church, it was the avenue to the tradition of Moses and the prophets, of Jesus and the apostles, of Cyprian and Augustine. Nevertheless, the Latin of the Vulgate was at the same time a wall of separation, dividing its adherents from those who were reading the Bible in Greek (the Christians of Constantinople, from whom they became separated around the eleventh century, 1054 being the date given in

the textbooks) as well as from those who were reading it in Hebrew (Jews but almost no Christians, not even scholars, except for a few daring souls and some occasional converts to Christianity from Judaism).

The need to have manuscripts of the Bible, or certainly of the lessons that were appointed for reading at Mass on Sunday or of the Psalms for the hours of prayer in the monastic houses, meant that manufacturing Latin Bibles became a major cottage industry—or, to be a bit more precise, a monastery industry. In the Middle Ages in the West, the transmission of the text of the Latin Vulgate—and of most other Latin texts, classical as well as Christian—was primarily the work of Benedictine monks throughout Western Europe. The monastic ideal of combining prayer and work, "the love of learning and the desire for God," found a splendid expression in the scriptorium, where scribes at their desks copied the text, usually as it was being dictated to them from a master copy. The scribes evolved an elaborate system of abbreviations, which we now have to learn to decipher. Unfortunately, they also developed the nasty habit of discarding the old copy once the new ones had been made: Who wanted a scruffy old manuscript when there were these bright and shiny new ones in clear ink on clean vellum? Alternately, they used the parchment of the old copy as the binding for a book, so that now we sometimes have to try to reconstruct a Vulgate manuscript from widely scattered remains, with half of a Psalm being found in Spain and the other half in Austria. And, of course, since "to err is human," as a Latin proverb they used to recite would remind them, they sometimes misheard what was being dictated, or what was being dictated was misread or mispronounced, or it was wrong in the first place, or they remembered an earlier version and substituted it for what had just been dictated, or they copied it twice—or they did all of the above. Therefore, alongside all the variants in the manuscripts that were responsible for the rise of the textual criticism of the Greek New Testament, the text of the Vulgate, too, gradually became confused and corrupt, and thus often separated still further from the original words of the Bible in Hebrew and Greek.

SEPARATE TRADITIONS OF INTERPRETATION

Even more divisive than the difference of languages (though not un-related to it) was the difference of the interpretations assigned to the text, particularly the difference between Jews and Christians now that the Tanakh had come to be regarded by Christians not as "your Scripture" but rather as "ours." The two systems of interpreting Tanakh or Old Testament, the Talmudic and the Christian as repre-sented by the New Testament, traveled on separate tracks with only occasional instances of influence across the chasm. Perhaps the best example of such an influence and of the contribution it could bring—or could have brought if there had only been a great deal more of it—can be seen in the work of the great Jewish biblical in-terpreter Rashi, who lived in the eleventh century CE, and two cen-turies later the great Christian biblical interpreter Nicholas of Lyra.

Rashi (which is an acronym constructed from "Rabbi Shlomo Ben Itzakh") combined a profound respect for the Jewish tradition of biblical interpretation, especially as represented by the Talmud, with a philologist's concentration on the original text of the Tanakh and a careful grammatical exposition of it, verse by verse and word by word. Thus the more fanciful and often extravagant elaboration of al-legories and other poetic interpretations that came from the rabbini-cal tradition was held in check by the primary insistence on what the text actually said. Rashi's work coincided with the very early begin-nings of an analogous shift of emphasis among Christian exegetes, an emphasis of which Thomas Aquinas in the thirteenth century is the best-known example. According to Thomas, the literal, grammatical sense of a passage of Scripture was the primary one to which any spiritual sense had to be attached and by which it was to be judged. "All the senses" of Scripture, he insisted in the opening chapter of his masterpiece, *Summa of Theology*, "are founded on one, the literal, from which alone any argument can be drawn, and not from those intended in allegory," which had much to contribute to spiritual un-

derstanding but only when based on the literal sense. As a homely modern argument has put it, a lamppost is intended primarily for illumination, but a drunkard uses it for support.

Logically carried to its conclusion, that insistence on the primacy of the literal sense would have led—that is to say, should have led—to a demand that the original text in the original language be primary, too; but Thomas never acquired a mastery of Greek, biblical or patristic. The one biblical scholar among the Christians in the later Middle Ages who more than any other carried out the logical conclusion from literal sense to original language was Nicholas of Lyra, a Franciscan at the University of Paris. So precise was his grasp of the nuances of Hebrew and so comprehensive was his knowledge of Rashi and the other Jewish exegetes—both of these being such rarities among Christian biblical scholars—that he was sometimes thought to have been a convert from Judaism, but that does not seem to have been the case. Rather, he seems to have mastered the language as a Christian and to have devoted a lifetime of research to the Jewish interpreters of the Tanakh. He was, for example, the principal source for rabbinical interpretations in Martin Luther's massive commentary on the Book of Genesis (eight volumes in the English translation of the American Edition of *Luther's Works*), in which he quotes Rashi and other rabbinical exegetes of Genesis, not at firsthand but from Lyra. It should be pointed out that this did not make Luther any more sympathetic to his Jewish contemporaries. Far from it. But it did indicate a recognition that, benighted though they still were because they did not read the Tanakh as a Christian book, rabbis such as Rashi did have something to teach Christian readers about the literal, grammatical sense of the Hebrew text, which the Christians were only beginning to repossess through the efforts of Christian Hebraists such as the Renaissance humanist Johannes Reuchlin.

MEDIEVAL CHRISTIAN INTERPRETATION

The Christian interpretation of the Bible in the Middle Ages took several forms. The most elementary, so elementary that later genera-

tions have often ignored it, was the production of explanatory notes to the Scripture written in the margin or at the bottom of the page, known as "glosses." Sometimes these were no more than paraphrases of foreign words or of difficult and obscure Latin words in the text, or etymologies (genuine or fanciful), such as an effort to explain the still puzzling word *Selah* in several of the Psalms, which has had to be explained even in the Jewish Publication Society Version as "a liturgical direction of uncertain meaning." But the glosses went far beyond that simple level to identify the doctrinal or moral meaning of the passage and, unavoidably, to correct the false meaning of the heretics. As glosses upon glosses grew into glosses upon glosses upon glosses, the size of the biblical text tended to become smaller and smaller on the page to accommodate all the marginal explanations surrounding it on every side. These often included quotations from earlier expositions of the text, some of the most precious of which have survived to our own time only in this form.

More ambitious was the exposition of the sacred text in sermons and homilies, sometimes for a lay congregation, sometimes for a monastic community, sometimes for a royal or noble court. The appointed readings from an Epistle and a Gospel for the Sundays and holidays of the church year ("pericopes") were collected in convenient form into a special liturgical book called a "lectionary" (from *lectio,* the Latin word for "reading"), and the homily would consist of expounding one or the other of these "lessons" (more usually the Gospel). Quite often, if truth be told, "expounding" the text really meant no more than reciting what someone else had said about it before, such as Augustine or Chrysostom or Jerome (which in many cases was probably just as well, considering the educational level of many of the preachers). Another format, called *lectio continua,* was, as this title indicates, a preached exposition not of the pericope for the day but of an entire book of the Bible, one verse after another at successive services, until finally these homilies constituted an entire biblical commentary. In clarifying the meaning of the text for their hearers, preachers would often refer to the topical issues and conflicts of the day. As a result, such sermonic commentaries have become a

valuable collection of source material not only about orthodox beliefs and pious practices but, in conjunction with other sources such as manuals of penance, about social customs, economic practices, and folk life—including the survival of a lot of superstition and paganism in officially "Christian" and "Catholic" Europe.

As Christian education and scholarship evolved, the *lectio continua* acquired academic status, too, and formal courses in Scripture took their place as a central part of the theological curriculum. For example, Thomas Aquinas, who is best remembered for his massive *Summa of Theology* in thousands of articles and questions, prepared for that assignment by working his way verse by verse through the books of the Bible; he was dictating a commentary on the Song of Songs when he died, probably before turning fifty. Thomas earned his master's degree in the process, as "Master of the Sacred Page." In most modern textbooks of the history of ideas in the Middle Ages, this biblical source of his thought, if it is mentioned at all, takes second or third place behind his study of Aristotle even though Thomas's own priorities were exactly the opposite. The deepening interest in the Bible eventually even stimulated attention to the Hebrew text of the Tanakh, especially in some centers such as the Abbey of Saint Victor in France. Negotiations with "the Greek church" of Constantinople during union councils held at Lyons in 1274 (the year Thomas Aquinas died) and at Florence in 1439, combined with the flight of Greek scholars to the West before the conquering armies of the Muslim Ottoman Turks, had a similar effect on the study of the Greek text of the New Testament, which eventually helped foster the literary humanism of the Renaissance in Italy and northern Europe.

As Beryl Smalley of Oxford said, "The Bible was the most studied book of the middle ages. Bible study represented the highest branch of learning. . . . Both the language and the content of Scripture permeate medieval thought." The method of biblical interpretation characteristic of the Christian Middle Ages proceeded typically on several levels, sometimes as many as seven, but stabilized at four: literal, allegorical, moral, and eschatological (usually called "anagogi-

cal"). These multiple interpretations were summarized in a Latin quatrain that has been translated to read:

> The letter shows us what God and our fathers did;
> The allegory shows us where our faith is hid;
> The moral meaning gives us rules of daily life;
> The anagogy shows us where we end our strife.

The standard example of the four senses was the biblical name "Jerusalem." In its literal sense it meant a locatable place on the map (which was usually placed at the top of the medieval map of "the world," not on the far right as in our maps). As an allegory it signified, as Saint Paul had said in the only genuine allegory in the New Testament, "the heavenly Jerusalem, the free woman; she is our mother." The moral imperative of "Jerusalem," the duty to construct a just society here on earth, would perhaps be expressed best centuries after the Middle Ages in the lines of William Blake:

> till we have built Jerusalem
> in England's green and happy land.

Its eschatological ("anagogical") meaning referred to "Jerusalem the golden, with milk and honey blest," the object of ultimate hope celebrated in a medieval hymn of that title by Bernard of Cluny as well as in countless hymns and spirituals ever since.

It says a great deal about the medieval Christian reading of the Tanakh that any interpretation which confined itself to the literal sense of a particular passage was criticized for its "Judaizing" tendency, because Saint Paul had differentiated himself from his Jewish past with the formula, "The letter killeth, but the spirit giveth life." The same criticism was likewise directed at the rare case of an interpretation that presumed to correct the translations of the Septuagint and the Vulgate by a reference (often borrowed) to the original Hebrew. For although there were four senses of Scripture, the most

avidly sought after was often the allegorical sense—or, as it was called, the "spiritual" sense—which of the four conveyed the richest meaning of a passage, often turning a prosaic reference to a "tree" into a celebration of the cross of Christ or the mention of a "rock" into a treatise on the authority of the pope, because Christ had said to Peter: "You are Peter, the Rock; and on this rock I will build my church, and the powers of death shall never conquer it."

"Holy Scripture," one medieval writer said in defending the spiritual interpretation, "is God's dining room, where the guests are made soberly drunk" with imaginative and allegorical interpretations. Sometimes it was the very exoticism of the language and imagery of the Psalms and the Prophets that encouraged such imaginations. In addition, allegory was, not incidentally, the best way to cope with the awkwardness of the imprecatory language in a vindictive passage like this one:

> Fair Babylon, you predator,
> a blessing on him who repays you in kind
> what you have inflicted on us;
> *a blessing on him who seizes your babies*
> *and dashes them against the rocks!*

Situated in the same Christian Bible that also contained the stern warning of Jesus, "It is not your heavenly Father's will that one of these little ones should be lost," these closing words had to have some other meaning than their literal sense. Therefore, according to one allegorical interpretation, this curse upon the "predator" of "Babylon," which in the Book of Revelation and elsewhere is the symbolic name for all that is evil and perverse, is really a vindication of the truth of the gospel and a denunciation of the heretics, whose "babies" are false doctrines and wicked books that deserve to be destroyed.

There is a special sense in which the person and life of Francis of Assisi can be said to embody the medieval Christian interpretation of the Bible. The very heart of his campaign to reform church and society was an appeal to the authority of the Bible, specifically the au-

thority of the Gospels as an imperative of humility and sincerity. Proceeding from the Gospels' preferential option for the poor, expressed for example in the opening verse of the Beatitudes in the version of Luke, "Blessed are you who are in need," and in the example of the one who said, "Foxes have their holes and birds their roosts; but the Son of Man has nowhere to lay his head," he celebrated poverty in his words and deeds, and in his deeds even more than in his words. The life of Jesus, primarily as this was narrated in the Gospels, became his norm. And for this he was rewarded with the *stigmata,* the New Testament word for the marks of the crucifixion on the body of Jesus. The program of biblical renewal for the church that came out of the Franciscan movement was a documentation of the power of the Bible to change lives—and, miraculously, sometimes even institutions.

THE SONG OF SONGS

An especially piquant documentation of the interpretation of the Bible in the Middle Ages, and of the difference between the Jewish and the Christian interpretation, can be found in their use of "the book which was most read, and most frequently commented in the medieval cloister, a book of the Old Testament: the Canticle of Canticles" or Song of Solomon. As it stands, the Song of Songs is a love poem of exquisite beauty, deeply evocative and sometimes quite explicit anatomically. But what is such a book doing in the Bible? Its lush erotic imagery was already being allegorized when the book was admitted into the canon of Jewish Scripture, where a prophet such as Hosea had denounced the infidelity of Israel to its God in the sexual imagery of betrayal, seduction, and harlotry. That allegorical interpretation of the Song was also characteristic of Jewish exegesis in the Middle Ages, notably in the commentary of Ibn Ezra. But was the bond of love expressed by the exchange of tender nothings between the Lover and the Beloved and "the voice of the turtledove" a typological figure for the covenant between God and the people of Israel; or for the self-sacrificing love that Christ has for the church, in keep-

ing with the use of the bridal metaphor for the church in the New Testament, which admonishes, "Husbands, love your wives, as Christ loved the church and gave himself up for it"; or for the intimate communion of the believer's soul with God or with Christ, as in the familiar hymn of Charles Wesley, "Jesu, Lover of my soul, / Let me to Thy bosom fly"? Of the countless expositions of the Song in the Middle Ages, one of the best known is the collection of the word-by-word commentary in the sermons of Bernard of Clairvaux, the twelfth-century monk and mystic, which allegorized every phrase into a celebration of Christ as the celestial Bridegroom. It is the same sacred text, equally revered by all and yet with such vastly different meanings: Which is the right one? Can all of them be right? Or could it be possible that none of them is?

As medieval manuscripts of the Canticle of Canticles in the Vulgate often show, some of them very strikingly, one additional difference between the Jewish and the Christian interpretation of the Bible was the development of graphic art within Christianity, both Eastern and Western. Its earliest beginnings are not historically identifiable, but many of the earliest surviving examples have been preserved in Saint Catherine's Monastery on Mount Sinai. Whenever the art first appeared, drawing pictures of Christ, of his mother, Mary, and of other saints, rather than merely abstract symbols such as a cross or a star, eventually became a central component of personal piety, of corporate worship, and of church architecture. Like almost everything else in the church, the painting of icons was attributed to biblical times and to the apostles. The apostle and evangelist Luke, who had written by far the most detailed word portrait of the Virgin Mary in the opening two chapters of his Gospel, was eventually said also to have been her first "icono-grapher," icon-writer. Yet everybody's Bible, not only the Tanakh of the Jews in Hebrew but the Old Testament of the Christians in Greek or Latin, minced no words in pronouncing within the very words of the Ten Commandments that were the Law of God to both Christians and Jews: "You shall not make for yourself a sculptured image, or any likeness of what is in the heavens above, or on the earth below, or in the waters under the

earth. You shall not bow down to them or serve them." To such biblical objections the church replied that images were "Bibles of the illiterate." An icon of Christ or Mary (especially in the Christian East) or a statue of Christ or Mary (especially in the West)—these were summaries of the Bible, particularly for the many who could not read the Bible in Greek or Latin or any other language. For example, the later Russian icon of the Holy Trinity by Andrej Rublev, based on Byzantine precedents, was anything but an effort to visualize the ineffable and transcendent mystery of the inner relation between Father, Son, and Holy Spirit in the undivided unity of the divine essence. Rather, like most icons, it was the portrayal of an event in the biblical history of salvation, the visitation to Abraham on the plains of Mamre of the one "LORD" who was nevertheless "three," by which mortals were given a glimpse of the mystery. From the illuminations of biblical manuscripts or the stained glass windows in medieval cathedrals it was possible to learn in great detail many of the stories of sacred history. This educational explanation of the role of images developed into a much more sophisticated biblical argument on their behalf: Christ himself was the authentic "image of the invisible God"; an icon of Christ, therefore, was nothing more than an image of the Image. Nothing could have illustrated more *graphically* how far apart Jews and Christians really were in their possession of a shared sacred text.

Dante's *Divine Comedy* is a compendium in poetic form of the Christian interpretation of Scripture in the Middle Ages. It celebrated Adam as the "ancient father of whom every bride is daughter and daughter-in-law," and David as "the cantor of the Holy Spirit." The entire history of ancient Israel and the narratives of the Gospels, "the plenteous rain of the Holy Spirit that is poured out on the old and new parchments," was an allegory of the history of the church. Its temptations and apostasies were symbolic of the crisis of the Papacy during the fourteenth century, its saints were a challenge and an inspiration to believers of every time and every place, and "the truth that rains down through Moses and the Prophets and the Psalms and through the Gospel" shaped the language and the imagery of Dante

the poet as he described the experiences of Dante the pilgrim in the Inferno, Purgatorio, and Paradiso of the world to come.

ISLAM AS A THIRD "PEOPLE OF THE BOOK"?

The rise of Islam as a third "people of the Book"—and of the Qur'an as a third Book—in the early seventh century CE complicated the relation of Judaism and Christianity to their common Book still further. The very term "people of the Book" in the title of the present chapter comes from the Qur'an, where most often it is a name for Jews but by extension applies also to Christians. The Qur'an admonishes:

> Do not argue with the people of the Book
> unless in a fair way, apart from those
> who act wrongly, and say to them:
> "We believe what has been sent down to us,
> and we believe what has been sent down to you.
> Our God and your God is one,
> and to Him we submit."

But "*the* Book" for Islam is in a unique sense only the Qur'an. It is normative Muslim doctrine that the Qur'an, just as it stands today in the original Arabic, came directly from God to the prophet Muhammad, who passed it on, undefiled, to those who have "submitted to the will of the One True God" (which is what the name "Muslim" means). The Muslim counterpart to the person of Jesus Christ, therefore, is not the person of Muhammad—despite the creed of Islam, "There is no God but God, and Muhammad is His prophet"—but the Qur'an, which, like the incarnate Logos, the Word of God, in the Christian creed, came down from heaven to abide on earth as the definitive revelation of the will of the One True God. The Prophet stands in service to the Book, not vice versa, and he is not in any

sense to be viewed as sharing in the essence of the One God, "Blessed be He."

With the Jewish Tanakh the Qur'an shared a starkly monotheistic faith and a profound antipathy to images. There is at least some reason to believe that one of the sources for the campaign of certain Christians, including several Byzantine emperors, against images from the eighth century onward in the East, the so-called iconoclastic controversy, was an acute embarrassment in response to Muslim criticism of the excesses in the Christian veneration of icons. Abraham is the father of believers also for the Qur'an, albeit through his son Ishmael rather than through his son Isaac, and Moses is the revealer of the Law and the will of God. The Qur'an's admonitions, "Commemorate Abraham in the Book" and "Commemorate Moses in the Book," follow in close succession. With Christianity the Qur'an shared a belief that the religion of the Book involved progressive revelation through history—not only from Moses forward to Jesus, but now from Jesus forward to Muhammad. And Mary, the mother of Jesus, named "Miriam" in the Qur'an with the sister of Moses, has been called "the heroine of the Qur'an," where she is more prominent than any other woman. With both the Tanakh and the New Testament the Qur'an shared the worship of the One True God: "Our God and your God is one." Surely any devout Jew or Christian would be able to pray to this One God in the words of a text from the suras of the Qur'an such as this poetic passage that has long been beloved of Sufis and other Muslim mystics:

> God is the light of the heavens and the earth.
> The semblance of His light is that of a niche
> in which is a lamp, the flame within a glass,
> the glass a glittering star, as it were, lit with the oil
> of a blessed tree, the olive, neither of the East
> nor of the West, whose oil appears to light up
> even though fire touches it not, — light upon light.
> God guides to His light whom He will.

So does God advance precepts of wisdom for men,
for God has knowledge of every thing.

In the Qur'an, therefore, Islam had a Book that was, at one and the same time, very much like the Jewish and Christian Bibles and yet very much unlike them: like them in the centrality of belief in one God and in the acceptance of the supreme authority of his revelation, but unlike them in the absence of historical narrative as the medium of that revelation. Did that make Islam "a *third* people of the Book"?

The great medieval laboratories for the relation of these three peoples of the Book to one another, and therefore for the relation of the three Books to one another, were the Near East and Spain. It was in Spain that some of the first Christian schools of Semitic languages were established. To a degree that is probably difficult even to imagine today, the three peoples of the Book coexisted there at least some of the time (and before the forcible expulsion of the Jews from Spain in 1492) in considerable amity and with a remarkable measure of toleration. One need only recall that one of the most important systems of Jewish theology from the Middle Ages (or any other time), *The Guide of the Perplexed,* the masterpiece of Moses Maimonides—"Rabbi Moshe ben Maimon," therefore commonly known by the acronym "Rambam," of whom it was said, "From Moses to Moses there was none like Moses"—was written in Spain in the twelfth century under a Muslim ruler and that it was written in Arabic. Again, one of the most important systems of Christian theology and philosophy ever produced in the Eastern Orthodox, Greek-speaking tradition, *The Orthodox Faith,* was written in Damascus in Syria in the eighth century by John of Damascus, also under the protection of a Muslim ruler. Significantly, John of Damascus listed Muslims—identified as "Hagarenes" because they traced their origins to Ishmael, the son of Abraham by his slave Hagar—not as pagans but as Christian heretics. Living in that social context, John of Damascus also composed one of the most influential of Orthodox Christian defenses of the use of icons, a practice that Muslims saw as one of the most offensive features of Christian worship and practice.

Even without importing all of our problems into the medieval scene, one cannot resist observing that it ill behooves an era of human history like this one to look back at the Middle Ages and think only of *jihad* or of the Crusades and pogroms without remembering these and similar encounters when, at least for an occasional moment, Jews, Christians, and Muslims, by the power of the Book and in the heritage of Abraham, the father whom they shared, managed to transcend their separations without losing their identities.

EIGHT

Back to the Sources

NOVVM IN

strumentũ omne, diligenter ab ERASMO ROTERODAMO
recognitum & emendatum, nõ solum ad græcam ueritatem, ue=
rumetiam ad multorum utriusq; linguæ codicum, eorumq; ue=
terum simul & emendatorum fidem, postremo ad pro=
batissimorum autorum citationem, emendationem
& interpretationem, præcipue, Origenis, Chry
sostomi, Cyrilli, Vulgarij, Hieronymi, Cy=
priani, Ambrosij, Hilarij, Augusti/
ni, una cũ Annotationibus, quæ
lectorem doceant, quid qua
ratione mutatum sit.
Quisquis igitur
amas ue=
ram
Theolo/
giam, lege, cogno
sce, ac deinde iudica.
Neq; statim offendere, si
quid mutatum offenderis, sed
expende, num in melius mutatum sit.

APVD INCLYTAM
GERMANIAE BASILAEAM.

CVM PRIVILEGIO
MAXIMILIANI CAESARIS AVGVSTI,
NE QVIS ALIVS IN SACRA ROMA=
NI IMPERII DITIONE, INTRA QVATV
OR ANNOS EXCVDAT, AVT ALIBI
EXCVSVM IMPORTET.

Title page of *Novum instrumentum,* edited by Desiderius Erasmus, 1516: the first officially published edition of the Greek New Testament.

n 1492, Columbus sailed the ocean blue" from Spain to the New World, eventually believing his voyage of discovery to have been nothing less than the fulfillment of biblical prophecy, on which he would later even write an apocalyptic treatise entitled *Book About the Prophecies*. In the same year, 1492, the Ladino-speaking Sephardic Jews, clutching their Torah scrolls, were expelled from Christian Spain, where only a few years later the newly invented technology of printing would make it possible for the first Greek New Testament ever printed to appear as part of a magnificent six-volume set that would include not only the Latin Vulgate but the entire Tanakh in Hebrew and in Greek, as well as the Targum of the Torah in Aramaic. These intertwining historical and linguistic threads are an apt symbol for the ambiguous place of the Bible at the end of the Middle Ages and in the period of the Renaissance. That helps to make the humanism of the Renaissance, both in Italy and in northern Europe and England, one of the most fascinating chapters in the entire history of the Jewish and Christian Scriptures.

By now it is probably a truism that the people of the "Middle Ages" had not been aware that they were living in the "middle" at all, except perhaps in the sense that they were standing between the First Coming of Christ and the Second Coming of Christ, the first in the flesh and the second in judgment. Our conventional concept of this as the "middle" period of the history of the West has come to us from the humanists of the Renaissance, who saw that period as a time of decline and decadence standing between them and a defining,

more or less "golden," age in the past. They disparagingly called its artistic creations "Gothic"—and the nickname has stuck—because the Visigoths and the Ostrogoths were barbarians. Those whom we now call "Renaissance humanists," as Anthony Grafton formulated their mission statement, "hoped that they could renovate education, literature, philosophy, and theology, not by looking to an uncertain future but by turning back to a perfect past" that was available, or had now at last become available through their work, in the Greek and Latin classics and in the Hebrew and Greek Bible.

Grafton's definition correctly puts education first among the areas that Renaissance humanists hoped to renovate and reform by turning back to the past. The other areas he lists—literature, philosophy, and theology—all needed to be renovated, too, and quite thoroughly, according to the humanists. In their judgment, literature and language were crude and amateurish, scholastic philosophy was a poor imitation of Aristotle, and scholastic theology was a poor imitation of scholastic philosophy. But they expected that the hoped-for renovation of literature, philosophy, and theology would happen through an educational revolution, the renewal of learning. This in turn was to be accomplished by "the revival of antiquity."

The Renaissance, whether in Italy or in the North, was much more than this revival of antiquity. For several generations now the interpretation of the Renaissance has been paying special attention to such sociological factors as the role of Florence and other cities in forming the spirit of "civic humanism" and to the creation of the modern banking system of early capitalism—the Medicis were bankers and then became popes—as a force that made possible the accumulation of wealth and the patronage of those cities, which were the political and social atmosphere within which literary humanism, music, and the visual arts were encouraged to flourish. These productive new emphases have only enriched and deepened the traditional attention to the revival of antiquity and to the humanists' motto of "Back to the sources!"

THE *RENOVATIO* OF CLASSICAL AND CHRISTIAN LATIN

Those ancient "sources" to which the humanists were urging their hearers to return were multiple. They were classical as well as Christian (and, within the Christian, not only biblical but postbiblical), Greek and Latin and Hebrew, prose and poetry, drama and rhetoric. It is sometimes easy to forget that with the Middle Ages out of which they had come the humanists of the Renaissance continued to share a primary reliance on Latin as the universal language for the communication of ideas. When, just before beginning his great epic poem, Dante wrote *On Vernacular Eloquence,* a spirited defense of the Italian vernacular, the language in which *The Divine Comedy* would appear, he was obliged to write the defense itself in Latin—but not, thank God, the poem, though he had originally planned to do so. Yet Latin, too, needed to be "renovated" by being taken back behind the corruption of the Middle Ages to the authentic literary sources of classical Roman antiquity. The humanists loved to poke fun at medieval Latin with its barbaric ignorance of basic grammar and proper syntax. There were anecdotes aplenty of monks who even on their deathbed did not know which Latin case was governed by which Latin prepositions, committing grammatical sins with their final breath. The model of perfect Latinity, and therefore the standard for the *renovatio* of the language, was the orator and philosopher Cicero. We still have copies of the lists of words from Cicero that the humanists compiled as the "controlled vocabulary" which writers of Latin were to consult as a model and norm, to be sure that no alien terminology or postclassical constructions had crept into their compositions. They vied with one another in preserving the supposed purity of their literary Latin even though it was, as a result, often antiquated and stilted.

Neither the Renaissance nor the Reformation would have made the difference it did for the historical career of the Jewish and Christian Scriptures if it had not been for the invention of printing from

movable metal type, which is usually attributed to Johannes Gutenberg. Today everyone uses the word "book" to refer almost exclusively to the printed book, and the history of the printed book began with the Bible. Like the translation of the Hebrew Bible into Greek, printing represents a major turning point in the history of the Bible. Ever since Gutenberg the history of the Bible is largely the history of printed Bibles, so that much of its worldwide dissemination is at the same time part of the history of the book and of printing (as well as of commercial publishing), in addition to being part of the history of evangelization and of missions.

But like the Bible as such, the printed Bible all began with Hebrew, Greek, and Latin texts—or (scrambling the historical sequence of these originals in order to be chronologically precise about the history of printing) with the Latin, Hebrew, and Greek versions. Except for a few minor jobs, which are usually dated earlier but are virtually unknown otherwise, Gutenberg's first major project was the *Biblia Latina* of 1454–55, usually called "the 42-line Bible" because it had forty-two lines per page. Therefore the *Cologne Chronicle,* published in German at the end of the fifteenth century, records under the year 1450: "That was a golden year. That was when men began to print, and the first book that was printed was the Bible in Latin"; and it attributes this invention of printing to "a citizen of Mainz . . . named Junker Johann Gutenberg." In 1462 there appeared what is usually called the Mainz Bible or "the 48-line Bible" (because it had forty-eight lines of text per page), published by Gutenberg's sometime partner Johann Fust and Fust's partner and son-in-law, Peter Schöffer. It carries a Latin colophon that bespeaks the consciousness of having achieved a technological breakthrough: "This little book was made in the city of Mainz by the artful invention of *printing or character-making, without the labor of a pen,* and it was completed for the glory of God, through the industry of Johann Fust, citizen, and Peter Schöffer of Gernsheim, clerk of the same diocese, in the Year of Our Lord 1462, on the Eve of the Feast of the Assumption of the Virgin Mary," thus on 14 August.

Taken simply as artifacts, these first printed Bibles in many respects resemble the bound manuscript Bibles that had preceded them more than they do the printed Bibles that were to follow. For one thing, the most precious copies of the Gutenberg Bible (perhaps as many as 45 out of the total print run of 270 copies, more or less, that made up the 1454–55 printing) are printed on vellum, a specially treated calfskin that was reserved for manuscript books, so that the page still has the feel of a manuscript even when one knows that it was printed with the innovative techniques of the printing press. The lingering influence of manuscript Bibles is evident above all from the physical design of the pages and from the type fonts. Both the Gutenberg Bible and the Mainz Bible appear in double columns of Latin text, just as the medieval manuscripts of the Latin Bible habitually did. The individual letters of the Gutenberg Bible are in the gothic font. Although they were applied to the page by combinations of metal type that had been daubed with ink, they still look in many ways as though some monk might have drawn or written them with a pen or stylus. In the Mainz Bible, however, the design of the gothic font has already been modified significantly. With the appearance in 1471 of the Latin Bible printed in Rome by Sweynheym and Pannartz, the Bible was printed for the first time in roman type (as this font is still called, to distinguish it from what we still call italic type, even in this age of the word processor).

Coinciding as it did with the drive "back to the sources," the invention of printing made it possible, indeed imperative, to circulate the Latin Vulgate Bible itself in the new form. To a degree that can often easily escape notice by someone who has never had responsibility for creating a critical edition of a historic text, the preparation of the text of the Bible for printing imposed on the editor or printer the obligation to make decisions about stabilizing the text, often for the first time ever. Over and over it became necessary to choose from among two (and often more) conflicting readings in the various manuscripts, of which only one could be the right one, and to decide which of them to print as *the* authoritative text. Once it was printed, the result of such choices achieved a certain measure of permanency.

Printe
endure ju
ous in the
name of l
criticisms
Protestant
8 April 15
Scriptures
thorough r
revision"
longer tha
case wher
it would
that had b
the counc
upon him
tion was
was so slo
ment a fe
copies in
cil, and a t
was carrie
for Sixtus
becoming
gate editic

THE RE

What was
was a sign
only dialo
the profou
translation
Dante kne

I

"]
o
p
n
p
tu
ti
e
s
E
p

v
t
c
I
b
a
b
t
r
I
c
r
i

glass and fresco; and narrative poems going back to *Heliand* and similar vernacular works—through all of these medieval channels the knowledge of the Bible had been far more extensive and thorough than Protestant propaganda usually gives it credit for being. Nevertheless, the Reformation did produce a growth in Bible-centered piety. The lives of the saints and the countless holidays and feast days devoted to their commemoration, especially the many days consecrated to legends of the Virgin Mary, slowly yielded to a church year and a devotional calendar shaped much more directly by the Bible. One index of the change was a gradual supplanting of saints' names by biblical names (especially the more colorful and plentiful ones in the Old Testament such as Jedidiah and Hephzibah) at baptism.

Medieval warnings about how difficult or even dangerous it was to read the Bible privately without the proper guidance of church and clergy yielded to earnest admonitions to read it between sermons, even to bring it to church—although those medieval warnings often seemed to be coming true whenever yet another sect arose, based on yet another idiosyncratic reading of the biblical text in the vernacular. The existing sources do give us occasional information about how biblically grounded the faith and life and everyday speech of common people became. It is difficult to imagine that any of this could have happened if the Bible had not been translated and printed for popular consumption.

A corollary effect of the printed Bible was the growth and improvement of biblical preaching. Whether or not lay people carried their personal Bibles to church on Sundays or weekdays (as they often did and still do in many denominations), they learned to expect and to demand that the preacher back up his message by constant reference to Holy Scripture, which they were able to check in their own copies. Then as now, people would sometimes complain that the sermons were boring or too long or too abstract and removed from everyday life. But they would also complain when they thought a biblical message was missing from a sermon. The biblical sermon became positively, in the hands of Luther or Calvin, religious oratory of

the highest order and a course in the events and personalities of the Bible. Its moral instruction was often based directly or indirectly on the Ten Commandments. The teaching of the New Testament, Luther insisted, was meant to be read and to be obeyed not only by the religious professional but by the artisan at his job and the mother at her household duties. That is part of what he meant by "the universal priesthood of believers" and was one reason that he devoted himself to producing a translation of the Bible which spoke to the people in their own language.

The translation and publication of the Bible by Martin Luther has been called "a moment of mythic proportions in German history." Therefore, when Germany's most idolized man of letters, Johann Wolfgang von Goethe, himself a figure of "mythic proportions," depicts the aged philosopher at his desk in part one of his poetic drama *Faust,* he has him reenact the scene of Luther in temporary exile at the Wartburg Castle in 1521. Faust tries to find the exact equivalent "in my beloved German" for the enigmatic Greek term *logos* in the opening verse of John's Gospel—"word," "sense," "power," "deed"? It was a challenge that Luther faced literally thousands of times translating the Bible into what was also for him "my beloved German." He suppressed his anti-Semitic feelings long enough to consult German rabbis about the names of the nonkosher species, which, according to Leviticus,

> you shall abominate among the birds . . . the eagle, the vulture, and the black vulture; the kite, falcons of every variety; all varieties of raven; the ostrich, the nighthawk, the sea gull; hawks of every variety; the little owl, the cormorant, and the great owl; the white owl, the pelican, and the bustard; the stork; herons of every variety; the hoopoe, and the bat.

(It is a measure of the difficulties Luther or any other Christian translator of the Torah faced that almost five centuries and entire libraries

of scholarship later, the late twentieth-century Jewish Publication Society translation of the Tanakh is still obliged to add the footnote to this passage in Leviticus: "A number of these cannot be identified with certainty.")

As he was translating the Bible for his several printings, beginning with the September Testament of 1522, Luther was able to draw upon an impressive range of linguistic resources. His little university at Wittenberg had suddenly become a magnet school to which students who spoke the various dialects of German brought their diverse vocabularies and ways of speaking. He himself had an uncanny ear for this diversity, which he could reproduce—or ridicule—at will. Above all he was, as even his adversaries grudgingly admitted, a magician with words across the infinite spectrum of ways of speaking in the Bible. The German Jewish poet Heinrich Heine once said of him that he could scold like a fishwife and whisper like a maiden. All of this he brought to the Bible, and just at a time when the German language was beginning to congeal, thanks in no small measure to the printing press. Germany would not be united politically until the nineteenth century, but Germany as a unified cultural force was in considerable measure the achievement of the stabilization and standardization of the German language through the printing of Luther's German Bible. "The Word they still shall let remain," he had sung in the final stanza of "A Mighty Fortress Is Our God." In a way that he could not have known, he proved this to be true and helped make it true.

As the Reformation erupted within one country after another or spread from one country to another, vernacular Bibles appeared. There were several Czech translations of the Bible by the Hussites, climaxing in the six-volume Bible of Kralice, completed in 1613. In France and French-speaking Switzerland, the Reformation led by John Calvin produced a number of vernacular Bibles, one of the most important being the translation of the New Testament by Calvin's cousin, who is usually called Robert Olivétan.

THE ENGLISH BIBLE

For the history of printed Bibles coming out of the Reformation there is a natural transition from the German Bible to the English Bible, from Luther's German translation to the English version of William Tyndale. Recent examinations of Tyndale's translations, the New Testament of 1526 and the Pentateuch of 1529–30, now including a handsome new publication of the complete text, have exonerated him of the usual charge of slavishly following or plagiarizing Luther's German translation, although it is obvious that in his introductions and notes Tyndale often did little more than translate Luther. On the other hand, those examinations have confirmed in detail how much of Tyndale there still is in later English Bibles, especially the King James Version. In 1535, ten years or so after Tyndale's New Testament, Miles Coverdale published the first English translation of the whole Bible, which was carried out on the basis of the Vulgate Latin, Luther's German, and Tyndale's English, but was not based independently on the Hebrew and Greek originals. Beyond its intrinsic importance as the first English Bible, Coverdale's translation of the Book of Psalms was the one that was incorporated into the Anglican *Book of Common Prayer,* where it has been retained even when the King James Version was substituted for earlier versions of the prescribed Epistle and Gospel lessons.

In 1539, five years after the Act of Supremacy had proclaimed Henry VIII the "supreme head" of the Church of England in defiance of the authority of the pope, the "Great Bible," which was, as its subtitle announced, "truly translated after the verity of the Hebrew and Greek texts," was issued for official use in church services. With a title page bearing a drawing by Hans Holbein that shows King Henry VIII distributing it to Archbishop Thomas Cranmer and Thomas Cromwell, it was so named because of its size, being intended for the lectern of churches, not for personal reading; it, too, was the work of Coverdale, though anonymously. By contrast, the

Geneva Bible was deliberately printed in a convenient size for the Protestant exiles from England under Queen Mary, who had found refuge in Calvinist Geneva. It was essentially a revision of Tyndale and the Great Bible, with contributions from the Protestant hosts who had given them shelter. Like several of its predecessors, the Geneva Bible not only achieved wide circulation among Anglicans, also after their return to England under Queen Elizabeth, but left a permanent mark on both religious language and its eventual successor.

By far the most important and influential of all was the Authorized Version of 1611, commonly known as the "King James Bible" because it was dedicated to King James I. Its celebrated preface, "The Translators to the Reader," justified not only its own rendering but the entire Reformation enterprise of translating the Bible, and it therefore spoke for the movement as a whole: "But how shall men meditate in that which they cannot understand? How shall they understand that which is kept closed in an unknown tongue? As it is written, 'Except I know the power of the voice, I shall be to him that speaketh a barbarian, and he that speaketh shall be a barbarian to me.'" Describing itself as having been "with the former translations diligently compared and revised," the Authorized Version was by far the most successful of all English translations of the Bible.

It has also proved to be, in its first edition or in various revisions up to the American Standard Version of 1901, the Revised Standard Version of 1952, and the New Revised Standard Version of 1990, the most durable of all the many translations into English, having been "the favorite text of the clear majority of post-Renaissance English authors, up to and including even modern authors such as D. H. Lawrence, James Joyce, Toni Morrison, and John Updike." Together with the earlier Anglican adaptation and revision of the traditional liturgy in the light of Reformation principles, *The Book of Common Prayer*, the King James Version stands as a monument of English prose and also as an abiding contribution of the English Reformation not only to the spirituality but to the culture of the entire English-speaking world, where it is (with good reason) usually grouped with the writings of Shakespeare for its language.

THE BIBLICAL "RULE OF THE SAINTS"
AND RELIGIOUS LIBERTY

The new emphasis of the Protestant Reformation on the authority of the Bible as the normative source for the knowledge of the will of God could not be without far-reaching political consequences. "Where there is no vision, the people perish": even a brief review of the Hebrew prophets will show that they did not address their denunciations of evil and exhortations to good only to private individuals one by one, but to the entire nation of Israel. The New Testament, written in the vastly different setting of the Roman Empire by those who were without political power, is far less clear in its social and political message. Paul's admonition, "Every person must submit to the authorities in power, for all authority comes from God, and the existing authorities are instituted by him," was written under the emperor Nero, who ended up persecuting Christians. Christ's distinction, "Pay to Caesar what belongs to Caesar, and to God what belongs to God," leaves unresolved the question of what can possibly belong to Caesar without belonging to God first—and last. Nor had any of this prepared Christians for what emerged in the fourth century when "Caesar" in the person of the emperor Constantine came to believe in the Christian God and to regard himself as (to use his own words) "bishop in externals" of the church.

When in Protestant eyes the authentic interpretation of the Bible as the will of God was restored—according to the most radical Protestants, for the first time since the days of the apostles—and now that the dominance of the Papacy over temporal rulers had been broken in Protestant territories, an entire new set of problems or opportunities came on the agenda. In the city of Münster in 1534–35 a radical Protestant apocalyptic group invoked the authority of the Bible to try to erect a theocratic "Kingdom of Zion," complete with the polygamy practiced by the biblical patriarchs and the community of property practiced by the primitive church of the Book of Acts.

This ended in debacle and continued to serve as a cautionary tale, but the idea of the biblical rule of the saints found a less extreme expression within mainstream Reformed or Calvinistic Protestantism and in English and American Puritanism. A Swiss confession of 1536 called upon the civil government "to exercise all possible diligence to promote and to put into effect *what a minister of the church and a preacher of the gospel teaches and sets forth from God's word,*" which therefore assigned direct political relevance to the message of the Bible (though only as correctly interpreted).

Several of the New England colonies served, in effect, as proving grounds for the ideal of the biblical rule of the saints. Moreover, that ideal of civil government in accordance with the will of of God as revealed in the Bible persisted even after the First Amendment of the United States Constitution and the disestablishment of the churches in the several states, which in some cases came long after the First Amendment—1816 in New Hampshire, 1818 in Connecticut, and 1833 in Massachusetts. At the same time, as court cases over Bible reading and prayer in the schools continue to indicate and as the profoundly biblical character of the message of Dr. Martin Luther King, Jr., shows, the Reformation question of the bearing of the Bible on the political order and the applicability of the Sermon on the Mount, or at any rate of some of the Ten Commandments, to a society where there is no established religion has continued to be an issue of serious attention and profound disagreement.

One unexpected and salutary by-product of the divisions and disputes of the Reformation was the development of religious toleration and the doctrine of religious liberty. "The one definite thing which can be said about the Reformation in England is that it was an act of State": This sentence would, with appropriate adjustments, apply also to Germany and Scandinavia, and even to Switzerland. But contrary to the intent of the state, religious pluralism and political dissent arose anyway; and thus, contrary to the intent of most of the combatants on all sides, the Reformation would lead eventually to religious liberty as the only way to maintain a civil society without civil war. Beginning with several groups in England, with its great variety

of religious beliefs, and then in the United States and most of the
West, the principle that the civil authorities "shall make no law . . .
prohibiting the free exercise" of religion has gradually impressed itself upon the conscience and the law as a matter not only of political
expediency but ultimately of moral and legal right—and of correct
biblical exegesis.

THE BIBLE AND CULTURE
IN THE REFORMATION

Political issues aside, the Bible in the period of the Reformation represented a major cultural force. No area of high culture during the
period of the Reformation was more profoundly affected by the
Bible than music. Luther was himself a gifted musician, and he strove
to compose singable hymns with a strongly biblical content. He did a
stanza-by-stanza recital of the Ten Commandments as a hymn, and
his best-known hymn, "A Mighty Fortress Is Our God" *(Ein' feste
Burg ist unser Gott),* familiar to concertgoers as the fourth movement
of Felix Mendelssohn's *Fifth Symphony,* is a free rendering of the biblical words "God is our refuge and stronghold." In the Calvinist and
then the Puritan tradition of Protestantism, application of biblical authority led to an eschewing of made-up poems in favor of "God's
hymnal," the Psalter, translated with meter and rhyme and set to
melodies for congregational singing. The translation and printing of
the Psalms and of the Bible as a whole resonated in poetic literature
far beyond the hymnal, as, in England, John Milton's *Paradise Lost* and,
in Germany, *Der Messias* of Friedrich Gottlieb Klopstock were to attest. The biblical hymn of the Reformation would blossom and
flower into the biblical cantata and biblical oratorio, which would
come into their own as musical forms just when the authority and ve-
racity of the Bible had come under attack.

In the visual arts, the centrality of the Bible in the culture of the
Reformation had a more mixed effect. For the first time since the
Byzantine iconoclastic controversies of the eighth and ninth cen-

turies, the very legitimacy of the visual depiction of the biblical narratives and personalities itself became an issue of major controversy,
with the Calvinist and Puritan campaign against "idolatry." Luther,
too, was highly critical of the superstition and excessive veneration
addressed to religious statues and pictures, as this was concentrated
above all in the Roman Catholic cult of the Virgin Mary and the
saints, but he did not advocate smashing the images as the rioting
Protestant radicals were doing in the 1520s. He could even see some
didactic value in such works of art; and his admirer, the artist Al-
brecht Dürer, employed woodcuts, metal engravings, and paintings to
put the Reformation interpretation of the Bible into pictorial form.
But in Protestant Switzerland and then in Puritan England, the Reformation led, by biblical authority, to the melting down of gold and
silver carvings and to the substitution of plain glass for stained glass.
The biblical depictions in the windows had to yield to the biblical
prohibition in the second commandment.

THE BIBLE IN THE CATHOLIC REFORMATION

The history of the Reformation and of the place of the Bible in the
Reformation is usually and appropriately concentrated on Protestantism, as the narrative in this chapter has also been. But both in reaction against the Protestant Reformation and in a continuation or
even an intensification of the reforming forces that had been at work
within Western Catholicism before Protestantism and quite apart
from it, the Reformation period must be seen as a major epoch for
the Roman Catholic history of the Bible, too.

As a result of the Reformation, differences over not only the interpretation of the Bible but over the scope of its canon helped divide
Western Christendom. The long-standing and—at least officially—
unresolved tension between the Palestinian canon of the Tanakh
(preferred by Jerome) and the more inclusive list of books contained ·
in the Septuagint and Vulgate translations (favored by Augustine)
broke into the open with the Protestant Reformation. Partly because

of their new appreciation for "the truth in Hebrew," the Protestant Reformers privileged the "original" Hebrew not only for its text but for its canon. Besides, such Catholic practices as prayers for the dead in purgatory and the invocation of the saints were (in the Elizabethan English of an Anglican confession of faith) "a fond [foolish] thing, and grounded upon no warranty of Scripture, but rather repugnant to the word of God." This was because the traditional "warranty of Scripture" for them had come not from the Hebrew of the Palestinian canon but from the Apocryphal Second Book of Maccabees. Both in defense of the authority of the Latin Vulgate against the dual insistence of the Protestant Reformers on the original texts and on vernacular translation of the Bible for the common people and in defense of a list of canonical books that included such passages as these from the Apocrypha, the council held by the Roman Catholic Church at Trent (1545–63) made the Vulgate official and authoritative both in its canon and in its text.

At the same time it becomes evident from a close reading of one decree of the Council of Trent after another that the biblical revival that we usually associate with the Renaissance and then with the Protestant Reformation was also resonating strongly there. The Council of Trent repeatedly took steps to curb the excesses and abuses that it acknowledged had arisen within the church and to apply the newly rediscovered authority of Holy Scripture to this task. One of the most glaring of these abuses, in the opinion of the Protestant Reformers but also of many leading prelates attending the Council of Trent, was the parlous state of biblical preaching in many sectors of the church. The council singled this out by decreeing that all bishops had it as their primary duty to preach the word of God, which, it is clear from the documents, some of them had never done before. It also addressed this need by requiring that each diocese establish a seminary for the training of priests. In the setting of the time, this led to reforms of the seminary curriculum that included more study of Scripture, at any rate more study than there had been before. Roman Catholic biblical preaching itself underwent a reformation. This was still far short of the dramatic upsurge in Roman Catholic biblical study brought

on by the encyclical *Divino afflante Spiritu* of Pope Pius XII in 1943 and the decree *Dei Verbum* of the Second Vatican Council, but it was enough to support the change in historical nomenclature by which what used to be called "the Counter-Reformation" has become "the Catholic Reformation."

The Vulgate Bible, so conceived and so dedicated, was, however, a part—the major part, to be sure, but still only a part—of a comprehensive system of authority in which the other components were, as the Council of Trent said, "traditions both written and unwritten" and the ongoing authority of the living church, including above all the authority of the pope. By embedding the Bible in that larger system of authority, the Council of Trent was also addressing a fundamental critique to the very idea of *sola Scriptura,* "the Bible only." As a matter of historical fact (and therefore of theological accuracy), the Christian *Scriptura* has never been *sola.* When the Christian movement began, it had the Tanakh (in most cases the Septuagint) as its *Scriptura* and, alongside it, the primitive proclamation of Jesus as its fulfillment. Then, by the time this proclamation had itself been written down and fleshed out into the New Testament *Scriptura,* the church also had the creeds and the liturgy, on the basis of which it decided what the New Testament, and behind it the Tanakh, meant for Christian faith and life. The very conflict over the biblical canon between the Protestant Reformers and the Council of Trent made it clear that even in a doctrine of *sola Scriptura* the authority of the Bible did not authenticate itself automatically (which would have required some kind of doctrine of repeated inspiration in each generation of the history of the church) but depended on its recognition by tradition and by the church for acceptance. Another aspect of the divine irony that we have seen repeatedly in the history of the use of the Bible within both Judaism and Christianity is that the Bible being used as a weapon against church and tradition had itself come from the arsenal of the church and had been preserved and protected by the tradition.

TEN

The Canon and the Critics

The

Life and Morals

of

Jesus of Nazareth

Extracted textually

from the Gospels

in

Greek, Latin

French & English.

Title page of *The Philosophy of Jesus of Nazareth*, by Thomas Jefferson (in his hand): Thomas Jefferson Papers, Library of Congress.

hen the invention of printing was combined with the zeal for biblical doctrine in Reformation theology and with the zest for literary and historical knowledge of the Bible in Renaissance humanism, the combination was responsible for an intellectual explosion and a scholarly revolution. Biblical scholarship as a field of study, indeed as a profession unto itself, came of age through the printed book because it became increasingly easy, as well as increasingly imperative, for scholars to publish the results of their studies, to draw upon and to criticize the publications of their colleagues, and to disseminate knowledge of the Bible to an ever-widening readership. One of the major eventual contributions of the invention of printing was the creation of the scholarly journal as a literary genre and of the proceedings of learned academies as a forum for the publication of the results of research. In each of the three major biblical constituencies—Jewish, Roman Catholic, and Protestant—this entire development would have been inconceivable without the medium of the printed book. In each of them a pattern was set that would continue to the present or, in some cases, reassert itself in the present. One outstanding example from each may be sufficient as a benchmark for our purposes here.

Perhaps because of its very isolation from the Christian establishment, whether Roman Catholic or Protestant, the biblical scholarship of Judaism was in a class by itself. Not only the first printed editions of the Hebrew Bible but postbiblical Hebrew and Aramaic texts began to appear very early: Targum Onkelos appeared in print about 1480 (and was later included by Christians in the Compluten-

sian Polyglot), and the Bible in Hebrew came out about 1488. The great scope and the high quality of Jewish biblical scholarship in the early days of printing are epitomized in the scholarly editions and other Hebrew publications that came from Daniel Bomberg. Probably in 1516–17 he published in four massive volumes the *Biblia Rabbinica,* which included not only the text of the Bible but the Targums and a wealth of rabbinical commentary. The work was heavily revised a few years later by Jakob ben Chayyim, who in 1524–25 produced an edition of the Massoretic text that achieved normative standing for many generations of Jewish and Christian scholars. The authority of the Torah in postbiblical Judaism was in many ways functionally the authority of the Talmud, so that it is even possible to put the Talmud and the New Testament side by side as the two major alternative systems—mutually exclusive in one sense but also, in another sense, interdependent—for reading the Tanakh. It was therefore a major scholarly achievement when Bomberg followed his *Biblia Rabbinica* with an edition of the Babylonian Talmud in 1519–22 and an edition of the Palestinian Talmud in 1522–23. Especially initially, the effect of all these publications on the learned study of the Bible was largely confined to Jewish scholars and even added to the separation of biblical scholars into Jewish and Christian—and, within the Christian, into Roman Catholic and Protestant.

Undeniably, Roman Catholic biblical scholarship in this period (and for a long time after this period) lagged behind the Protestant in many respects—and the Eastern Orthodox lagged far behind the Roman Catholic. A notable exception to this was the attention of Roman Catholic scholars to publishing the results of biblical archaeology, especially for the Old Testament. Nevertheless, it bears mentioning that one of the first great monuments of biblical scholarship in the age of printing and one of the greatest of all times was a Roman Catholic work that owed absolutely nothing to the Reformation or to Protestantism (though it owed a great deal to the Renaissance): the sumptuous and erudite Complutensian Polyglot of 1514–17, published in Alcalá, Spain, in six volumes, with the support and patronage of a remarkable churchman and humanist, Cardinal Francisco

Ximénez de Cisneros, archbishop of Toledo and grand inquisitor. It has been tersely described by David Price:

> There are four volumes of the Old Testament, with Jerome's Vulgate in the center of the page between the Hebrew text (with roots printed in the margin) and the Septuagint (with an interlinear Latin translation); the Targum Onkelos is printed for the Pentateuch along with a Latin translation. Volume 5 is the New Testament in Greek, and volume 6 includes various indices and study aids, including a Hebrew and Aramaic dictionary, a Hebrew grammar, and interpretations of Greek, Aramaic, and Hebrew names.

Both the Greek text of the Septuagint and the Greek text of the New Testament (1514) were the first ever to be *printed*—although, as mentioned earlier, the New Testament of Erasmus was first to be *published,* in 1516. Inclusion of the Targum Onkelos was a recognition—coming, perhaps by more than chronological coincidence, on the twenty-fifth anniversary of the expulsion of the Jews from Spain in 1492—that a sound Christian interpretation of the Torah had to be informed also by the Jewish exegetical tradition. This massive collection of scriptural learning was based on the principle, as voiced by Cardinal Ximénez, that the Bible in translation, including even the precious Vulgate, "cannot be understood in any way other than from the fount of the original language." Although the Council of Trent thirty years later legislated a juridical authority for the Latin Vulgate, that dedication, in the spirit of the Renaissance, to scholarship derived "from the very fount of the original language" was to persist, especially in the centers of study that would be directed by the Society of Jesus. The twentieth-century affirmation of the primary authority of "the original text of the sacred books" by Pope Pius XII and then by the Second Vatican Council may be seen as an ultimate vindication, more than four centuries later, of the sacred philology of the Renaissance as this had been embodied in Cardinal Ximénez, grand inquisitor of Spain, and as it had been made possible by the invention of printing.

Especially in the Protestantism of northern Europe and Great Britain, biblical scholarship was also the product of the further development of the medieval university into the modern university as the primary engine of intellectual change in modern culture and, therefore, the central focus of both discovery and controversy. In the political, cultural, and educational organization of Europe that came out of the national conflicts and the Wars of Religion, Roman Catholic and Protestant—and even Reformed Protestant and Lutheran Protestant—universities were separate; and Jewish academies of biblical learning were separate even more from them. One great exception to the isolation between Jewish and Christian scholarship was the remarkable Buxtorf family of Reformed Basel (all with the given name Johann), which for several generations cultivated not only Hebrew learning but rabbinical learning as well. Its founder, Johann Buxtorf, has been called "the greatest of all Protestant scholars of rabbinic literature." His many scholarly publications, perhaps above all the four-volume *Biblica Hebraica* with Targum and other rabbinical commentaries, were for generations the principal access to the Jewish exegetical tradition, not only for his Calvinist cobelievers but for other Christian interpreters of the Old Testament; and they have not lost their usefulness even now. This reverence for the Massoretic text was responsible for extending to the vowel points, added centuries after the consonants were written down, the same inerrant authority and verbal inspiration by the Holy Spirit that were predicated of the consonantal text.

CRITIQUE OF TRADITIONAL
VIEWS OF THE BIBLE

In 1779, at the height of what has been described as "the antidogmatic, antienthusiastic temper of an age tired and disgusted with religious controversies," the German man of letters Gotthold Ephraim Lessing published a philosophical drama entitled *Nathan the Wise.* It is set in the time of the Crusades, and its three main characters are Nathan, a wise and tolerant Jew; Saladin, a Muslim sultan; and a

member of the Christian Knights Templar—therefore adherents, respectively, of the Jewish Tanakh, the Muslim Qur'an, and the Christian Bible. In the course of the drama Nathan tells Saladin the following legend (based in part on Boccaccio). There was once a man in the East who possessed a ring of inestimable value that conferred on its owner great blessings and favor with both God and man. In each generation the current owner would bestow it on that one among his sons who was the most worthy of it. The system was working well until in one generation there were three sons of equal virtue and ability, so their father could not bear to single out one of them as the recipient of the miraculous ring. What was to be done? The father took the ring to a master artisan and ordered him to make two more so completely like the original that no one, not even the artisan or the father, would ever be able to tell them apart. As he was dying, the father called each son to him and gave him one ring as though it were the only ring. After his death the inevitable quarrels arose among the brothers over which of the three had the one true ring, and the case went before a judge. The only solution was for each one to acknowledge that there were indeed two other rings and act accordingly but at the same time behave morally as though his were the true one, whether Tanakh or Old and New Testament or Qur'an.

> They search, dispute, lament,
> In vain; the proper ring could not
> Be found; 'twas hid as well almost
> As—the true faith from us today,

as Nathan the Wise explains the real point to Saladin. The key to the dilemma was for all three of them, each in his own special way, to find and practice toward one another a "love that's free from prejudice, as promised by the ring."

Exactly twenty-five years after Lessing's *Nathan the Wise* in 1804, another distinguished man of letters, who happened also to be the president of the United States, Thomas Jefferson, found his own solution to the absolute claims of biblical religion. Working, as he himself put

it, for "2. or 3. nights only at Washington, after getting thro' the evening task of reading the letters and papers of the day," Jefferson in *The Philosophy of Jesus of Nazareth* set about the daunting task of separating—literally with a straight razor—the authentic teachings of Jesus, as he perceived them, from the "rubbish" in the traditional Gospels. After leaving the presidency and at greater leisure, he returned to the assignment, producing the more comprehensive *The Life and Morals of Jesus of Nazareth* in parallel columns of Greek, Latin, French, and English. During most of the twentieth century the English version would be presented, usually under the title *The Jefferson Bible,* to each incoming member of the United States Senate. In this enterprise both Lessing and Jefferson were expressing and embodying the spirit of their time, the Enlightenment; but they were also continuing and carrying out a task to which many of their contemporaries were devoting themselves: the critical-historical study of canonical Scripture. It was a literary and theological assignment that cut across the traditional confessional boundaries—between Catholic and Protestant, between Protestant and Protestant, between Jew and Christian.

HASKALAH-ENLIGHTENMENT-AUFKLÄRUNG

The appealing character of Nathan the Wise in Lessing's play was modeled after the eminent German Jewish philosopher and leading figure of the Haskalah or Jewish Enlightenment, Moses Mendelssohn, Lessing's friend and the grandfather of the composer Felix Mendelssohn. But unlike his grandson, who converted to Christianity and composed the oratorio *Paulus* as well as the *Reformation Symphony* in 1830, Moses Mendelssohn remained loyal to the tenets of Judaism (as he understood them). He was the author of books and tracts arguing for better understanding and toleration between Jews and Christians, and to that end he translated the Torah and the Psalms into German for both a German Jewish and a Gentile readership. Whether it was called "Haskalah" in Hebrew or "Aufklärung" in German or "Eclair-

cissement" in French, the Enlightenment was a complex movement that included many ideas and theories. But in the quest for a rational "religion of nature," many who came from the Jewish tradition or from the Christian tradition, whether Catholic or Protestant, were hoping to find a common faith that stood within and behind—and yet somehow beyond—the competing historical faiths. This common faith would be the "true ring" of Nathan's legend. In theory such a reduction of these faiths to what could be called a "least common *inter*denominator" seemed to hold the promise that the bitter controversies of the past could be transcended by discovering what the sacred books of all the traditions all share. The five points of Deism propounded by Lord Herbert of Cherbury became a kind of theme with variations for Enlightenment thinkers of various backgrounds: the existence of a God, the duty to worship that God, the centrality of virtue in that worship, the obligation of repentance for any departure from that virtue, and the prospect of a life to come with rewards for virtue and punishments for sin. Everything else in their sacred scriptures and holy traditions—cultus, doctrine, authoritative institution, and even the founder, be he thought of as human or as divine— was secondary to these five tenets and therefore a superfluous addition or a historical accident or both.

What stood in the way of such reductionism, of course, was the institutionalism of organized religion, and above all the massive credentials for organized religion that were provided by the Bible whether Jewish or Christian. Synagogue, church, and sect as well as individual believers had all been appealing to these credentials through the centuries for the vindication of their own dogmatic or ethical or liturgical particularities. That was why Thomas Jefferson, straight razor in hand, took it upon himself to excise from the text of the Christian Gospels such stories as the virgin birth and the resurrection and the other miracles, and also the many sayings of Jesus, above all in the Gospel of John, in which he claimed for himself some sort of unique relation to God. There was, at least in principle, nothing about Jefferson's portrait of Jesus and of his teachings at

which non-Christian readers, whether Jewish or Gentile, could justifiably take offense, and Jefferson's opponents wondered just why such a person as this denatured Jesus would ever have been crucified.

Whether it should be seen as a surgical instrument or as a cosmetic tool (or as a lethal weapon), Jefferson's razor did cut into the long-standing tension or contradiction in the Christian (and Jewish) view of the Bible as an authoritative and divinely inspired text that it was nevertheless legitimate and even obligatory to study with the best philological tools available. As divinely inspired and therefore authoritative, it stood apart from all other books, and it was traditionally so designated on its cover or spine as *Holy* Bible, *Sacra* Scriptura, *Heilige* Schrift. The leading statement in English of the doctrines of the Reformation spoke for a Protestant consensus when it declared that "the supreme judge by which all controversies of religion are to be determined, and all decrees of councils, opinions of ancient writers, and private spirits are to be examined, and in whose sentence we are to rest, can be no other than the Holy Spirit speaking in the Scripture," which it defined as "the Old Testament in Hebrew and the New Testament in Greek, being immediately inspired by God, and by his singular care and providence kept pure in all ages." Some adherents of this doctrine of divine inspiration went so far as to claim that the well-known and (at least to a student of classics) often shocking deviations of the Greek New Testament from even the absolute minimum of the grammatical and literary standards of classical Greek were the result of the deliberate will of the inspiring Spirit to write the Bible in "Holy Ghost Greek" and thereby set it apart from its pagan past, even though the evidence from the papyri and other sources would show in the nineteenth and twentieth centuries that the Greek of the New Testament was basically the everyday Greek (usually labeled "Koiné") that was spoken and written at the time throughout the Hellenistic Mediterranean world.

But because "Enlightenment," as defined by Immanuel Kant in a celebrated essay entitled "What Is Aufklärung?" was seen as "man's exodus from his self-incurred tutelage, [which had meant] the inabil-

ity to use one's understanding without the guidance of another person," liberation from that tutelage meant the willingness to subject every authority and all tradition, however cherished they might be, to a critical examination. During the period of the Enlightenment, therefore, such critical examination was addressed to many forms of authority, whether political (for example, monarchy) or ecclesiastical (for example, the Papacy) or intellectual (for example, the absolute claim of Judaism or Christianity to be the only divine revelation), and to many texts of the tradition, whether legal or literary—or biblical.

But as it moved back through time, such a study of history could not stop short of the privileged sanctuary of the first century, so that it soon became clear that the crucial question was: May we apply to the documents of the Bible the same methods of historical-critical study that are appropriate to other components of our tradition? At one level it had been a fundamental assumption of literary scholarship ever since the Renaissance and the Reformation that the answer had to be yes. Erasmus had compared existing manuscripts of the Greek New Testament to produce his first edition of 1516, following the same procedures that his humanist colleagues were employing in preparing the first critical editions of the pagan Greek and Roman classics. Moreover, the meaning of an obscure Greek vocable in the New Testament or the significance of a puzzling grammatical construction was to be arrived at by the same kind of painstaking research that a scholar would use in parsing the Greek of Sophocles or the Latin of Cicero. All of this was part of what eventually came to be called "lower" criticism. But Enlightenment scholars of literature were not content with leaving it at that. Following precedents going all the way back to Antiquity, Friedrich August Wolf in his *Prolegomena to Homer* of 1795 probed the traditional authorship and the literary unity of classics such as the *Iliad* and the *Odyssey*, coming to the conclusion that "Homer" was the traditional designation for several different authors whose work had been stitched together and in this form had been handed down as those two epic poems that were supposedly the work of a single writer, Homer, the blind bard. Could (or

should) this "higher" historical-critical method lead to similar conclusions about the authorship of the books of the Bible, and what would happen if it actually did?

THE RISE OF THE HISTORICAL-CRITICAL METHOD

Within both Judaism and the two major branches of Western Christianity, the Roman Catholic and the Protestant, Enlightenment scholars in this period undertook the historical-critical study of the Jewish and Christian Scriptures. Three figures in the three religious traditions of this history stand out as pioneer critics of canonical Scripture: Benedict Baruch de Spinoza for Judaism, Richard Simon for Roman Catholicism, and Johann Salomo Semler for Protestantism. The patterns in which the controversy over the historical-critical method of handling the Bible played itself out in each of these three traditions are a key to the understanding both of that particular tradition itself and of the place that the Bible occupies in modern culture and modern religion. At one level each of these traditions initially had reason not to be afraid of the consequences of historical criticism, and yet it turned out to be perceived as a major threat to each of them, not only in the seventeenth and eighteenth centuries but long afterward.

On the basis of the central importance of the Talmud it can be argued that a historical-critical approach to the study of the Torah and the Tanakh is as legitimate as is a similar method of studying the Talmud. Everyone who knows anything about the history would be obliged to acknowledge, first, that there was a time when the Talmud did not exist; second, that it arose under specific historical circumstances; third, that it did not arise all at once but grew and developed over a long period of time and in various cultural settings; and fourth, that therefore we are to study it by assembling as much information about each of these assumptions as is historically possible (which is in fact a large body of information). In one sense Spinoza and the other

Jewish practitioners of the historical-critical method could claim to be doing no more than applying these same four assumptions also to the text of the Torah and the Tanakh, which had preceded the Talmud and on which the Talmud had been based. This might in itself seem innocuous enough. But Spinoza's historical and literary hypotheses questioning the traditional ascription of the authorship of the Pentateuch to Moses were not purely literary and historical; such hypotheses rarely if ever are. Instead, they seemed to be functioning in the total context of Spinoza's thought as the cutting edge for his magnificent but heretical metaphysical system, often labeled "pantheistic," in which the terms "God" and "Nature" became interchangeable and the transcendent Creator was seen as indistinguishable from the immanent Universe. It was for these and similar philosophical doctrines that the Great Synagogue of Amsterdam excommunicated Spinoza in 1656. But because such doctrines fundamentally contradicted the traditional teaching of the very first chapter of the Torah about God the Creator and the world as creature, "In the beginning God created heaven and earth," and because Spinoza's historical-critical theories contradicted the traditional Jewish belief about how Moses had written the Torah under divine inspiration, the condemnation for heretical departure from normative Judaism was applied to Spinoza the literary critic as well as to Spinoza the philosophical theologian (or theologizing philosopher).

As a committed defender of Roman Catholic teaching and a member of the Congregation of the Oratory, Richard Simon joined in the attack on Spinoza's speculations about the Tanakh. But in his *Critical History of the Old Testament,* which was published in 1678, Simon set forth his own interpretations based on his study of the Old Testament in the context of the ancient Near East. Bringing his impressive command of the linguistic equipment and his knowledge of parallel documents to bear on the biblical text, especially the Pentateuch, Simon argued that the "Five Books of Moses" could not have been written by him or by any one author but were derived from multiple earlier sources. Although these views did get him into trouble with church authorities, there remained much to be said for the

position that the Roman Catholic understanding of the coordinate relation between Scripture and tradition, as this understanding had been codified by the Council of Trent in 1546 against the *sola Scriptura* of the Protestant Reformation, was far less vulnerable to the historical researches of the critics than was the Protestant understanding, where everything stands or falls with the authority of the letter of Scripture. Not only the Roman Catholic reliance on holy tradition as, in some sense, a "second source of revelation" alongside the Bible but also the dedication of Roman Catholic exegesis to the spiritual and allegorical interpretation of the Bible could be seen as putting it beyond the reach of the critics. None of this, however, could hold off the challenge of the critics from such increasingly untenable Roman Catholic biblical tenets as the normative authority of the Latin Vulgate (with all its mistranslations) or the claim that the apostle Paul was the author of the Epistle to the Hebrews (which had been doubted by many eminent and orthodox authorities already in the ancient church) or the authenticity of various textually dubious readings in the Greek New Testament (as the manuscript evidence against them began to accumulate, though it was assembled largely by Protestant biblical scholars).

It definitely was the case that in the ranks of the historical critics Protestant biblical scholars greatly outnumbered all others. The polymath Johann Salomo Semler investigated many problematic chapters in the history of the church, including the checkered story of the gradual stabilization of the canon of the Bible. Like many of the Protestant critics who followed him, Semler could claim to be following in the footsteps of Luther and the Reformation, and to be doing so with greater consistency than the political situation of the sixteenth century had permitted the first Protestant Reformers themselves to do. The same kind of historical-critical scrutiny to which Luther and his fellow reformers had subjected the cherished traditions and doctrines of the medieval church, such as the claims of the Papacy or even the sacramental system, could and should be rolled back to the very first centuries of the history of the church. Even the first century, revered as "apostolic," must not be beyond the reach of

historical criticism. The important outcome to which such probing led Semler and other Protestant critics was not this or that specific radical conclusion about the Bible, which may not withstand a similar historical scrutiny today, but the permanent justification of this as a method—or as *the* method—for the scholarly study of Scripture. During the nineteenth and twentieth centuries, nevertheless, several Protestant denominations were torn apart over its legitimacy, with those who eventually acquired the somewhat loose designation of "fundamentalist" rejecting not only the answers but even the very questions of the historical-critical method.

From one perspective, the question of who wrote down one or another individual book of the Bible might seem to be of secondary importance for the eyes of faith. If the Holy Spirit of God is the real Author of the whole of Scripture, why should it matter as much as it obviously did whether it was Moses himself who actually wrote the account of how "Moses the servant of the LORD died in the land of Moab, at the command of the LORD," which the defenders of the Mosaic authorship of the entire Pentateuch, in order to be consistent, have been obliged to maintain? The rabbis had felt constrained to come up with elaborate explanations of just how Moses, even with the assistance of divine inspiration, could have written his own obituary. For Christians, whether Roman Catholic or Protestant, the question was bound up with the consistent practice by Jesus himself, at least according to the Gospels, of referring to the Pentateuch, in whole or in part, as "the book of Moses." Was it permissible even to ask whether Jesus could have been mistaken in following uncritically the views of Old Testament authorship shared by his Jewish contemporaries or whether perhaps he was accommodating himself to their ignorance? And what did that imply for orthodox Christian belief and doctrine not only about the Bible but eventually about the person of Jesus Christ? Was this question of the authorship of the books of the Bible, therefore, the first domino which, once toppled, would bring about in turn the collapse of the entire traditional authority of faith and morality?

Authorship of the Bible was, to be sure, not an isolated issue. What was ultimately at stake was the credibility of the Bible, to

which the successive scientific discoveries and scientific theories of the modern period have repeatedly represented a challenge. If Galileo was correct in using his telescope to identify the sun, not the earth, as the center of the universe, and therefore in teaching that the earth revolves around a sun that does not move, what was one to make of the long day of Joshua when, according to the Tanakh, "the sun stood still and the moon halted"? If Charles Darwin in *The Origin of Species* of 1859 truly discovered that species had evolved from other species and were not permanently fixed, and in *The Descent of Man* of 1871 that the human species was not an exception to this universal rule but shared in the evolutionary process, what happened to the accounts of creation in the first and second chapters of the Book of Genesis and, above all, to the theologically and ethically momentous teaching that "God created man in His image, in the image of God He created him; male and female He created them"? If marriage was not instituted in the Garden of Eden by a special act of God but had itself evolved, it appeared to many that the very foundations of monogamous marriage and of the nuclear family were being shaken.

Similar challenges shook the credibility of the Bible on questions of history. The fundamental truth claims of the biblical record were historical claims about things that were believed to have happened, not "once upon a time" in a fairy tale or somewhere outside of time and space, but at specific times and places that belonged to the total history of the human race and that could be located on a map. The message of the Bible about morality or even about doctrine was grounded in narrative. "I the LORD am your God who brought you out of the land of Egypt, the house of bondage": this was not only the literary preface but the historical and the theological presupposition to each of the Ten Commandments in the Torah. "If Christ was not raised, then our gospel is null and void, and so too is your faith": this "gospel" and "faith" were basically not a series of doctrinal tenets or ethical precepts but a historical claim. And therefore if the history of the resurrection of Christ had not really happened, the message and faith in the message, according to the authority of the apostle Paul, had to be "null and void."

Thus, the New Testament reported that on Good Friday during the crucifixion of Jesus, "it was about the sixth hour, and there was a darkness *over all the earth* until the ninth hour." And yet in the bitterly sarcastic comment of the unbelieving historian Edward Gibbon, "even this miraculous event, which ought to have excited the wonder, the curiosity, and the devotion of mankind, passed without notice in an age of science and history" and did not receive so much as a mention from any contemporary Greek or Roman pagan writer. The Christmas story in the Gospels makes a special point of locating its events in the context of "a decree issued by the emperor Augustus for a census to be taken throughout the Roman world. . . . [I]t took place when Quirinius was governor of Syria"; but historical investigation of independent sources was unable to verify this imperial "census" or to identify this "Quirinius." In spite of the detailed account in the Book of Exodus and even after intense archaeological excavations in the historic sites of ancient Egypt, it continued to be impossible to verify, much less to date, the event from Egyptian sources or to answer the simple question: "Who was the Pharaoh of the exodus?"

The eighteenth and nineteenth centuries became the great time of confidence in the historical method as the key to the understanding of many areas of human life. The study of literature was the examination of the history of a national literature, from *Beowulf* to Shakespeare to Milton. The key to law was the historical relation between Roman law and the barbarian law codes of the Germanic peoples who came into the Roman Empire. In the hands of a thinker such as Georg Wilhelm Friedrich Hegel, the history of philosophy was the best way to put philosophical doctrines and systems into the right perspective. Similarly, the history of Christian doctrine was seen as the right means for coming to terms with theology so that, as Karl Barth observed, "in the history of Protestant theology the nineteenth century brought with it the none too dignified sight of a general flight, of those heads that were wisest, into the study of history." It is to this "historicism" that we owe the assumption that tracing such a phenomenon century by century was the best way to understand it. But instead of corroborating the ac-

counts in the Bible, this historiography now became a major force in promoting doubts about the truthfulness of the biblical record.

In many ways the Tanakh was simultaneously more immune and yet more vulnerable than the New Testament. Of all the books of the Bible, Koheleth (the Book of Ecclesiastes) came closest to the rationalism and skepticism of the Enlightenment philosophers, who saw in it a kindred spirit. Yet the lingering anti-Jewishness in Christian thought also made the historical criticism of the Old Testament seem somehow less dangerous, and it is significant that the historical-critical method did begin with the Pentateuch rather than with the Gospels. The long history covered by the Torah, the Nevi'im, and the Kethuvim, with its many echoes of all the Near Eastern religions with whom Israel came into contact, was a fertile field for historians, comparativists, and critics. As Peter Gay has summarized Enlightenment attitudes toward it, "The Old Testament, even at its most rationalist, overwhelmed law by charisma, orderly cosmology by creation myths, moral injunctions by word and number magic, the conception of the ethical individual by the myth of the Chosen People and the Promised Land, history by eschatology." It was not difficult to dismiss much of this by referring condescendingly to a narrow Jewish national religion that had supposedly been transcended by the more spiritual message of Jesus. Less than two weeks before his death, Goethe said: "Beyond the grandeur and the moral elevation of Christianity, *as it sparkles and shines in the Gospels,* the human mind will not advance."

Initially, therefore, the historical-critical study of the Bible did not appear to threaten the person of Jesus Christ "as it sparkles and shines in the Gospels," or even the orthodox doctrine about him. But once it had been spilled from the bottle, the corrosive acid of rationalistic criticism could not be kept away from even the most precious chapters of the Christian Bible and the person of Jesus Christ himself. Working quietly and writing anonymously, apparently with no intent of publishing the results, at least during his own lifetime, Hermann Samuel Reimarus left behind a manuscript entitled *Apologia or Defense for the Rational Worshipers of God.* It was, perhaps not surprisingly, Gotthold Ephraim Lessing, the author of *Nathan the Wise,* who first published

portions of it in 1774–78; it would not be until 1972 that the entire manuscript was published. Here it was not only the miracles of Moses but the miracles of Jesus that were exploded. Jesus had predicted, had led his followers to await, and had himself expected the coming of the end of the world and the arrival of the kingdom of God. When that hope was brought to a bitter end by his crucifixion, he cried out in despair, quoting the twenty-second Psalm (in Aramaic), "'Eli, Eli, lama sabachthani?' which means, 'My God, my God, why have you forsaken me?'" The entire edifice of New Testament religion, beginning with the Epistles of Paul, and after it the whole development of traditional Christianity, with the evolution of the creeds and the rise of the episcopate, was an elaborate attempt to make up for or to rationalize that fundamental disappointment. Far from being the incarnate Son of God and the risen Savior of the world, as Christians regardless of denomination had long been confessing him to be, Jesus was the defeated leader of the aspirations of his followers, himself misled and misleading others. It was therefore appropriate that Albert Schweitzer opened his *Quest of the Historical Jesus* with the work of Reimarus.

To the extent that they were even aware of all this, Jewish and Christian believers by the millions went on reading their Scriptures, praying their Psalms, and teaching their Bible diligently to their children. It is no exaggeration to say that a chasm developed between pew and study, which was sometimes even a chasm between pew and pulpit. Like Dostoevsky's Grand Inquisitor, parish pastors who had been educated to treat the Bible with skepticism went on reciting the creed and teaching the catechism as though the orthodox faith of the church were true when they themselves no longer believed it. Reimarus was just one example of this schizophrenic approach. This chasm was probably most pronounced within Protestantism, where it would lead to several controversies and schisms during the nineteenth and twentieth centuries in several denominations. But the anti-Rationalist protests within Judaism and the anti-Modernist decrees of several popes, including the anti-Modernist oath imposed by Pope Pius X in 1910, also documented the severity of the perceived danger. Nevertheless, it would be a mistake— and one into which many historians of Christianity and Judaism during

the eighteenth and nineteenth centuries have found it altogether too easy to fall—to treat this struggle between criticism and anticriticism as though it were the whole story of the Bible in this period. It was at this very same time that there occurred an unprecedented increase in the dissemination and translation of the Bible quite literally throughout the world as the books of the Bible were brought to more parts of the earth than ever before in their history.

Meanwhile, through several masterworks composed during the seventeenth and eighteenth centuries, of which we shall select only three here, "their sound is gone out into all lands, and their words unto the ends of the world," as one of them put it, quoting Tanakh and New Testament together.

Although his posthumously published *Christian Doctrine,* in which he had "decided not to depend upon the belief or judgment of others in religious questions" but "to puzzle out a religious creed by myself by my own exertions," showed how far he had deviated from the orthodox consensus about the Trinity and the person of Jesus Christ that had been shared with the rest of Christendom also by his own Puritan party within the Church of England, John Milton in *Paradise Lost* of 1667 and *Paradise Regained* of 1671 gave the sweep of biblical history a literary expression that had been unmatched since Dante. Invoking the same Holy Spirit to whose inspiration the composition of the Torah by Moses was attributed as the

> Heavenly Muse, that on the secret top
> Of Oreb, or of Sinai, didst inspire
> That shepherd, who first taught the chosen seed,
> In the beginning how the heav'ns and earth
> Rose out of chaos,

Milton prayed

> That to the height of this great argument
> I may assert eternal Providence,
> and justify the ways of God to men.

The answer to that prayer for inspiration was a retelling of the biblical narrative by this contemporary of Spinoza in which many generations of readers have found their own form of inspiration, both artistic and religious.

Johann Sebastian Bach and George Frideric Handel were both born in 1685, a decade after Milton's death. The vast body of Bach's sacred compositions and cantatas, and above all his *Mass in B Minor* and his *Passions,* can be taken as a documentation of how a countryman and near contemporary of Hermann Samuel Reimarus was reading the same Bible that Reimarus was, not to undermine its authority but to celebrate its message. At the hands of Bach in the *Saint Matthew Passion,* even "My God, my God, why have you forsaken me?" (rendered by his librettist, for some reason, in the Hebrew of the Tanakh rather than in the Aramaic quoted by Matthew) becomes not a cry of despair from a disillusioned Messiah who had been expecting the coming of the kingdom of God on earth, but a mysterious expression of the believer's trust in the atoning sacrifice of Christ. With its blending of intensely private reflection on Holy Scripture, somber retelling of the biblical narrative of the passion, and soaring doxology, Bach's *Saint Matthew Passion* has made the Gospels live for generations to whom the work of the critics might have seemed otherwise to pose an impenetrable barrier. As Alexander Schmemann, the Russian American Orthodox theologian, said of it, "Every time I listen to it, especially passages like the cry of the daughters of Zion and the final chorale, I come to the same conclusion: How is it possible, in a world where such music was born and heard, not to believe in God?"

Less profound perhaps than the *Saint Matthew Passion* but more than making up for that in its instant accessibility to any hearer and its universal appeal to all hearers, Handel's *Messiah* is, during its innumerable performances in the Christmas season, the longest sustained exposure that many modern listeners ever experience to a substantial chunk of the Bible. It is also a dramatic embodiment of the ambiguous place of the Bible in the context of relations between Jews and Christians. Its best-known chorus, familiar enough to be caricatured more often than it is performed, is "Hallelujah," the Christian musi-

cal setting of a Hebrew word and a Jewish hymn of praise. Its present association with the Christmas season is not part of its original intent: The work was performed for the first time on 13 April 1742 in Dublin, and "Part the First," associated with the nativity of Christ, is only (as it is in the Gospels themselves) a large-scale introduction to the accounts of the passion and of the resurrection. This is what the Hallelujah Chorus celebrates, not the nativity as such. Around the motif of prophecy and fulfillment, *Messiah* skillfully interweaves texts from the Old Testament and the New Testament in the King James Version, as in the aria following the Hallelujah Chorus and opening the third part:

> I know that my Redeemer liveth, and that He shall stand at
>   the latter day upon the earth:
> And though worms destroy this body, yet in my flesh shall I see
>   God;
> For now is Christ risen from the dead, the first-fruits of them that
>   sleep.

Even some preachers, who ought to know better, have quoted this as though it were a single passage from the New Testament.

Once again, as in the age of the Reformation, the period of Haskalah-Enlightenment-Aufklärung raised the possibility and the hope that new perspectives on reading the Book that they had in common might finally manage to bring Jews and Christians closer together. But in spite of Moses Mendelssohn and the almost irresistible appeal of Lessing's *Nathan the Wise,* the tone for much of the Enlightenment attitude toward Judaism was set instead by the anti-Semitism of Voltaire. This anomaly was an eerie anticipation of twentieth-century Germany, where post-Christian Gentiles and assimilated Jews were living side by side in relative peace and toleration until they were overwhelmed by the forces of hate who were wearing new uniforms but reciting age-old slogans. Among those slogans, many of which came from a new paganism, were some garbled words of Jewish-Christian Scripture.

ELEVEN

A Message for the Whole Human Race

MAMUSSE
WUNNEETUPANATAMWE
UP-BIBLUM GOD
NANEESWE
NUKKONE TESTAMENT
KAH WONK
WUSKU TESTAMENT.

Ne quoſhkinnumuk naſhpe Wuttinneumoh *CHRIST*
noh aſoowesit
JOHN ELIOT·

CAMBRIDGE:
Printeuoop naſhpe *Samuel Green* kah *Marmaduke Johnſon.*
1 6 6 3.

Title page of the Natick-Algonquin Bible, the first Bible printed in America
(Cambridge, Massachusetts, 1663, 1661). (By permission of the Houghton Library,
Harvard University)

ust as the defenders of the old faith had taken the rapid expansion of Catholicism to Spanish America and French Canada during the seventeenth century to be a kind of divine reparation for the heavy losses to the Reformation in Great Britain and northern Europe suffered by the Papacy during the sixteenth, so there might seem to be some sort of law of compensation at work in the standing of the Bible in the culture of the eighteenth, nineteenth, and twentieth centuries. For every scholarly or speculative deconstruction of its message and diminution of its authority by critics in Europe and the United States there was yet another translation of Holy Scripture into some new language in Asia or Africa and a net gain of thousands or millions of additional Bible readers.

As was evident from the debates in the Talmud about "the universality of the Torah," it had long been the prophecy and the hope of the Hebrew prophets that all the nations would eventually be illumined by the light of the Torah, which was intended to be a message not for Israelites alone but for the whole human race:

> O Lord, my strength and my stronghold,
> My refuge in a day of trouble,
> To You nations shall come
> From the ends of the earth and say:
> "Our fathers inherited utter delusions,
> Things that are futile and worthless."
> Once and for all I will teach them

My power and My might.
And they shall learn that My name is LORD;
People and the inhabitants of many cities shall yet come;
My name is honored among the nations.

But the historical fact is that the name of the Lord and the message of his word have gone beyond the boundaries of the Near East and of Europe and have now finally reached "all races and tribes, nations and languages" of the human race primarily through the agency of the Christian missionary enterprise, which brought the Word "to every part of the world."

"AWASH IN A SEA OF BIBLES"

The English-speaking world since the Reformation has been an especially fruitful garden for the growing of Bibles. With the issuance of the *Bay Psalm Book* in 1640, book publishing began in the English colonies of the New World. It contained all 150 Psalms, done in metric lines by Richard Mather, John Eliot, and others. By an extension of the Reformation principle of *sola Scriptura* to the realm of worship and hymnody, Puritans and some other Calvinists insisted that the book of Psalms, "God's own hymnbook," was so completely preferable to any poems and hymns of human composition that it was best to obey the commandment of the New Testament, "With psalms and hymns and spiritual songs, sing from the heart in gratitude to God," by sticking to the Psalms, translated literally but turned into singable verse. It is to such metrical adaptation of the Psalter that we are indebted for some of the best-known hymns in the English language. John Eliot was also responsible for the production of *Mamusse Wunneetupanatamwe Up-Biblum God* (1661–63), a translation of the Bible into "Massachusetts," as the Natick-Algonquin language was called. Cotton Mather said of it, with justifiable pride: "Behold, ye Americans, the greatest honor that ever you were partakers of. The Bible

was printed here at our Cambridge, and is the only Bible that ever was printed in all America, from the very foundation of the world."

It would certainly not be "the only Bible that ever was printed in all America" for very long. Of the hundreds of millions of Bibles that have been printed in all America since then, by far the most have been the King James Version, which would therefore deserve to be called "*the* American Bible" in a special sense. In fact, in the decision of the Supreme Court forbidding the ritual practice of Bible reading in the schools as a violation of the establishment clause of the First Amendment to the United States Constitution, *Abington School District* v. *Schempp* of 1963, the Court itself pointed out that "the only copies furnished by the school are the King James version, copies of which were circulated to each teacher by the school district," although other versions, including the Roman Catholic Douai-Reims Bible, were permitted to be used. But several other American versions of the twentieth century should at least be mentioned. Significantly, all but one of them are revisions of the King James. The American Standard Version of 1901 was the text produced by the American members of the British committee for the Revised Version of 1881–85, which was intended to eliminate archaic language and to incorporate changes made necessary by critical study of the original texts and by modern advances in knowledge of biblical Hebrew and Greek. The Revised Standard Version of 1946–57, by far the most successful of these versions, revised the American Revised Version still further while striving to keep the translation in a liturgically appropriate form. A further revision of this revision of a revision, the New Revised Standard Version of 1989, is notable for its substitution of "inclusive language" for masculine nouns and pronouns, translating "brothers *and sisters*" where the original text has only "brothers." In a class by itself because of its individualism and even colloquialism (as when Jesus, appearing to the disciples after the resurrection, greets them with "Good morning!" rather than "Peace be with you!"), *The Bible: An American Translation* of 1923–35 is often identified by the name of the translator of the New Testament, Edgar J. Goodspeed.

The most recent major edition of a "new Bible" is at the same time very ancient in form and conception: The Saint John's Bible, produced by the Benedictine Abbey of Saint John the Baptist in Collegeville, Minnesota, long a center of liturgical and biblical renewal within the Roman Catholic Church and beyond. As it has been described by the monastery, "When finished, The Saint John's Bible will be the first commissioned completely hand-written Bible in 500 years, since the advent of movable type by Johann Gutenberg revolutionized the printing industry nearly 550 years ago. Prior to that, all Bibles were copied by hand. Since then, virtually all have been printed." Using quills and other traditional instruments as well as processes and materials that only modern technology could have made possible, the ancient and medieval arts of calligraphy, illumination, and illustration are being employed to copy the text of the Bible in ink and in color, including pure gold for representations of the Divine. The pages themselves follow the ancient example by being made of vellum, which has been carefully burnished and smoothed. As the portions that have already been produced demonstrate, the end result will be a truly unique adaptation of living tradition to contemporary life, a fitting expression of the Bible as "a message for the whole human race."

In America, as in Great Britain since the King James Version and even earlier, the cultural dominance of the Bible makes itself evident even in everyday speech (although the speakers are often unaware that they are quoting the Bible): "I am escaped with [not "by"] the skin of my teeth," Job says in the King James Version. "There is no new thing under the sun" is not a piece of "folk wisdom," as a recently published textbook identifies it, but the word of Koheleth the Preacher. "The powers that be" is the apostle Paul's term for government, in this case the rule of the emperor Nero. And "If a house be divided against itself, that house cannot stand" originally came from the Gospels, not from Abraham Lincoln (who must have known large sections of the King James Bible by heart). Especially in the nineteenth and twentieth centuries, the Bible has served as the source of countless historical novels and films. In historical perspective what

stands out about these novels and films is the amount of acquaintance with the biblical stories they were able to take for granted in their readers and viewers, not only because so many Americans regularly attended church and Sunday school but because even those who did not go to church often made a point, sometimes quite vociferously, of reading the Bible at home. When the set of *Great Books of the Western World* was published in 1952, its editor, Robert Maynard Hutchins, longtime president and chancellor of the University of Chicago, explained: "Readers who are startled to find the Bible omitted from the set will be reassured to learn that this was done only because Bibles are already widely distributed, and it was felt unnecessary to bring another, by way of this set, into homes that had several already"; but references to the Bible are included in its *Syntopicon* or index.

Bibles were so "widely distributed" in America during the nineteenth and twentieth centuries that the United States was "awash in a sea of faith," which means, among other things, "awash in a sea of Bibles." American churches (especially Protestant churches) and synagogues were persistent in urging their members to own and read the Bible, often making the presentation of their first Bible to children a rite of passage in connection with confirmation or bar mitzvah. But the distribution of Bibles to the widest possible public became a religious vocation for the Bible societies that began in Great Britain in 1804 with the British and Foreign Bible Society, and more than a hundred arose in the United States after the War of Independence. During the Colonial period the university presses of Oxford and Cambridge enjoyed a monopoly in the distribution of the Authorized Version, also in North America. Now that this monopoly was broken, together with other vestiges of British rule such as the authority of Anglican bishops in England over American "Episcopalian" parishes, the Bible societies in the several states, and then in 1816 the American Bible Society for the nation as a whole, became an immediate success. As reported by one reference work in 1996, the statistics of the American Bible Society over the years are remarkable: "It distributed nearly 100,000 Bibles in the first four years of operation. In the three-year period between 1829 and 1831, moreover, the

ABS printed and distributed more than one million copies of the Scriptures, at a time when the total population of the United States was only around 13 million. Still strong today, the ABS reported that in 1986 it had distributed nearly 290 million Bibles and portions of the Scriptures in a single year." The other leading Bible society in the United States, the Gideons, who are best known to travelers for their campaign to place a copy of the (Protestant) Bible in every hotel room, reported that in 1992–93 they had disseminated more than 38 million copies.

These statistics are only one measure of the central position that is occupied by Holy Writ in the culture and piety of Protestant America, matching or surpassing what the depiction and veneration of the Virgin Mary were in Latin Catholicism on both sides of the Atlantic, and the devotion to the holy icons in the Orthodox Christianity of Byzantium and its daughter churches. Like the image of the Virgin and the ubiquitous icons, it has sometimes seemed that the Bible has become more of a totem than a sacramental. Witnesses in court and presidents at their inauguration took the oath "So help me God!" with their right hand on the Bible; Psalm 23 (in the King James Version, of course) was for a long time part of the opening exercises of public schools; the Ten Commandments were prominently displayed in courthouses and other public places; and in every war there were stories circulating of how a soldier was miraculously saved from death when the New Testament in the breast pocket of his uniform stopped a bullet—a miraculous power that had been attributed in earlier periods of Christian history, back to the days of swords and arrows, to the relics of the saints. Not only was the Bible present for the opening of school each day, but repeatedly it reached into the classroom. One of the most notorious illustrations of its authority in the schools was the famous "Scopes trial" of July 1925 over the teaching of evolution in the public schools of Tennessee, which was forbidden by the laws of that state. The trial pitted William Jennings Bryan, a former secretary of state who was known as a vigorous advocate of the literal interpretation of the Bible, specifically of the creation story in Genesis, against Clarence Darrow, a renowned defense attorney and a pro-

fessed atheist. The clash between these two public figures became, and probably still is, emblematic of the dominant authority of Scripture literally interpreted in the region of the United States that a journalist and man of letters covering that trial, H. L. Mencken, labeled "the Bible Belt" in sharp contrast to the attitude toward the Bible of the more radical segments of the intellectual elite.

This "monkey trial" was only the most widely publicized manifestation of the phenomenon in "the Bible Belt" and far beyond it that came to be called "fundamentalism." In the secular public and in the media to this day the label "fundamentalism" has come to be a way of lumping together and dismissing any kind of religious orthodoxy or authoritative tradition at all, so that the term finally seems to have little or no specific meaning. The name itself came from a series of pamphlets, *The Fundamentals* (1910–15), in which the embattled defenders of the literal interpretation of the Bible made their case against the "modernists" in the Protestant churches for such doctrines as creation in six days of twenty-four hours each and the virgin birth. To the extent that the term remains useful, fundamentalism originated as a movement within several Protestant denominations to make the inspiration and inerrancy of the Bible the doctrine by which all Christian faith stands or falls. It therefore involves a resistance to any scholarly interpretation of the Bible that seems to jeopardize its absolute uniqueness and authority or to require an accommodation of its teachings to a scientific worldview.

Yet in the very region where much of this biblical resistance was going on, the Bible had become a powerful force in a quite different direction. Historically speaking, it is difficult to imagine a more Bible-saturated culture than the experience of African slaves in America. Slaveholders often regarded it a duty (and put it forth as a flimsy justification for the system) to Christianize their slaves, in some cases because it would teach them obedience and make them submissive. The one book of the Bible to be devoted to the issue of slavery, Paul's Epistle to Philemon, is anything but an emancipation tract, telling Philemon to take back his runaway slave Onesimus "no longer as a slave, but as more than a slave: as a dear brother," therefore as

more than a slave, though not less of a slave, but, significantly, not urging or requiring Philemon to set Onesimus free. But the white evangelization of African slaves turned out to be more successful than the slave owners could ever have expected. They surely could not have reckoned with the possibility that the Bible would become as integral to the life of the slaves as it did, as this was profoundly expressed in the indigenous music of the "spiritual." Not only did the poignant subjectivity of the Psalms shape the poetry of lament in such lyrics as "Sometimes I feel like a motherless child, a long way from home," and the drama of the passion story in the Gospels become starkly contemporary in the challenge of the question, "Were you there when they crucified my Lord?" But the themes of captivity and liberation in the book of Exodus came to voice in this tradition with pathos and power as they never had before, at any rate in Christian history:

> Go down, Moses,
> 'Way down in Egypt lan';
> Tell ole Pharaoh
> To let my people go.

Despite all its language about "submitting to the authorities in power, for all authority comes from God, and the existing authorities are instituted by him," the Bible also carried the promise of freedom even as it provided consolation to those, black and white alike, who were living lives not of freedom but of what Henry David Thoreau called "quiet desperation."

Not only the Africans who had been brought to the New World in chains but those who were still in Africa, together with the inhabitants of Asia and the islands of the sea, became in this same period a vast new potential audience for the Bible. The nineteenth century has been called "the great century" for Christian missions, taking up three of the seven volumes of the monumental *History of the Expansion of Christianity* by Kenneth Scott Latourette. The centrality of the Bible in the theology and piety of the Protestant churches that came

out of the sixteenth-century Reformation makes it understandable that the Bible translator replaced the monk as the principal agent also of their strategy of evangelization and missions. At a time when Western culture was expanding its power over the rest of the world, in the process associated with such terms as "imperialism" and "colonialism," Christian missions were bringing the gospel message and therefore the books of the Gospels and the rest of Scripture to those same places. At a level unmatched anywhere else in its long history, the Bible appeared in what eventually became hundreds and even thousands of new languages. Many of these were ancient and venerable literary languages with an indigenous poetry and literature already in place. Others had existed only in spoken form and had to be reduced to an alphabet for the first time. It would be impressive, as several such catalogs show, to list these hundreds and even thousands of modern translations of the Bible alphabetically, from Albanian and Athabaskan to Zulu. But more interesting for our purposes here is a consideration of what this new program of bringing the Word to the world—to the whole world—meant for the history of the Word.

The linguistic accident and overwhelming historical reality that the New Testament was written in a later (though seemingly corrupted) version of the same language which had been spoken and written by Sophocles and Plato and that, two centuries or so earlier, the Tanakh had been translated into Greek meant that through most of its history the exposition of the Bible, both Jewish and Christian, had concerned itself primarily with its relation to Hellenism. The Christian missionaries arriving in Asia and Africa with their Bibles during the seventeenth, eighteenth, and nineteenth centuries carried in their luggage prayers and liturgies, creeds and catechisms—and standard translations of the Bible into Latin or English or German— that had been shaped in a multitude of subtle and invisible ways by the problematics and the assumptions of the dialogue that has been called in the title of more than one twentieth-century book *Christianity and Classical Culture*. These were, as the British American philosopher Alfred North Whitehead described them, "fundamental assumptions which adherents of all the variant systems within the

epoch unconsciously presuppose. Such assumptions appear so obvious that people do not know what they are assuming because no other way of putting things has ever occurred to them"—until, that is, they are suddenly put down into a culture where no one has ever heard of these assumptions.

The novelty of the situation created enormous difficulties in the evangelistic and pastoral administration of Christian missions, with such issues as polygamy becoming a major source of confusion and controversy. Must a convert give up all his wives except the first one? But then what about the polygamy of Abraham, who is nevertheless the only Old Testament figure whom the New Testament adorns with the title "the father of all who have faith"? The assignment of translating the Bible into a new language and therefore into a new culture was especially fraught with such difficulties. Ulphilas, the fourth-century "apostle to the Goths," was reported to have omitted the Books of Kings from his translation of the Bible, on the grounds that the Goths were already warlike enough and did not need any more encouragement in that direction from the bloody battles described in the Scriptures of their new religion. Each new translation could become the occasion for problems of this kind. Even without the benefit of the conventions of capitalization that have become standard in all English Bibles regardless of their provenance, biblical language, both Hebrew and Greek, has a generic term for "a god" or "gods" as distinct from the very specific Name YHWH, which is not only unique to God but so holy for pious Jews that it may not even be pronounced but must be replaced by "the LORD" even in Greek (and English) translation. But how was the missionary to render this fundamental distinction in a language like Chinese, which seemed to have only proper names for its various deities but no generic word for "god"? Similarly, the New Testament speaks about "immorality such as even pagans do not tolerate, the union of a man with his stepmother." But what would happen to this element of what was supposed to be "natural law" in a culture where other brands of "pagans" seem not only to "tolerate" such a "union" but even to require it, as well as more obviously incestuous ones?

It was also possible that a newly converted culture could manifest hitherto unknown affinities with the biblical message. An extraordinary example of such affinities is a creed composed for the Masai people of Africa in the 1960s. Its second article, about Jesus Christ, affirms:

> We believe that God made good his promise by sending his Son, Jesus Christ, a man in the flesh, a Jew by tribe, born poor in a little village, who left his home and *was always on safari* doing good, curing people by the power of God, teaching about God and man, showing that the meaning of religion is love. He was rejected by his people, tortured and nailed hands and feet to a cross, and died. He lay buried in the grave, *but the hyenas did not touch him*, and on the third day, he rose from the grave.

After nineteen centuries of the Christian reading of the Gospels in the original Greek and in many new languages all over the globe, it took the fresh experience of a new culture in Africa to discover there the message that Jesus, after having been "always on safari doing good," was buried in a stone sepulcher sealed by a rock to protect his body from the danger of the scavenging hyenas, a danger that first-century Palestine and twentieth-century Africa both knew very well.

A book in which a grandiose phrase like "all the world" really meant no more than the Greco-Roman world surrounding the Mediterranean Sea, or at most the "corpus of Christendom" in the Middle Ages, became through the missionaries of the nineteenth and twentieth centuries truly a message for the whole human race, not only for Europe and America. But coming at a time when the reverence for the Bible and the all but universal acknowledgment of its uniqueness and authority had begun to decline sharply, above all in Europe and America, and particularly among the intelligentsia, this changed context meant that the Bible also had to take its place in a veritable pantheon of sacred scriptures.

Two events in the final quarter of the nineteenth century may stand as symbols of this new situation. In 1875 the celebrated Sanskrit

scholar and pioneer of the study of comparative religion Friedrich Max Müller launched the publication in English translation of *The Sacred Books of the East,* which by its conclusion at the end of the century came to a total of fifty-one volumes. As he had foreseen, the availability of this set, standing on library shelves alongside editions of the Jewish Tanakh and the Christian Bible—which were in their origins sacred books of the East, too, as was the Qur'an—stimulated a method of comparative study that stressed the obvious similarities and the supposed borrowings among the various holy scriptures. And in 1893, in connection with the Columbian World Exposition, which was held in Chicago to commemorate the four-hundredth anniversary of Columbus's discovery of the New World in 1492, a World Parliament of Religions was convoked, bringing together the traditions represented by most of the sacred books, including both Judaism and Christianity for the Bible. Such a grouping implied that the Bible, like the Rig-Veda, could legitimately be an object of reading and study "from the outside" by adherents of some other scripture (or of none) who sought to "learn *about* it" as a body of anthropological and historical data, not necessarily to "learn it" as believers had been doing within both Judaism and Christianity for so many centuries. This way of studying and printing the Bible has become a standard part of publishing and teaching.

A good illustration of how such a comparativist method could shape the reading of the Bible is the familiar story of the *Aqedah,* "the binding of Isaac." In a rabbinical Targum on that passage, it is an account of faith as faithfulness and faith as obedience in which an almost superhuman loyalty to God and his commands led the father of the covenant to be willing to make the ultimate sacrifice, praying: "And now, when his sons find themselves in a time of distress, remember the *Aqedah* of their father Isaac and hear the voice of their supplication. Hear and answer them and deliver them from all tribulation." In Christian exegesis, in addition to those elements, the story is read typologically as an anticipation and prophecy of the crucifixion of Christ in which God "did not spare his own Son, but gave him up for us all." But set against the broader background of the ancient

Near East, the story of the *Aqedah* comes out sounding like an echo of the widely practiced child sacrifice that is condemned elsewhere in the Torah.

HATRED OF THE BIBLE

Even as these attitudes of historical objectivity or scholarly neutrality toward the Bible were becoming fashionable in some circles in the West, the twentieth century also witnessed some of the most virulent expressions of hatred toward the Bible at any time in its long history. The triumph of Marxism-Leninism in Orthodox Russia after World War I and eventually in the rest of Eastern and East-Central Europe after World War II launched a campaign to eliminate the Bible from the collective memory of entire generations, from schools and homes and churches. In spite of the Soviet constitution, which theoretically guaranteed religious liberty, the printing of Bibles was prohibited, the reading of Bibles was punished, and Bibles together with icons, "the Bibles of the illiterate," were relegated to a superstitious past. Supposedly anti-Communist in its inspiration, National Socialism in Germany, in an unholy collusion with residual anti-Semitic elements in the various churches, went even beyond Communism in undertaking through the "German Christians" to purge the biblical tradition of its "Jewish" qualities and to create a heretical "Aryan Christianity" under which anyone of identifiably Jewish ancestry would not be ordained to the clergy and the "Jewish tribalism" of Scripture would yield to a method of interpreting the New Testament that did not depend on the Old Testament. Although the German Bible continued to be printed with an Old Testament included, it had lost its authority. And among the other victims of the Nazi Holocaust, holy books and scrolls of the Torah together with the Talmud also perished.

THE GOLDEN AGE OF BIBLICAL SCHOLARSHIP

Nevertheless, the nineteenth and twentieth centuries—even and especially in Germany—were at the same time the golden age in the history of biblical scholarship, both within and beyond the historic communities of "peoples of the Book." Beginning with a revival of Near Eastern archaeology that was attributed (more or less accurately) to the inspiration of Napoleon, whose troops were the ones who discovered the Rosetta stone in 1799, the excavation of biblical sites continued under the many regime changes of the region, including the establishment of the State of Israel in 1948. Among the new discoveries, not all of them by professional archaeologists, none affected the study of the Bible more profoundly than the Dead Sea Scrolls at Qumran in the 1940s and 1950s, which contained nonbiblical manuscripts but also biblical ones. For the first time there became available a substantial body of manuscripts of the Tanakh that were earlier than our existing texts and that predated the Massoretic vowel points. This discovery has redefined the textual study of the Hebrew Bible and provoked far-reaching controversy about the Torah, Nevi'im, and Kethuvim, as well as the New Testament.

For the Jewish study of the Bible, this study and controversy came after a period of intense scholarly debate. In the 1920s, coinciding with the earliest beginnings of the Nazi movement, the Institute for the Scholarly Study of Judaism in Berlin was engaged in applying to the Torah, Talmud, and other texts of the tradition some of the same methods of analysis and interpretation that were prevalent in the academic milieu of the Weimar Republic. As the charming account in Gershom Scholem's *From Berlin to Jerusalem* (1980) has shown, this rational, sometimes downright rationalistic methodology led counterintuitively to a deeper appreciation of the nonrational elements in the Jewish tradition. The mystical biblical speculations of the Kabbalah, the extravagant imagery of the medieval commentators on the Song of Songs, even the excesses of Messianic apocalypticism as associated

with the movement founded by Shabbetai Tzevi—these systems of thought and spirituality were fascinating, historically and phenomenologically, to "the scientific study of Judaism." One salutary outcome of this revival of the scholarly study of Torah and Talmud within twentieth-century Judaism was a marked increase in the knowledge of Jewish interpretation among non-Jewish scholars. Although it has sometimes been criticized by both Jewish and Christian exegetes, the four-volume *Commentary on the New Testament from Talmud and Midrash* by Paul Billerbeck has meant that there is no longer any excuse for the ignorance of the Jewish tradition of commentary that had characterized the church's reading of the Bible for so long.

Within Protestantism, where the scholarly study of the Bible in the original Hebrew and Greek had been endemic since the Renaissance and the Reformation and had entrenched itself in the faculties of divinity at the universities of Great Britain, Germany, and elsewhere, and then in the theological seminaries of the United States, research and publication about the Bible continued to grow, producing editions, journals, monographs, and monumental series. B. F. Westcott and F. J. A. Hort in Great Britain and Eberhard Nestle in Germany brought the science of textual criticism to new heights, which, among other results, made both necessary and possible the new translations of the Bible. The volumes of the *International Critical Commentary,* with each book of the Bible assigned to a scholar with specialized competence, brought these achievements together in a verse-by-verse exegesis; some of these volumes, such as John Skinner on Genesis and Alfred Plummer on Luke, contain grammatical and philological insights that present-day students of the Bible still find indispensable. The most influential such reference work is probably Gerhard Kittel's *Theological Dictionary to the New Testament,* originally published in German and subsequently translated into English. The format of the lexicon facilitated the use of word study as a means of examining biblical concepts and doctrines, helping to establish—with great benefits but sometimes also with great oversimplifications—a new "biblical theology" in which the allegedly philosophical framework of classical systematic theology was supposed to yield to cate-

gories that came from the biblical text itself rather than being super-imposed on it. Among the innumerable biblical commentaries of the twentieth century, the *Anchor Bible* was notable for the collaboration of Jewish, Protestant, and Roman Catholic scholars in its production.

Such collaboration became possible for Roman Catholics through what must be called, without exaggeration, a biblical renaissance, if not indeed a biblical revolution, within the Roman Catholic church in the twentieth century. The charter of that renaissance was the encyclical *Divino afflante Spiritu* issued by Pope Pius XII on 30 September 1943. While continuing to honor the "juridical" authority of the Latin Vulgate in the Latin church, which the Council of Trent had elevated as a bulwark against the Protestant doctrine of *sola Scriptura,* the encyclical urged—or, rather, mandated—careful study of the biblical text "through a knowledge of languages," above all the original Hebrew and Greek. In such study, moreover, the Catholic exegete was to pay special attention to the literary genre characteristic of Near Eastern literature, avoiding a literalism that could not tell the difference between poetry and prose or that read biblical historiography as though it were a modern newpaper. From this study should come translations of the Bible into vernacular languages for the common people, which the church did not forbid but encouraged so long as they were accompanied by comments and helps to explain the text. All these admonitions of *Divino afflante Spiritu* received powerful reinforcement in *Dei verbum,* the *Dogmatic Constitution on Divine Revelation of the Second Vatican Council* of 18 November 1965. "Easy access to Holy Scripture," the council decreed, "should be available to *all* the Christian faithful," not only to the clergy and the theologians, because "there is such force and power in the word of God that it stands as the church's support and strength."

It does seem safe to hazard the guess, in the absence of hard statistical data, that not only within the Roman Catholic church but all over the world the Bible has been studied by more people during the past century than during the preceding nineteen. But it is sobering to remember that the same century has also been the century of two world wars, of widespread persecution and genocide, and of the Holo-

caust. Sometimes it seems that the dominant biblical metaphor of the age has been not the liberating exodus of the people of Israel from captivity in Egypt but the four horsemen of the Apocalypse—war, famine, pestilence, and death. To stay with the issue that has stood at the center of our attention throughout this book, the relation between the two "peoples of the Book," Jews and Christians, attained in the Nazi Holocaust what must be counted the lowest point in its miserable history. Yet the twentieth century, as this chapter has been suggesting, was also a high point in the history of the Bible. The dimensions of that historical paradox will be the subject of the next and final chapter.

TWELVE

The Strange New World Within the Bible

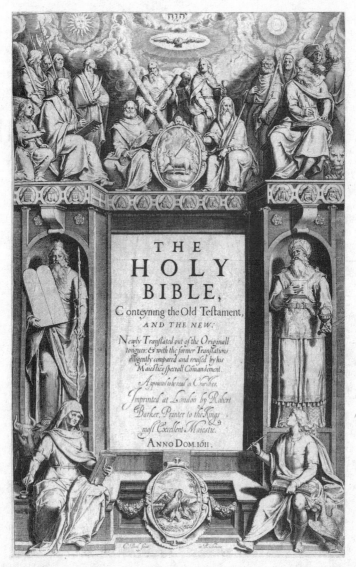

Title page of the first edition of the King James Version (1611). (From the collection of the Bridwell Library, Perkins School of Theology, Southern Methodist University)

Paul, as a child of his age, addressed his contemporaries. It is, however, far more important that, as Prophet and Apostle of the Kingdom of God, he veritably speaks to all men of every age. The differences between then and now, there and here, no doubt require careful investigation and consideration. But the purpose of such investigation can only be to demonstrate that these differences are, in fact, purely trivial.

hese are the opening words of the most influential, or at any rate the most explosive, biblical commentary of the twentieth century, *The Epistle to the Romans,* issued by Karl Barth in 1918. It was called "a bombshell that dropped into the playground of the theologians," rudely interrupting their games. The first sentence aptly summarizes the historical-critical method of interpreting the Bible, as the scholars of the eighteenth and especially the nineteenth century, including some of Barth's own professors, had brought it to unprecedented heights, showing the many respects in which Paul—or Moses or Jeremiah or even Jesus of Nazareth—had to be seen as "a child of his age addressing his contemporaries," sharing in their outlook on the world and being limited by it. But then the sentences that follow go on to trump that historical-critical method of "careful investigation" by pointing beyond it and beyond all of its results to the transcendent reality that Barth had called "the strange new world within the Bible." At about the same time the Jewish theologian Martin Buber, author of *I and Thou,* which has been widely read also by Christians, was composing translations

of the Torah and comments on it that in similar fashion made the usual modern antitheses between the Talmud and critical method seem irrelevant and quite obsolete.

There was—and there is—no going back behind the historical, textual, literary, and philological investigation of the Tanakh and the New Testament. But we can and we must go beyond it, for the Tanakh is more than a museum piece or the surviving artifact of a Near Eastern tribal cult or the only available piece of literature written in the Hebrew language to be used as a lexicon for the modern revival of the language. It is not less than any of these, but it must be more. And in the same way it is not adequate to describe the New Testament as the literary deposit of just another Hellenistic mystery religion or as a remnant of a mythological cosmology or as the struggle of an apocalyptic community to redefine its identity after its hope of the Second Coming, as this was promised (and expected) by Jesus, had been so cruelly disappointed.

A "BEAUTY EVER ANCIENT, EVER NEW"

Every year in the modern world, and even in a culture that calls itself postmodern, performances of Handel's *Messiah* and Bach's *Saint Matthew Passion* continue to draw appreciative audiences consisting of believers and unbelievers alike. Though with some effort, undergraduates still manage to learn to read, and even in some measure to comprehend, the *Divine Comedy* and *Paradise Lost*. The sayings and narratives in the Bible, with all their rich and varied tapestry, retain their beauty and charm. As the Psalm says, "There is no speech nor language, where their voice is not heard. Their line is gone out through all the earth, and their words to the end of the world." Even in a secular age—especially in a secular age—the Bible proves to be *the* unique antidote to cynicism and the source of inspiration for poets and philosophers, artists and musicians, and the countless millions all over the globe who turn to it every day and in their times of need. Book by book, sometimes chapter by chapter, the Bible provides the

subtext, also in the twentieth and the twenty-first centuries, for how we deal with life and death and how we define our deepest hopes. It is, to paraphrase a maxim of the early church, a river in which a gnat can swim and an elephant can drown.

In 1959 the American poet Archibald MacLeish, who served as Librarian of Congress from 1939 to 1944, received the Pulitzer Prize for Drama for his play *J.B.*, which is an evocative and existential retelling of the story of the Book of Job. Toni Morrison, who received the Nobel Prize in Literature for 1993, has taken her inspiration from the Song of Solomon in her novel of that title, published in 1977, and again in *Beloved* of 1987. But the outstanding literary example in the twentieth century of how the ever ancient beauty of the Bible can become ever new is almost certainly the massive four-volume epic *Joseph and His Brothers* (1933–44) by Thomas Mann, who won the Nobel Prize for Literature in 1929. He himself called it "this pyramidlike piece of work." Begun in Nazi Germany and completed in the United States, the novel bears the marks of this experience: Abraham, Isaac, and Jacob, as the patriarchs of the Jewish people, become here the spiritual ancestors of us all; and in the fourth and final part, *Joseph the Provider*, which deals with Joseph's rescue of the Egyptian people from starvation, Thomas Mann, as he himself acknowledged, was using President Franklin D. Roosevelt and the New Deal as a model. On the basis of painstaking research in the Talmud and other rabbinical commentaries, he was able to expand the dozen or so chapters of the Torah that are devoted to the dramatic story of Joseph into nearly two thousand pages of profound characterization, psychological analysis, spectacular pageantry, and intricate plot, which a reference work on the Bible and literature calls "the definitive modern rendering of the Joseph story [and] perhaps the greatest single commentary on the life of the biblical Joseph" ever written.

Modern translations of the Bible, which continue to appear in a steady stream, especially in English, have proved to be ever new in their literary beauty as well as accurate in their rendering of the ever ancient text. An outstanding example is the New English Bible of 1970, whose versions of the Apocrypha and of the New Testament in

a subsequent revision underlie this book, together with the Jewish Publication Society Version of the Tanakh. It began with a literal translation prepared by scholars in the biblical languages, which was then revised by a commission of authors to put it into the best possible literary English, and then it was reviewed by the scholars to be sure that these revisions had not done violence to the originals. The result is a rendering of genuine power and beauty. Poetry sounds like poetry, the Anglo-Saxon idiom has supplanted the Latinisms and the "dainty English" of earlier translations, and the native force of English parts of speech comes through with new clarity. For example, because prepositions in English tend to be so weak-kneed, the more literal translation of the Epistle to the Romans in the King James Version, "of him, and through him, and to him are all things," is replaced with monosyllabic nouns: "Source, Guide, and Goal of all that is—to him be glory for ever!"

An appalling ignorance of the Bible seems to have become epidemic in our time, as is evident from the nervous laughter when on a stage or at a dinner party someone mentions the subject of angels or prayer or the immortality of the soul. Nevertheless, one of its positive features (although it is hard to think of what the other positive features may be) is the thrill of discovery that comes to otherwise fairly educated people when they confront it for the first time, whether in a college classroom or in private reading. All of a sudden it speaks to them as though it had never spoken to anyone else before: "beauty ever ancient, ever new." It has always possessed that power, and those whom it strikes have always been at a loss about how to cope with it.

Yet like the beauty ever ancient, ever new of a Byzantine icon or of Gregorian chant, the stately cadences of the Book of Psalms and the haunting beauty of the Bible do run the constant danger of getting in their own way. The very familiarity of the Bible after all these centuries can dull its sharp edges and obscure its central function, which is not only to comfort the afflicted but to afflict the comfortable, including the comfortable who are sitting in the pews of their synagogue or church as they listen to its words. If it is true that every age manages to invent its own particular heresies, our own age seems

especially vulnerable to an aestheticism (represented with special poignancy by the worshipful audiences who listen to Richard Wagner's *Parsifal* on Good Friday, as he seems to have intended) that finds the ultimate mystery of transcendence, "the mystery that awes and fascinates," in the beauty of art and music, which have the magical capacity to transport us into an otherworldly realm without at the same time calling us to account for our sins in the presence of the holy God and righteous Judge of all mankind.

To invoke a Kierkegaardesque figure of speech, the beauty of the language of the Bible can be like a set of dentist's instruments neatly laid out on a table and hanging on a wall, intriguing in their technological complexity and with their stainless steel highly polished—until they set to work on the job for which they were originally designed. Then all of a sudden my reaction changes from "How shiny and beautiful they all are!" to "Get that damned thing out of my mouth!" Once I begin to read it anew, perhaps in the freshness of a new translation, it stops speaking in clichés and begins to address me directly. Many people who want nothing to do with organized religion claim to be able to read the Bible at home for themselves. But it is difficult to resist the suspicion that in fact many of them do not read it very much. For if they did, the "sticker shock" of what it actually says would lead them to find most of what it says even more strange than the world of synagogue and church.

A FOREIGN LANGUAGE

Translations of the Bible, be they ancient or new, beautiful or pedestrian, can also run the danger of artificially domesticating the language of the Tanakh or the New Testament. At one level that is their very purpose: "that he may run that readeth it," as the prophet says. It is the genius of Luther's translation of the Bible into German that much of the time it does not sound like a translation at all but like the German that Isaiah or Matthew might have spoken and written if they had lived in sixteenth-century Saxony. Anyone who has done a

great deal of translating of any text from any language has had to learn over again the seemingly obvious principle that the reader of a translation should not have to use a foreign language lexicon to comprehend it. At the same time, the translator of any text, and to a special degree the translator of the Bible, will run into many words and phrases that are difficult to translate. The liturgical instruction *Selah* in the Book of Psalms is described by the Jewish Publication Society Version of the Tanakh as "a liturgical direction of uncertain meaning," and *Raca* in the Gospels is identified in a footnote by the Revised Standard Version of the New Testament as "an obscure term of abuse." Both of these technical terms have stubbornly resisted the effort and the learning of centuries and entire millennia, after which they still remain quite "foreign" to us.

But the language of the Bible is "foreign" in a far more profound way, too. Every teacher of Hebrew school or Sunday school has to discover that much of the Bible, whether it be the Tanakh or the New Testament, often speaks in an agricultural idiom that children of the modern city find quite incomprehensible. The words "The LORD is my shepherd" may be familiar, but they really do not say very much to a student of the Bible, young or old, whose only association with shepherds and their work is a wool sweater or an occasional lamb chop. Nor does it mitigate the foreignness when, as in certain forms of religious art, the shepherd is sentimentalized into a figure that no ancient shepherd and no sheep whether ancient or modern would be able to recognize. And lest the Christian reader of the Bible seek to dismiss this as a problem that is peculiar to "the Old Testament": When Jesus says of himself, "I am the good shepherd; the good shepherd lays down his life for the sheep," he is invoking the same agricultural metaphor, not for some peripheral element of the Christian message, but for its central affirmation that Christ died for the world. Perhaps the most foreign of all the foreign language in the Bible is the language of apocalyptic, as in the books of Ezekiel and Daniel and then in the Revelation to John. In one chapter after another these books describe a kaleidoscope of beasts and stars and colors and processions, all of it presumably meaning something to the

writer and intended to mean something to the reader, then and even now. The divergent and sometimes bizarre interpretations to which biblical apocalypticism, both Jewish and Christian, has been subjected confirm this impression of foreignness even by their efforts to clarify and explain it.

And yet is it not the very foreignness of the language of the Bible that makes it command our attention? As Kierkegaard said once, this message is not something that you can tell me about while I am shaving! The language of the Bible is a language to be read and reread, to be pondered and scrutinized. To the eyes and heart of faith, after all, it is a love letter, one long love letter. When I receive a letter from a friend whom I love, I cannot simply read it once and then discard it. Rather, I will think about what it means, what this or that phrase is intended to say. And when that letter is written to me in another language, I am compelled by its very language to read it more slowly. The great commentators on the sacred text have been set apart from the run-of-the-mill exegetes by their having learned to exploit its very strangeness to probe beneath the surface. That is also part of the rationale behind the practice of allegorical interpretation, of finding "the spiritual sense." Because so many of the words and phrases of the Bible are not how we usually talk or what we always talk about, the allegorical interpreter looks for the "key" in this text, or in some other text, or in the inspiration of the Spirit of God in answer to prayer. Even apart from allegory, the language of the Bible constantly rings the changes, turning an idea to this angle or that one, saying the same thing over and over until it is not quite the same. The Psalms are an especially fertile collection of such seemingly repetitive language. The successive verses of Psalm 1 pick up theme and variations with an inner logic of development that does not fit the categories of our conventional ways of thinking. Psalm 119, the longest chapter in the Bible, plays these variations on its theme by employing some name for the Bible in every verse—"decrees, ways, precepts, commandments, testimonies," and so forth. If that way of speaking were not so foreign to the language that I speak and write, I would be tempted to dismiss it. Because the apocalyptic language in the Tanakh and the

New Testament is in many respects the most foreign of all, the poetry and the art of William Blake, which are often no less foreign, can speak in a language that is loud and clear (though "clear" in an unusual way).

AN ALIEN UNIVERSE

As the interminable and tiresome quarrels of the nineteenth and twentieth centuries about the first chapter of Genesis have shown in at least sufficient detail, it is not easy to square the picture—or "pictures" in the plural—of the universe in the Bible with modern physics or biology. We have great difficulty even with the help of Coleridge's "suspension of disbelief" transporting ourselves by imagination into a natural order in which demons, not microbes, are regularly seen as the cause of disease. Whether or not "our dear friend Luke, the doctor" was actually the author of the Gospel that now bears his name and of the Book of Acts, there is not a single act of healing in either of those books or in the rest of the New Testament that is unambiguously attributed to a human physician or to a natural cure. Because "the sky hung low in the ancient world," supernatural forces, both sinister and benign, were never far away, whereas it is instinctive for us, even if we are Jewish or Christian believers, to treat reports of such forces with suspicion and skepticism. Again, when the apostle Paul, in the climax to his great hymn about the humiliation and exaltation of Christ, says "that at the name of Jesus every knee should bow—in heaven, on earth, and in the depths," he does seem to be operating with the three-story picture of the universe that was current among many of his contemporaries but that even the most literalistic of biblical interpreters would not affirm today.

The presence in the Bible of attitudes toward nature and the universe that are, in our judgment, "prescientific" is, moreover, not simply a nutshell that can be discarded to find the eternal kernel inside. As Paul's hymn shows, these attitudes are bound up with its funda-

mental message. Nevertheless, when seen in the light of the history of biblical commentary and interpretation, whether Jewish or Christian, this "prescientific" picture of the universe is in fact one that it has been possible for widely divergent "scientific" pictures, as they have succeeded one another through the ages, to accommodate. It is a fair generalization that there is no scientific or philosophical cosmology with which the biblical message has been unable to come to terms at least in some measure, and at the same time none with which it has been entirely comfortable. What is more, the accommodation of the biblical message to this or that cosmology has often reached its completion at just about the same time that the cosmology was yielding to its successor. It is impossible to make up an alternate formulation, using the vocabulary of any scientific or philosophical worldview ancient or modern, that could have the eternal staying power of the sublime opening words of the Book of Genesis, "In the beginning God created heaven and earth." The very irrelevance of biblical cosmology has made it relevant over and over.

A "PECULIAR PEOPLE"

When the King James Version of the New Testament describes the new community of the Christian church as "a chosen generation, a royal priesthood, an holy nation, *a peculiar people,*" it is not using the English word "peculiar" in the modern colloquial sense of "eccentric" or "weird," and the Revised English Bible correctly renders these titles as "a chosen race, a royal priesthood, a dedicated nation, *a people claimed by God for his own.*" But on second thought, "peculiar" in the modern sense may not be entirely inappropriate, either.

Anti-Jewish readers of the Tanakh, even when they have been Christians, have taken a certain glee in pointing out the stereotypically Jewish characteristics of the people who inhabit its pages. Sometimes the requirement of circumcision seemed to be more important than the divine call for a pure heart. As a Byzantine treatise against the

Jews argued, why should you object to eating pork and yet be willing to eat a chicken, which is filthier than a pig in where it goes and what it eats? More generally, so many of the commands and promises in the Tanakh pertain to this present life and to the body, rather than to the eternal life of the soul. A hymn like this,

> Sons are the provision of the LORD;
>   the fruit of the womb, His reward.
> Like arrows in the hand of a warrior
>   are sons born to a man in his youth.
> Happy is the man who fills his quiver with them,

gives the impression that earth, not heaven, is where the ultimate blessing of God is located and that eternal life means living on through our descendants. All of this, moreover, sometimes seems very ethnocentric: This "peculiar people" is the chosen people and no other. It is not to the individual, even the pious individual, but to the nation that so many of the promises of God are addressed. God's arbitrary selection of his "chosen people" sometimes appears to violate even an elemental sense of fairness.

In the New Testament these qualities seem, if anything, to have become worse. While it teaches an otherworldly religion, with the promise of eternal life in heaven, both the arbitrariness and the collectivism have been compounded. The tortured argumentation of Paul's exposition of predestination by the sovereign will of a God who "not only shows mercy as he chooses, but also makes stubborn as he chooses" leads to this troubling declaration:

> But if it is indeed God's purpose to display his retribution and to make his power known, can it be that he has with great patience tolerated vessels that were objects of retribution due for destruction, precisely in order to make known the full wealth of his glory on vessels that were objects of mercy, prepared from the first for glory? *We are those objects of mercy.*

The "chosen generation" is a peculiar people indeed. It is also very much of a collective and corporate entity. The New Testament can speak about individuals, as when it promises in the singular "that everyone who has faith in him may not perish but have eternal life." But it reaches the summit of its language about this promise in the metaphor of the church as "the body of Christ." As the hand or the eye amounts to nothing by itself but must belong to a body to perform its function, so it is with the "members" of the church. The very term "members," which we now use regularly and rather blandly for those "individuals" who are parts of a Boy Scout troop or a labor union, really means "limbs" or "body parts" and is the antithesis of any language about "individuals."

Even more than the Tanakh, therefore, the New Testament consistently addresses not individuals but churches and *the* church: "*Ye are* the light of the world." This has to be quoted in the King James Version because in the centuries since its appearance the English language has lost the second person singular "thou" and "thee" when dealing with human beings, and "you" serves both as singular and as plural (except in the recently developed colloquial term "You guys," which apparently does not have sexist connotations). As a result it is often impossible to tell, as in the Revised English Bible for that same passage, "You are light for all the world," whether this "you" refers to a collective or an individual subject. But it does mean a collectivity, a community, not an individual.

Repeatedly in Jewish and Christian history, however, the discovery that the proper framework for understanding the Bible is nothing less than a total community has proved to be not an obstacle to reading it but a liberating force. It is in fact one of the great advances in biblical study during the twentieth century that such a definition of religion as the one propounded by the philosopher William James—"the feelings, acts, and experiences of *individual men in their solitude,* so far as they apprehend themselves in relation to whatever they may consider the divine," which described many interpretations of the Bible—has yielded to the recognition that in the Tanakh "the people of God" is the proper context for the promises and the commands of

God. The Decalogue addresses itself not to individual Jewish believers "in their solitude" but to Israel as the people of God, whom "the LORD your God brought out of the land of Egypt," in every succeeding generation. For Christianity the initially problematic collectivism of such a metaphor as "the body of Christ" has become part of the inspiration for the renewal of the ecumenical imperative to realize the prayer of Jesus just before his crucifixion, "May they all be one; as you, Father, are in me, and I in you, so also may they be in us," and to read the Bible, both Old Testament and New Testament, in that light. The oneness between the Father and the Son, as this is expressed in that prayer, is so close, according to the insistence of the orthodox doctrine of the Trinity, that it does not at all threaten biblical monotheism, as critics of that doctrine past and present have frequently charged, but actually confirms it. The basic confession of the doctrine of the Trinity, the Niceno-Constantinopolitan Creed of 381, opens with the words "We believe in one God." And that is the kind of oneness, beyond individualism and even beyond individuality, that is the divine pattern for the relation among Christ's disciples, a relation for which the metaphor "the body of Christ" is singularly appropriate.

AN OBSESSION WITH SACRED GEOGRAPHY

For Judaism this twentieth-century recognition has been bound up, especially in the twentieth century, with the problem of the relation between "the people of God" and "the land." The presupposition for much of the language of the Torah was the life of Israel as the people of God dwelling in the Holy Land. So recurrent is the theme of "the land" throughout the patriarchal narratives of the Torah from beginning to end as to seem downright obsessive. Uncounted centuries before the exodus of the people of Israel from Egypt under Moses, God appears to Abram (as his name was initially pronounced and spelled), saying,

> Fear not, Abram,
> I am a shield to you;
> Your reward shall be very great,

and meaning, "[I shall] assign this land to you as a possession. . . . To your offspring I assign this land, from the river of Egypt to the great river, the river of Euphrates," providing the geographical boundaries. At the conclusion of the patriarchal narratives, Joseph, now reunited and reconciled with his brothers, promises them: "God will surely . . . bring you up from this land [of Egypt] to the land that He promised on oath to Abraham, to Isaac, and to Jacob."

The conquest of the promised land is the theme of the Book of Joshua, and the successes and failures of its defense are the subject matter of most of the Historical Books of the Tanakh, but always it is *the* land that stands at the center of the account. Once again, as though He were drawing a map for Joshua, the LORD all but specifies latitude and longitude to him: "Every spot on which your foot treads I give to you, as I promised Moses. Your territory shall extend from the wilderness and the Lebanon to the Great River, the River Euphrates [on the east]—the whole Hittite country—and up to the Mediterranean Sea on the west." At the opening of the book of Judges, therefore, "an angel of the LORD came up from Gilgal to Bochim and said, 'I brought you up from Egypt and I took you into the land which I had promised on oath to your fathers.'" In the books that appear last in the Kethuvim and therefore in the entire Tanakh, the Books of Chronicles, the same theme still resounds:

> Be ever mindful of His covenant,
> the promise He gave for a thousand generations,
> that He made with Abraham,
> swore to Isaac,
> and confirmed in a decree for Jacob,
> for Israel, as an eternal covenant,
> saying, "To you I will give the land of Canaan
> as your allotted heritage."

The covenant and the land are complementary terms; indeed, in passages like this they seem to have become almost interchangeable.

The loss of that land led not only to the exiles' prayer at the Passover, "Next year in Jerusalem!" but to the struggle of the biblical commentators in the Talmud to find a way of faithfully obeying the commandments in some other land. Basically, that struggle can be seen as a way of transcending the obsession with geography and of defining the "eternal covenant"—not the land, "holy" and "promised" though it is—as the key to continuity. The end of so many centuries of landlessness came with the creation of the State of Israel in 1948 CE (AH 5708), which religious Zionism has justified on the basis of these biblical promises. But it was not the end of the struggle—that year did not mark the coming of Messiah—which has found its modern counterpart in those commentators of the Diaspora who still seek to define the "observance" of Halakhah in a manner that is not bound to "the land." The debates within the world community of Judaism about the case for and against Zionism have frequently called attention to the geographical inconsistencies, within the several "map-making" passages of the Torah and the Tanakh, about exactly where the boundaries of the promise stand. Meanwhile, the neighbors of the State of Israel, who also claim descent from Abraham through Ishmael, his older son, do not accept the territorial claims purporting to be based on a divine covenant and promise. Christians, who read the Tanakh as their Old Testament, began from the first not only to go on drawing the distinction between land and covenant but to give a "spiritual" sense to the promised land and to Jerusalem. As "the land" was the theme for the closing books of the Tanakh, so the final book of the New Testament, in its next-to-last chapter, announces the vision of a promised land beyond all geography: "I saw the Holy City, new Jerusalem, coming down out of heaven from God, made ready like a bride adorned for her husband."

A CONTRARY LIFESTYLE

"Your word is a lamp to my feet, a light for my path": for a book that has been used for thousands of years as a guide to life, the Bible, on closer examination, sets forth both in precept and in example a contrary lifestyle, or several contrary and mutually contradictory lifestyles, that cannot easily be squared with how its adherents actually live.

Particularly in the Kethuvim, the Writings and Historical Books, the Tanakh describes the way of life of a people in a perpetual state of war. Joshua was a field marshal, as Moses charged him and the people of Israel in his farewell discourse: "The LORD your God Himself will cross over before you; and He Himself will wipe out those nations from your path and you shall dispossess them.—Joshua is the one who shall cross before you, as the LORD has spoken.—The Lord will do to them as He did to Sihon and Og, kings of the Amorites, and to their countries, when He wiped them out." So ruthless was this charge that King Saul received the command from God: "Now go, attack Amalek, and proscribe all that belongs to him. Spare no one, but kill alike men and women, infants and sucklings, oxen and sheep, camels and asses!" When Saul was not conscientious and thorough enough in carrying out this ruthless charge, actually sparing some of his victims, he was punished by being deposed from his throne by God. Contrary to the kitschy image of angels that most people seem to have today, the title "the LORD of hosts" in the Tanakh means "the LORD, valiant in battle," the commander of the heavenly armies of whom in one night a single "angel of the LORD went out and struck down one hundred and eighty-five thousand in the Assyrian camp, and the following morning they were all dead corpses."

Already in some passages of the Tanakh, and then with greater thoroughness in the Jewish commentators, the militarism of this biblical language became an allegory for what was eventually called the war between the flesh and the spirit. Near the end of his life, "the

word of the LORD came to [David], saying, 'You have shed much blood and fought great battles; you shall not build a House for My name for you have shed much blood on the earth in my sight.'" The builder of the Temple was not to be a man of war, not even a man of war who had fought his many wars for God. Therefore "the LORD of hosts . . . puts a stop to wars throughout the earth." That antithesis to the biblical language and lifestyle of war reaches its zenith in the vision of the prophet Isaiah:

> Thus He will judge among the nations
> And arbitrate for the many peoples,
> And they shall beat their swords into plowshares
> And their spears into pruning hooks:
> Nation shall not take up
> Sword against nation;
> They shall never again know war.

Therefore, when the angels in the Christmas story of the New Testament, instead of slaying 185,000 enemy soldiers apiece in the Assyrian (or even the Roman) camp, proclaimed "on earth peace," they were continuing this vision of Isaiah in the Tanakh. And when the apostle Paul specified that "the weapons we wield are not merely human" and listed the component parts of "the full armor provided by God," he was carrying out the "spiritual sense" of the traditional militaristic language.

The lifestyle set forth in the New Testament, however, raises its own problems, of which two should suffice to make the point. There is no gainsaying the obvious expectation of the New Testament community that the end of the world was near, and the teaching that this expectation was to shape how they lived. Paul voiced that expectation when he wrote of "those of us who are still alive when the Lord comes. . . . First the Christian dead will rise, then we who are still alive will join them, caught up in clouds to meet the Lord in the air." The motivational force of this expectation runs through all of New Testament ethics: "The end of all things is upon us; *therefore* to

help you to pray you must lead self-controlled and sober lives." But the end of all things did not come, and it still has not. How are Christians to deal with a New Testament definition of the moral life that is, in greater or lesser measure but certainly in a significant measure, based on the premise that "the end is upon us" and that the presence of Christ is about to break in on human history? An entire school of New Testament interpretation and of early Christian historiography has been built on the thesis that "the delay in the end" was the motivation for the invention of elements of stability and continuity such as the authority of the bishop and the creed, to compensate for the disappointment.

An important part of the orthodox Christian answer to this aspect of the question about the strange world of the Bible has been a sacramental one. The eschatological promise and prayer with which the New Testament concludes, "He who gives this testimony says, 'Yes, I am coming soon!' Amen. Come, Lord Jesus!" is, already in the second century and probably earlier, being transposed into the liturgy of the Eucharist, where Christ comes to every celebration. It is in that constant and continuing presence that believers have found the fulfillment of the promise of Jesus—"I will not leave you bereft; I am coming back to you"—in great cathedrals and in remote villages, always in anticipation of the great and final Day of the Lord, but meanwhile not in any sense "bereft" because, as promised in another saying that was interpreted sacramentally, "where two or three meet together in my name, I am there among them."

Closely related to the expectation of the end, but if anything even more "strange" though not "new," in the lifestyle of the Bible is its asceticism. It is at least in part on account of the eschatological "time of stress" and because "the world as we know it is passing away" that Paul counsels: "He who marries his betrothed does well; and *he who does not marry does better.*" Whatever the enigmatic saying of Jesus about "eunuchs who have made themselves eunuchs for the kingdom of heaven's sake" may mean—and there have been those in various periods of Christian history who have obeyed it with a chilling literalness—it does give, like the words quoted from Paul, a privileged position to

the unmarried and celibate estate. So do the words of the Book of Revelation about "the hundred and forty-four thousand who have been redeemed from the earth . . . who have kept themselves chaste and have not defiled themselves with women, for they are virgins." Lest asceticism be dismissed (as it sometimes is) as a New Testament aberration from the supposedly more healthy lifestyle inculcated by the Tanakh, it bears mentioning that one of the greatest of all the heroes of the Tanakh was the mighty Samson, whom it describes as a "Nazarite," the adherent of "a special vow" of asceticism laid down in the Torah forbidding use of the fruit of the vine in any form and any cutting of the hair.

At the same time the Nazarites also represent the eventual Christian system for dealing with the imperative of an ascetic lifestyle, namely, by institutionalizing it. As the general requirement of self-denial continued, "Anyone who wishes to be a follower of mine must renounce self; he must take up his cross and follow me," the more extreme requirements of asceticism became the code of conduct for the professionals, the nuns and monks who bound themselves by Nazarite-like vows—and a great deal more—to a life of poverty, celibacy, and obedience. Through most of Christian history and even today ordinary believers have been living their lives in the awareness that there are some of their sisters and brothers who have pledged themselves to a life of chastity and prayer. Even when I myself am too busy with the important business of life and the life of business to take time off for "prayer and fasting," there are these athletes of asceticism, who actually live as though the biblical command to "pray continually" means what it says. Yet at the same time that it was systematizing the ascetic lifestyle in the rules and practices of monasticism, the church was taking the biblical reference to marriage as a "mystery" to mean "mystery" as "sacrament" and was therefore teaching that the entire life together of a man and a woman in marriage was one of the seven sacraments of the church—and in a way that the monastic life was not.

A "WHOLLY OTHER" GOD

Above all (quite literally or, more than literally, *above* all), the Bible is a strange new world because it confronts us with a God who speaks but who in the very act of self-revelation is and remains the Wholly Other One—

> My plans are not your plans,
> Nor are My words your words
> > —declares the LORD.
> But as the heavens are high above the earth,
> So are My words high above your words
> And My plans above your plans

—a God whose very being and acting is "immeasurably more than all we can ask or conceive." The only way to speak accurately about the God of the Bible is to employ such negative terms, as Moses learns when at the burning bush he asks the God who speaks from the bush, "When I come to the Israelites and say to them, 'The God of your fathers has sent me to you,' and they ask me, 'What is His name?' what shall I say to them?" and learns that unlike the idols of the nations, this God has no name. Therefore, one of the great heresies combated in the early centuries of the church was the presumptuous claim that we can know the Being of God as well as God knows it. The Being of God, according to the Bible, is Wholly Other.

Yet if that is all there is to be said about the God of the Bible, then, as the New Testament puts it, "we of all people are most to be pitied." For it is about this Wholly Other God, the transcendent one, that the prophet Isaiah can proclaim: "Immanuel, with us is God." And paraphrasing these words of Isaiah, the seer of the Apocalypse in the final book of the Christian Bible can continue the vision just quoted: "I heard a loud voice proclaiming from the throne: 'Now

God has his dwelling with mankind! He will dwell among them and they shall be his people, and God himself will be with them. He will wipe every tear from their eyes. There shall be an end to death, and to mourning and crying and pain, for the old order has passed away!'"

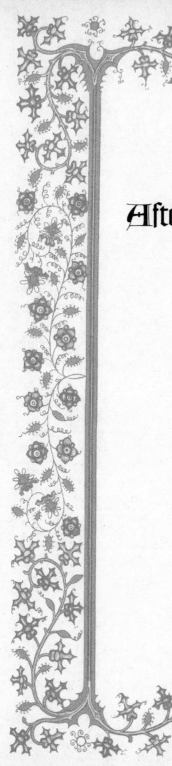

Afterword

fter all this—

    after all the commentaries;
    after all the controversies;
    after all the sermons;
    after all that biblical scholarship, whether Jewish or
        Christian or secular;
    after all the heresies and all the orthodoxies, whether
        Jewish or Christian or secular;
    after all the other books (including this one);
    after all the prayers and all the tears;
    after all the forced conversions and all the pogroms;
    and after the Holocaust

—after all this, the question with which this book began still remains: Whose Bible is it?

In an ultimate sense it is presumptuous for anyone to speak about "possessing" the Bible. As both the Jewish and the Christian communities of faith have always affirmed, the Bible is the Book *of God* and the Word *of God,* and therefore it does not really belong to any of us. Psalm 119, which is one long hymn of praise about the word of God, insists throughout that it is speaking about "*thy* statutes," "*thy* testimonies." And when Jesus defines what it means to be his disciple, he does this with the same insistence: "If ye continue in my word, then

are ye my disciples indeed. And ye shall know the truth, and the truth shall make you free." Throughout Jewish and Christian history, whenever believers, whether individually or collectively, have made proprietary claims about Holy Scripture as though they were sovereign over it, the sovereignty of God over them and over Holy Scripture has eventually found a way, sometimes a dramatic way, of vindicating itself, as the voices of Hebrew prophets and Christian reformers have repeatedly demonstrated. Because the purpose of the Tanakh is, as the New Testament attests, "for teaching the truth and refuting error, or for reformation of manners and discipline in right living," and because the purpose of the New Testament also is, as it testifies concerning itself, "that you may believe," it follows that I am not the subject but the object in my encounter with the word of the Bible: "O LORD, You have examined me and know me." To speak of possessing the Bible or even to ask "Whose Bible is it?" is, in the light of that encounter, not only presumptuous but blasphemous. At most we are, as Edmund Burke says of tradition, not "entire masters" but only "temporary possessors and life-renters" of it.

On the other hand, that status of "temporary possessors and life-renters" is one that Jews and Christians now share with the whole of humanity. In part this is due to the unprecedented distribution and circulation of Bibles during the nineteenth and twentieth centuries, so that now there is virtually no language—and there should be (though there is, but for other reasons) virtually no library—in which the Tanakh and the New Testament are not available. But the change is qualitative as much as it is quantitative and goes back to the Septuagint translation of the Tanakh into Greek during the centuries immediately preceding the Common Era. Once that first step had been taken, "the nations" (which is what gentiles or *goyim* means) could and did read the Bible even without believing it, and they have been doing so ever since. For if it is profoundly true that there are truths in the Bible that only the eyes of faith can see, it is also true that the eyes of unfaith have sometimes spotted what conventional believers have been too preoccupied or too bemused to acknowledge. It is difficult

to imagine that the modern consensus among Jews and Christians about the Bible not being a textbook of science or of history, for example, would have taken the form it has without the rude questions that came from the outsiders. The appreciation of the Bible as literature and the sensitivity to its "literary genres" are the by-products of the new and catholic (lowercase "c") audience that it has acquired in going forth to those who want only to learn *about* it. Each in their own way, both Jews and Christians have had to learn to live with this more catholic readership of a text that they had thought of as exclusively their own.

Yet it would be fatuous in the extreme to pretend that the primary and special readership of that text even now can be anything but the Jewish and Christian communities. From the Septuagint to the most recent translation into some exotic tongue, the fundamental impulse for making the Bible available has always come from within those communities. The historical or literary or philological desire to comprehend what it says has been and is vastly less important than the religious need to understand it in order to obey it. For that reason the study of the biblical text must always be the special business of (using the medieval terminology) *Synagoga* and *Ecclesia*. Within both of those traditions, moreover, "those who are charged with the responsibility of teaching," as Thomas Aquinas calls them, must also take special responsibility and special care not only to teach the Bible but to learn it before they teach it. The vagaries of theological fashion or the disciple-making of theological professors or the desire to be relevant to contemporary society can sometimes overshadow the permanent hold that commentary on the sacred text has and must have in the preparation of those who will be the professional interpreters of the faith tradition. Every new breakthrough of insight and every new breakout of relevance in Jewish and Christian history has been accompanied by "new light breaking forth from the holy Word." Not the only prerequisite for this to happen, but an authoritative prerequisite nonetheless, is the requirement that those who speak to and for the community in interpreting the Bible be competent to do so on the

basis of the original texts. As this applies to the teaching of Vergil and Dante, so it applies to the Hebrew and Greek originals of the Bible.

Reverting to Handel's *Messiah:* "Since by man came death, by man came also the resurrection from the dead" is a text about the series of testaments or covenants that God has made with the human race. It speaks about two such, the one through Adam and the one through Christ. But there are as well covenants made with humanity through Noah and through Abraham and through Moses. Christians have also put each of these into a dialectical relation with the covenant through Christ: death through Adam, life through Christ; promise through Abraham, fulfillment through Christ; law through Moses, gospel through Christ. Yet the more deeply we study the Hebrew Scriptures, the more clearly we must recognize that, taken by itself, this dialectic can greatly oversimplify the case. For there is also "life" through Adam by the sheer fact of our being human, "fulfillment" in Abraham for all who are his children, be they Jews or Christians or Muslims, and "gospel" through Moses by the liberation from chaos that Torah confers. Ultimately, we need therefore to look to a doctrine of multiple testaments, according to which the one God—the God of Abraham, Isaac, and Jacob, who is also the Father of Jesus Christ—has throughout the history of salvation formed a series of covenants but has not broken covenants or repudiated them.

The Jewish tradition and the Christian tradition are "two distinct religious communities with a common commitment to Scripture and its interpretations," but with two distinct, though not necessarily contradictory and sometimes even complementary, methods of honoring that commitment and carrying out those interpretations. The new situation created by our fundamentally altered perceptions of both the distinctness and the complementarity calls for the modern recovery of a very old methodology of interpretation: the multiple senses of Scripture. To put it directly, a passage of the Bible does not mean only one thing, and the vain dispute over whether these are "your Scriptures" or "our Scriptures" is often an argument between two (or more) of these multiple senses. Any of the many passages from the Tanakh / Old Testament that have been cited in the preced-

ing chapters could serve as an illustration, but so can one that has not been cited: "Is it nothing to you, all ye that pass by? behold, and see if there be any sorrow like unto my sorrow, which is done unto me, wherewith the LORD hath afflicted me in the day of his fierce anger." As it stands and according to its literal and historical sense, it is a plea of the prophet Jeremiah against the callousness of the inhabitants of Jerusalem in the sixth century BCE. As both the Lamentations and the Book of Jeremiah (with or without the additions to it that are classified as Apocrypha) describe in great detail, they ignored the word of the Lord and of his prophet and went on with their everyday business as though it did not concern them. Although it is not quoted anywhere in the New Testament as a messianic prophecy, this cry from the Book of Lamentations becomes for Christians, according to its spiritual and prophetic sense as incorporated in Handel's *Messiah,* an accompaniment to "My God, my God, why hast thou forsaken me?" as a word spoken under the First Testament which has acquired additional specific meaning under the Second Testament. And it is surely not an unwarranted further extension of its multiple senses, in the light of the enormity of the Holocaust and the massive indifference to it in much of the world, including the Christian world, to apply it there as well. Nor does any of these multiple senses preclude the possibility or the likelihood that in this fallen world new situations will arise to which its words will be the only fitting response.

If the history of the Jewish and Christian Scriptures teaches us anything, it is that neither of these communities would be anything without it. The Scriptures depend on the communities not only to preserve and transmit their texts, which has never been a trivial assignment, but to interpret them and reinterpret them over and over again—and ever more studiously to do so together. The Tanakh and the New Testament are agreed: "What therefore God hath joined together, let not man put asunder!"

Appendix I: Alternative Canons of the Tanakh / Old Testament

Tanakh (Judaism) and Protestant Bibles

(Numbers indicate order in the Hebrew Tanakh [JPS].)

Genesis (1)
Exodus (2)
Leviticus (3)
Numbers (4)
Deuteronomy (5)
Joshua (6)
Judges (7)
Ruth (18)
I and II Samuel (8)
I and II Kings (9)
I and II Chronicles (24)
Ezra ⎫
          ⎬ (23)
Nehemiah ⎭
[Apocrypha]
[Apocrypha]
Esther (21)
Job (16)
Psalms (14)
Proverbs (15)
Ecclesiastes (20)
Song of Songs (17)
[Apocrypha]
[Apocrypha]
Isaiah (10)

Vulgate (Roman Catholicism) and Septuagint (Eastern Orthodoxy)

(Numbers indicate order in the Septuagint [Rahlfs ed.].)

Genesis (1)
Exodus (2)
Leviticus (3)
Numbers (4)
Deuteronomy (5)
Joshua (6)
Judges (7)
Ruth (8)
I and II Kings (9–10)
III and IV Kings (11–12)
I and II Chronicles (13–14)
I Esdras ⎫
           ⎬ (16)
II Esdras ⎭
Tobit (19)
Judith (18)
Esther (17)
Job (29)
Psalms (24)
Proverbs (26)
Ecclesiastes (27)
Song of Songs (28)
Wisdom of Solomon (30)
Ecclesiasticus / Ben Sirach (31)
Isaiah (44)

Jeremiah (11)	Jeremiah ⎫
Lamentations (19)	Lamentations ⎬ (45)
[Apocrypha]	Baruch ⎭
Ezekiel (12)	Ezekiel (46)
Daniel (22)	Daniel (47)
Hosea ⎫	Hosea (31)
Joel ⎮	Joel (34)
Amos ⎮	Amos (32)
Obadiah ⎮	Obadiah (35)
Jonah ⎮	Jonah (36)
Micah ⎮	Micah (33)
Nahum ⎬ (13)	Nahum (37)
Habakkuk ⎮	Habakkuk (38)
Zephaniah ⎮	Zephaniah (39)
Haggai ⎮	Haggai (40)
Zechariah ⎮	Zechariah (41)
Malachi ⎭	Malachi (42)
[Apocrypha]	I and II Maccabees (20–21)
[Apocrypha]	III Maccabees [East only] (22)

Appendix II: New Testament

(Italies indicate that a book was still being disputed into the 4th century, but eventually adopted.)

Matthew
Mark
Luke
John
Acts
Romans
I Corinthians
II Corinthians
Galatians
Ephesians
Philippians
Colossians
I Thessalonians
II Thessalonians
I Timothy
II Timothy
Titus
Philemon
Hebrews
James
I Peter
II Peter
I John
II John
III John
Jude
Revelation

Notes and Further Reading

"The making of many books is without limit, and much study is a wearying of the flesh," Koheleth the Preacher laments in the Tanakh (Ecclesiastes 12.12). The first half of his lament (as well as, often enough, the second half) applies above all to books about the Book, which do seem to be "without limit" already and yet to be increasing exponentially. There have been entire monographs on every chapter, sometimes on every paragraph, of this brief history—as I have reason to know, having written books and articles about the subject matter treated in almost every one of these chapters. At the risk of quoting myself, I am citing some of these books at the appropriate places in the notes that follow, though not copying from them; and (with permission) I have also recycled in chapters 2 and 6 some material that originally appeared in my comprehensive article "Bible" in the fourteenth edition of the *Encyclopaedia Britannica*. Although books about the Book are seemingly "without limit," only a few have attempted to present the subject matter of this book: *The Cambridge History of the Bible* (3 vols.; Cambridge, England, 1963–69), scheduled to appear in a second edition, to which I have been invited to contribute a chapter on "The Authority of the Septuagint"; and Christopher De Hamel, *The Book: A History of the Bible* (London, 2001). After completing the manuscript for this book, I read (and reviewed) the two volumes of F. E. Peters, *The Monotheists* (Princeton, N.J., 2003), which cites a number of the same texts. Even a brief examination will show how my book differs from all three of these. The titles that follow supply background for, or continue the discussion from, the preceding pages.

Except for the two dozen or so places where the King James Version—as the Authorized Version of 1611 is almost universally identified in American usage and is usually called here—is so firmly established that it would have been artificial to deviate from it, titles and translations of scriptures and scriptural quotations are from the versions that are assembled in *Sacred Writings*, edited by Jaroslav Pelikan (6 vols.; New York, 1992): volume 1, *Tanakh* (Jewish Publication Society translation, and following its design of setting prose as prose but verse as verse); volume 2, *Apocrypha and New Testament* (Revised English Bible

translation); and occasionally (particularly in chapter 7) volume 3, *Qur'an* (translation by Ahmed Ali, originally published by Princeton University Press). (I have sometimes italicized words in quoting the Bible.)

Among the many Bible dictionaries from many theological and literary perspectives, *The Anchor Bible Dictionary* in six volumes, edited by David Noel Freedman (New York, 1992), is balanced, well-informed, and user-friendly. For most of the topics discussed here, it also contains extensive suggestions for further reading.

Preface

ix   "A Virgin shall conceive": Isaiah 7.14.

ix   "For unto us a Child is born": Isaiah 9.6.

ix   "He hath borne our griefs": Isaiah 53.4.

xi   "A fluent though curious English": Patrick O'Brian, *The Mauritius Command* (New York, 1991), 89.

INTRODUCTION: The Bible, the Whole Bible, and Nothing but the Bible?

The relation of Jewish and Christian interpretations is one of the themes of Julio Trebolle Barrera's *The Jewish Bible and the Christian Bible: An Introduction to the History of the Bible* (Grand Rapids, Mich., 1998). My *Interpreting the Bible and the Constitution* (New Haven, Conn., 2004) draws parallels and contrasts between the methods of interpreting these two normative texts and "great codes." Robert M. Grant's *The Bible in the Church* (New York, 1948) is a sprightly account of the history of interpretation. A more ambitious treatment is being edited by Alan J. Hauser and Duane E. Watson, *A History of Biblical Interpretation* (Grand Rapids, Mich., 2002 ff.).

4   "discernible [only to] ecclesiastical scholars": William Manchester, *The Death of a President* (New York, 1967), 324n.

4   "I will raise up a prophet": Deuteronomy 18.18–19; quoted in New Testament: Acts 3.22.

5   "you are Peter": Matthew 16.18–19.

ONE: The God Who Speaks

Two radically different discussions of language and literature are: Northrop Frye, *Great Code: The Bible and Literature* (New York, 1982), and George Steiner, *After Babel: Aspects of Language and Translation* (New York, 1992). Robert Alter and Frank Kermode, in *The Literary Guide to the Bible* (Cambridge, Mass., 1987), look at many of the questions being discussed

throughout this book. Alexander Heidel, *The Gilgamesh Epic and Old Testament Parallels* (Chicago, 1946) is a criticism of the facile drawing of "parallels" to the Bible in much of modern criticism.

9   God *said,* "'Let there be light'": Genesis 1.1, 3

9   "In the beginning": John 1.1.

9   "They have mouths": Psalm 115.5.

9   Eleven times: Genesis 1.3, 6, 9, 11, 14, 20, 22, 24, 26, 28, 29.

9   the God who speaks does not write: Exodus 31.18

10   "children" . . . "stones": Matthew 3.9.

10   "Eben-Ezer": 1 Samuel 4.1.

10   Voice from the bush: Exodus 3.4–6.

10   "The LORD said to Abram": Genesis 12.1.

11   "the LORD appeared to Isaac and *said*": Genesis 26.2–5.

11   "the LORD was standing beside Jacob": Genesis 28.10–15.

11   "the prophet Jesus": Matthew 21.11.

11   "Never did We send a message": Qur'an 21.7.

12   "the word of God came": 1 Samuel 15.10; 2 Samuel 7.4; 2 Samuel 24.11; 1 Kings 6.11; 1 Kings 20.4; 1 Chronicles 17.3; 2 Chronicles 11.2.

12   "to the prophet": Isaiah 38.4; Ezekiel 11.14; 12.1, 7, 21, 36; 13.1; Jeremiah 1.1, 2.

12   "Word of God in person": John 1.1–14.

12   "The word of God came to John": Luke 3.2.

12   "It was there from the beginning:" 1 John 1.1.

12   "The word which came to Jeremiah": Jeremiah 30.1–4.

13   "Now that this": Isaiah 6.6–7.

13   "There were indeed many other signs": John 20.30; 21.25.

16   John Stuart Mill, *On Liberty,* ch. 2.

17   "Today in your hearing": Luke 4.16–30.

17   Jesus writing on the ground: John 8.6, 8.

17   "studying the scriptures diligently": John 5.39.

17   "No one ever *spoke*": John 7.46.

17   "Unlike their *scribes*": Matthew 7.29.

18   "This is my body": 1 Corinthians 11.24–25.

18   "many [other] writers": Luke 1.1–2.

18   Cyril of Jerusalem: *Catechetical Lectures* 5.12.

19   "Happiness lies more in giving than in receiving": Acts 20.35.

20   Basil of Caesarea: *On the Holy Spirit* 6.6.

21   "For the leader; with instrumental music": Psalm 4.1.

21   "*Shiggaion* of David": Psalm 7.1.

21   "Hallelujah. Sing to the LORD a new song": Psalm 149.1.

21   "Go to every part": Mark 16.15.

22   "God *said*": Genesis 1.1.

22   "In the beginning the [spoken] Word already was": John 1.1.

22   "How I wish I could be with you now": Galatians 4.20.

22   Plato *Phaedrus*: 275D–276A.

23   "Because Koheleth was a sage": Ecclesiastes 12.9–10.

23   "The scriptures written long ago": Romans 15.4.

23   "all inspired scripture": 2 Timothy 3.16–17.

23   Conversion of Augustine: Augustine *Confessions* 8.12.29.

24   "Let us behave with decency": Romans 13.13.

25   "So then faith does come from *hearing*": Romans 10.17.

25   "In the beginning": John 1.1–3, 14.

TWO: The Truth in Hebrew

My reading of the Tanakh in the context of the history of Judaism is greatly indebted to the two-volume work edited by Louis Finkelstein, *The Jews: Their History, Culture, and Religion* (New York, 1960), and to *The Prophets* by Abraham Joshua Heschel (New York, 1962). My discussion in this chapter will show the influence of the work of Brevard S. Childs, *Introduction to the Old Testament as Scripture* (Philadelphia, 1979).

29   "In the beginning God": Genesis 1.1.

29   "and the stars": Genesis 1.16.

29   stars without number: Genesis 15.5.

29   "When I behold": Psalm 8.4–6.

29   Covenant with Noah: Genesis 9.8–17.

30   "all the families of the earth": Genesis 12.3.

30   "the father of all who have faith": Romans 4.11.

30   "Go forth": Genesis 12.1.

30   "a scribe expert in the Teaching of Moses": Ezra 7.6.

31   "the God of Abraham": Exodus 3.6.

32   "when God began to create": Genesis 1.1.

32   "God in search of man": Abraham Joshua Heschel, *God in Search of Man: A Philosophy of Judaism* (New York, 1955).

33   "I Am That I Am": Exodus 3.14.

33   Song chanted: Song of Miriam: Exodus 15.20.

33   "I the LORD": Exodus 20.2–3.

34   "This is your god": Exodus 32.4.

34   "the creatures that you may eat": Leviticus 11.1.

34   "census of the whole": Numbers 16.2.

35   tribes occupying the land of Canaan: Judges 3.5.

35   "O happy Israel": Deuteronomy 33.29.

36   "As I was with Moses": Joshua 1.5.

36   "You may view the land": Deuteronomy 32.52.

36   Gideon: Judges 8.

36   Samson: Judges 13–16.

37   "We must have a king": 1 Samuel 8.19–20.

37   David and Jonathan: 1 Samuel 18–19.

37   David's adultery and murder: 2 Samuel 11–12.

37   "wisdom and discernment" of Solomon: 1 Kings 5.9.

37   David had not been allowed: 2 Samuel 7.13.

38   "my Lord seated on a high and lofty throne": Isaiah 6.1.

38   "Here am I": Isaiah 6.8–9.

38   "Rod of My anger": Isaiah 10.5.

38   suffering servant: Isaiah 53.11.

38   Christian interpretation of Isaiah 53: Acts of the Apostles 8.30–36.

38   "Before I created you": Jeremiah 1.5.

39   "a new covenant": Jeremiah 31.31–33.

39   Ezekiel's vision of the wheels: Ezekiel 1.15–21.

39   Ezekiel's vision of the valley filled with dry bones: Ezekiel 37.

39   "a wife of whoredom": Hosea 1.2.

39   Plague of locusts: Joel 2.2.

40   "You alone have I singled out": Amos 3.2.

40   "I will make you least": Obadiah 1–2.

40   "a huge fish": Jonah 2.1.

40   "He has told you": Micah 6.8.

40   "I will make your grave": Nahum 1.14.

41   Marauding bands of Babylonians: Habakkuk 3.

41   "the day of the LORD's wrath": Zephaniah 1.18.

41   "set to work on the House": Haggai 1.15.

41   "Behold, I am sending My messenger": Malachi 3.1.

42   "wine is a scoffer": Proverbs 20.1.

43   "Who is this": Job 38.2–4.

43   "Eat, lovers, and drink": Song of Songs 5.1.

43   "Wherever you go": Ruth 1.16.

43   "Take us back": Lamentations 5.21.

44   "Utter futility": Ecclesiastes 1.2.

44   "Nothing new under the sun": Ecclesiastes 1.9.

44   festival of Purim: Esther 9.24–26.

44   "sent His angel": Daniel 6.23.

45   List of the families and decrees: Ezra 4.8–22.

45   "I have found a scroll": 2 Kings 22.8.

46   "Ezra and Nehemiah": Ezra 7, Nehemiah 7–10.

46   "the books": Daniel 9.2.

47   "the father *of all* who have faith": Romans 4.11.

47   "Abraham was overjoyed to see my day": John 8.56.

47   firstborn son, Ishmael: Genesis 25.12–18.

47   "remember when Abraham prayed": Qur'an 14.35.

47   "And he believed": Genesis 15.6.

THREE: Moses Speaking Greek

Henry Barclay Swete's *An Introduction to the Old Testament in Greek* (New York, 1968) originally published in 1900, has stood for over a century as a helpful introduction, and Sidney Jellicoe, in *The Septuagint and Modern Study* (Oxford, 1968), identifies the issues that the Septuagint also raises for the nonspecialist. In my Jerome Lectures at the American Academy in Rome, *What Has Athens to Do with Jerusalem?: "Timaeus" and "Genesis" in Counterpoint* (Ann Arbor, Mich., 1997), I have described the verbal and philosophical effect of the Septuagint in both Judaism and Christianity. Most modern translations of the Tanakh into English incorporate numerous readings from the Septuagint in their notes.

51   "Greek-struck Rome": Juvenal *Satires* III.59–67.

53   informs us that Timothy: Acts 16.1–3; 2 Timothy 3.15–16.

54   an unknown poet: Psalm 137.

54   quoting the inscription: John 19.19–20.

56   "to its cultured despisers": Friedrich Schleiermacher, *Religion: Speeches to Its Cultured Despisers* (1799).

57   "the God of Abraham": Exodus 3.6.

58   "Hear, O Israel": Deuteronomy 6.4.

58   On the Targums, see chapter 4.

59   "He makes the winds": Psalm 104.5; Hebrews 1.7.

59   "virgin": Isaiah 7.14; Matthew 1.22–23.

59   "And I saw two mounted horsemen": Isaiah 21.7; Matthew 21.5.

60   It had long been: Isaiah 18.7.

60   account of Pentecost: Acts 2.5–11.

60   "from the northernmost palm tree": Fernand Braudel, *The Mediterranean and the Mediterranean World* (New York, 1972).

60   The theme of emerging: Plato *Republic* Book VII.

61   "And so to Rome": Acts 28.14.

63   "The Father and Maker of all": Plato *Timaeus* 28C.

63   "And God saw that this was good": Genesis 1.4, 10, 12, 18, 21, 25, 31.

64   "a true and perfect version": *Response to Pope Pius IX* 21.

66   "In the beginning": John 1.1–3.

66   "The Lord made me": Proverbs 8.22–30.

FOUR: **Beyond Written Torah:**
Talmud and Continuing Revelation

The three-volume *Encyclopedia of Judaism,* edited by Jacob Neusner and others (New York, 1999), contains highly informative articles about all the texts discussed in this chapter. There is a great deal of information collected in H. L. Strack, *Introduction to the Talmud and Midrash* (Edinburgh, Scotland, 1991). Jacob Neusner, *The Formation of the Babylonian Talmud* (Leiden, Netherlands, 1970) condenses a vast body of learning. Louis Ginzberg's *Legends of the Jews* in seven volumes (Philadelphia, 1909–38) is an inexhaustible source, and Gershom G. Scholem's *Major Trends in Jewish Mysticism* (Jerusalem, 1938) has become a modern classic. C. D. Ginzberg, in *Introduction to the Massoretico-Critical Edition of the Hebrew Bible* (New York, 1966), gives an idea of the dimensions of the achievement of the Massoretes.

71   "not . . . to establish any doctrine": *Thirty-Nine Articles of the Church of England,* article 6.

72   "not spake but speaketh": *The Selected Writings of Ralph Waldo Emerson* (New York, 1992), 80–81.

75   "inspired scripture": 2 Timothy 3.16.

75   "any Hebrew text retroverted": *The Anchor Bible Dictionary,* 5:1102.

75   "*Your people*": Psalm 110.3.

75   "My God, my God": Psalm 22.1. 16; Matthew 27.46.

77   "Please, speak to your servants": 2 Kings 18.26.

77   Jesus in Nazareth: Luke 4.16–21.

77   Paul in Antioch: Acts 13.15.

77   "They read [in Hebrew]": Nehemiah 8.8.

78   "The descendants of Japheth": Genesis 10.2.

79   "The LORD reigns": Psalm 96.10; Justin Martyr *Dialogue with Trypho* 73.

79   enforceable . . . to the point of death: Leviticus 10.6–9.

79   "I have hurried": Psalm 119.60.

79   "by the rivers of Babylon": Psalm 137.1.

80   "the Law . . . earlier version of the Ten Commandments": Exodus 20.8–11.

80   "On six days": Exodus 35.2–3.

81   "You are not permitted": Deuteronomy 16.5–7.

81   But an earlier passage: Exodus 12.1–28.

81   "In joining the two": Jacob Neusner, *The Encyclopedia of Judaism,* 1:361.

81   "The LORD said to Moses": Exodus 12.1, 9.

81   But after the exodus: Deuteronomy 16.7.

81   "They roasted the passover sacrifice": 2 Chronicles 35.13.

83   "Ehyeh-Asher-Ehyeh": Exodus 3.14.

83   "To me, O Israelites": Amos 9.7.

84   Shem, Ham, and Japheth: Genesis 10.1, 32.

85   "Anyone who knows": Leon Wieseltier, "Center Conversations" of the Ethics and Public Policy Center (Washington, D.C., 2004), 27:7–8.

FIVE: The Law and the Prophets Fulfilled

Raymond E. Brown, in *The Sensus Plenior of Sacred Scripture* (Baltimore, Md., 1955), and Jean Daniélou, in *From Shadows to Reality: Studies in the Biblical Typology of the Fathers* (Westminster, Md., 1960), chart the various forms that the concept of "fulfillment" took in the Christian interpretation of prophecy and fulfillment. The first volume of my *The Christian Tradition: A History of the Development of Doctrine,* which bears the title *The Emergence of the Catholic Tradition (100–600)* (Chicago, 1971), examines the transition from Judaism (and Hellenism) to normative Catholic Christianity. George W. E. Nickelsburg, *Ancient Judaism and Christian Origins: Diversity, Continuity, and Transformation* (Minneapolis, 2003), with its masterful grasp of a vast body of both Jewish and Christian texts, could as well have been cited for the preceding chapter.

89   "Christianity enters the world" : Reinhold Niebuhr, *The Nature and Destiny of Man* (New York, 1941–43), 2:35, quoting Luke 4.21.

89   "The spirit of the Lord": Isaiah 61.1–2.

90   "happened in order to fulfill": Isaiah 7.14 (King James Version); Matthew 1.22–23.

90   His escape to Egypt: Matthew 2.15.

90   "Out of Egypt I have called": Hosea 11.1.

90   In one of the earliest traditions: Luke 24.25–44.

91   the apostle Philip, and "a high official": Acts 8.26–39.

91   "Like a sheep": Isaiah 53.7–8.

91   Paul's miniature autobiography: Galatians 1.13–14.

92   Conversion of Paul: Acts 9.1–9.

92   Paul the "chosen instrument": Acts 9.15.

92   In his first public appearance: Acts 9.20.

92   Paul in Athens: Acts 17.17–31.

92   Paul in Rome: Acts 28.17–23.

92   In the earliest recorded: Justin Martyr *Dialogue with Trypho the Jew* 29.

93   Eusebius *Church History* 1.4.14.

93   "tested in every way": Hebrews 4.15.

94   Temptation of Jesus: Matthew 4.1–11; F. M. Dostoevsky, *The Brothers Karamazov*, book 5, ch. 5.

94   "Scripture says": Deuteronomy 8.3; 6.16; 6.13; Psalm 91.11–12.

95   "The scriptures written long ago": Romans 15.4.

95   Ten Commandments: Exodus 20.2–14.

95   "there is not one good man on earth": Ecclesiastes 7.20; Romans 3.9–10.

95   "You have heard how Job": James 5.11.

95   But the Torah . . . cautionary tales: 1 Corinthians 9.7–9, citing Exodus 32.6, Numbers 25.1–9, Numbers 21.5–6, Numbers 16.11–25.

96   First and Second Adam: Romans 5.12–17; 1 Corinthians 15.45.

96   First and Second Eve: Irenaeus of Lyons *Demonstration of the Apostolic Preaching* 33–34; Luke 1.38 (King James).

96   "shadow" and "reality": Colossians 2.16–17; Daniélou, *From Shadows to Reality*.

96   "a priest for ever": Psalm 110.4; Hebrews 5.6; "Lamb of God": John 1.29.

96   "in accordance with the scriptures": 1 Corinthians 15.3–4.

97   "For a child has been born to us": Isaiah 9.6.

97   "This is an allegory": Galatians 4.22–26; Genesis 21.1–21.

98   "the term 'anointed'": *Anchor Bible Dictionary,* 4:777.

98   "Suffering Servant": Isaiah 53.

98   "King of glory": Psalm 24.9.

98   "despised, shunned by men, a man of suffering": Isaiah 53.3.

98   Reign of the Roman emperor Augustus: Luke 2.1.

SIX: Formation of a Second Testament

Bruce M. Metzger, *The Text of the New Testament* (New York, 1968), by the current leader of the team who produced the Revised Standard Version, is judicious and packed with information. *Introduction to the New Testament* (New York, 1997) by Raymond E. Brown, a leading Roman Catholic biblical scholar, and *Introduction to the New Testament* (New York, 2000), by Helmut Koester, a German American Protestant scholar, carefully summarize the present state of New Testament study.

103   books of The New Testament were composed . . . to bear witness: John 20.30–31.

104   genealogy of Jesus: Matthew 1.1–17.

104   the Sermon on the Mount: Matthew 5–7; commentaries on it: Jaroslav Pelikan, *Divine Rhetoric: The Sermon on the Mount as Message and as Model in Augustine, Chrysostom, and Luther* (Crestwood, NY, 2000).

105   "A prophet never lacks honor": Matthew 13.57.

105   "great commission": Matthew 28.19–20.

105   his baptism at the hands of John the Baptist: Mark 1.9.

106   "They said nothing": Mark 16.8.

106   Genealogy in Luke: Luke 3.23–38.

106   the parable of the prodigal son: Luke 15.11–32.

106   "he set his face resolutely": Luke 9.51.

106   especially the encounter: Luke 24.13–32.

106   the otherwise unknown Theophilus: Luke 1.1; Acts 1.1.

107   The Gospel of John prologue: John 1.1–14.

107   "Peace is my parting gift": John 14.27; "highpriestly prayer": John 17.

107   "Let not your hearts be troubled": John 14.1–2; "The Lord is my shepherd": Psalm 23.1 (King James).

107   "many" who had already: Luke 1.1.

109   The ascension of Christ: Acts 1; coming of the Holy Spirit: Acts 2.

109   "You are Peter": Matthew 16.18; also Luke 22.32 and John 21.15–20.

109   The preaching and martyrdom of Stephen: Acts 7.

109   Conversion of Paul: Acts 9; Peter's vision: Acts 10.

109   Paul in Athens: Acts 17.16–34.

109   A council at Jerusalem: Acts 15.

109   Paul . . . appeals to his Roman citizenship: Acts 22.25–29.

109   "And so to Rome!": Acts 28.14.

110   doctrine of justification: Romans 3.28; new life: Romans 5.1; Paul's struggles: Romans 7.

110   "the whole of Israel will be saved": Romans 11.26.

111   a defense of Christian liberty: Galatians 5.1.

111   "fellow-citizens": Ephesians 2.19; ethical life: Ephesians 5.21–23.

111   a vision of the cosmic Christ: Colossians 1.17.

111   humility of Christ: Philippians 2.5–11.

111   mourning the death: 1 Thessalonians 4.13–18.

112   rise of the Antichrist: 2 Thessalonians 2.3–12.

112   "keep safe": 1 Timothy 6.20.

112   "the hour for my departure": 2 Timothy 4.6.

112   superior to the priests: Hebrews 5–7.

112   "the roll call of the saints": Hebrews 11.

113   makes good works unnecessary: James 2.14-26.

113   their prerogatives: 1 Peter 2.9–10; loyalty to Christ: 1 Peter 3.13–22.

113   their heresies: 2 Peter 2.

113   discussion about love: 1 John 4.7–21.

114   "a new heaven": Revelation 21.1; thousand years: Revelation 20.1–3.

115   Accepted and disputed books of the New Testament: Eusebius *Church History* 3.25. See also p. 255.

115   Collected letters of Paul: 2 Peter 3.16.

SEVEN: The Peoples of the Book

A comprehensive and reliable guide to this chapter and also to the materials discussed in chapter 4 is J. W. Bowker, *The Targums and Rabbinical Literature: An Introduction to Jewish Interpretations of Scripture* (Cambridge, England, 1969). Moshe Idel, in *Kabbalah: New Perspectives* (New Haven, Conn., 1988), illuminates many problems. Herman Hailperin, in *Rashi and the Christian Scholars* (Pittsburgh, Pa., 1963), shows how much of rabbinical learning managed to penetrate the church. J. N. D. Kelly, *Jerome* (New York, 1975) is a thoughtful portrait of the Christian translator of the Bible into Latin. Jean Leclercq, *The Love of Learning and the Desire for God* (New York, 1982) is a guide to the biblical topography of monastic culture. Beryl Smalley, *The Study of the Bible in the Middle Ages* (Oxford, 1952) is a standard of scholarship. Henri de Lubac's two-volume *Medieval Exegesis* (Grand Rapids, 1998–2000) is learned and brilliant. My *Eternal Feminines* (New Brunswick, N.J., 1990) examines Dante's use of the Bible.

123   Therefore the same Hebrew verb: Psalm 121.2.

123   "whether Augustine be the greatest": Alexander Souter, quoted in G. G. Willis, *Saint Augustine and the Donatist Controversy* (London, 1950), xi.

125   "Ciceronian" than a "Christian": Jerome *Letters* 22.

125   the Ave Maria: Luke 1.28: Luke 1.42–33.

127   "All the senses": Thomas Aquinas, *Summa Theologica*, I.Q 1, art. 10.

130   Beryl Smalley of Oxford: Smalley, *Study of the Bible in the Middle Ages*, xi.

131   "The letter shows us": Grant, *The Bible in the Church*, 101.

131   "the heavenly Jerusalem": Galatians 4.26.

131   Blake, *Milton,* preface.

131   "The letter killeth": 2 Corinthians 3.6 (King James).

132   "You are Peter": Matthew 16.18.

132   "Fair Babylon, you predator": Psalm 137.8-9.

132   "It is not your heavenly": Matthew 18.14.

132   "Babylon" in the Book of Revelation: Revelation 14.8.

133   "Blessed are you who are in need": Luke 6.20.

133   "Foxes have their holes": Luke 9.58.

133   *stigmata:* Galatians 6.17.

133   "the book which was most read": Leclercq, *The Love of Learning and the Desire for God*, 90.

133   "the voice of the turtledove": Song of Songs 2.12.

134   bridal metaphor: Ephesians 5.25.

134   "You shall not make": Exodus 20.4–5.

135   Abraham on the plains of Mamre: Genesis 18.1–2.

135   "image of the invisible God": Colossians 1.15.

135   "ancient father of whom": *Paradiso* 26.92–93.

135   "the cantor of the Holy Spirit": *Paradiso* 20.38.

135   "the truth that rains down": *Paradiso* 135–38.

136   "Do not argue with the people": Qur'an 29.46.

137   "Commemorate Abraham in the Book" and "Commemorate Moses": Qur'an 19.41, 51.

137   named "Miriam": Exodus 15.20-21.

137   "the heroine of the Qur'an": Jaroslav Pelikan, *Mary Through the Centuries* (New Haven, Conn., 1996), 67–79.

137   "Our God and your God is one": Qur'an 29.46.

137   "God is the light": Qur'an 24.35.

138   the son of Abraham by his slave Hagar: Genesis 16.11.

EIGHT: Back to the Sources

Deborah Kuller Shuger, *The Renaissance Bible* (Berkeley, Calif., 1994) is a portrait of biblical humanism. Paul Oskar Kristeller, in *Renaissance Thought: The Classic, Scholastic, and Humanist Strains* (New York, 1961), puts the Renaissance study of the Bible into context. Roland Bainton, *Erasmus of Christendom* (New York, 1969) is a sympathetic and moving account of the greatest biblical scholar of his age. Jerry H. Bentley, in *Humanists and Holy Writ* (Princeton, N.J., 1983), examines "sacred philology," as do Jaroslav Pelikan, Valerie R. Hotchkiss, and David Price in *The Reformation of the Bible / The Bible of the Reformation* (New Haven, Conn., 1996), with many illustrations of Renaissance and Reformation Bibles or books about the Bible. Elizabeth Eisenstein, in *The Printing Press as an Agent of Change* (Cambridge, England, 1979), sees the work of Gutenberg as a revolutionary force, and Janet Thompson Ing, in *Johannes Gutenberg and His Bible* (New York, 1988), carries on the investigation. C. A. Patrides and Joseph Wittreich, *The Apocalypse in English Renaissance Thought and Literature* (Ithaca, N.Y., 1984), to which I contributed a chapter, is a case study of how one book of the New Testament fared in the Renaissance. Joseph L. Blau, *The Christian Interpretation of the Cabala in the Renaissance* (New York, 1944) led to a new (and continuing) interest in this subject.

144   "Renaissance humanists": Anthony Grafton, *Rome Reborn: The Vatican Library and Renaissance Culture* (New Haven, Conn., 1993), 10–11.

144   "the revival of antiquity": Jacob Burckhardt, *The Civilization of the Renaissance in Italy* (1860; New York, 1958), 1:175–278.

150   "When a man knows he is to be hanged": Boswell's *Life of Johnson* for 19 September 1777.

151   "Then felt I like": John Keats, "Upon First Looking into Chapman's Homer."

154   characterized the believer and "peacemaker": Matthew 5.9.

156   "built on the foundation of the apostles": Ephesians 2.20.

156   text of the First Epistle of John: 1 John 5.7–8 (King James).

157   "Babylon the great": Revelation 17.5.

158   "we have two swords": Luke 22.38.

158   "My kingdom": John 18.36.

159   "the Old Testament in Hebrew": *Westminster Confession* 1.8.

NINE: The Bible Only

The Bible in the Sixteenth Century, edited by David Steinmetz (Philadelphia, 1990), surveys the field. Heinrich Bornkamm, in *Luther and the Old Testament* (Philadelphia, 1969), points out that in a modern faculty Luther would be a professor not of doctrinal theology but of the Old Testament. W. Schwarz, in *Principles and Problems of Biblical Translation* (Cambridge, England, 1955), studies Luther's methods as a translator. My *Luther the Expositor* (Saint Louis, Mo., 1959) is a companion volume to the American Edition of *Luther's Works,* thirty volumes of which consist of his commentaries on the Bible. David Price and Charles C. Ryrie, *Let It Go Among Our People* (Cambridge, 2004) is a history of the publication of the English Bible from its beginnings, which can be read in conjunction with Adam Nicholson, *God's Secretaries: The Making of the King James Bible* (New York, 2003). I read J. Michael Reu, *Luther's German Bible* (Columbus, Ohio, 1934) as I was growing up, and I still turn to it now. I have learned much from Edward A. Dowey, *The Knowledge of God in Calvin's Theology* (New York, 1952) and from H. Jackson Forstmann, *Word and Spirit: Calvin's Doctrine of Biblical Authority* (Stanford, Calif., 1962). George Tavard, in *Holy Writ or Holy Church* (New York, 1959), relates the connection between Scripture and tradition at the Council of Trent to broader questions. George Huntston Williams, in *The Radical Reformation* (Kirksville, Mo., 1992), documents exhaustively how the Bible could be pitted against tradition.

163   Second Vatican Council, *Decree on Ecumenism,* 21.

164   "When our Lord and Master Jesus Christ said 'Repent'": Matthew 4.17.

170   Jedidiah: 2 Samuel 12.25; Hephzibah: Isaiah 62.4.

171   "a moment of mythic proportions": David Price in *The Reformation of the Bible / The Bible of the Reformation,* 135.

171   *logos:* John 1.1.

171   "you shall abominate": Leviticus 11.13–19.

174   "the favorite text": David Lyle Jeffrey, ed., *Dictionary of Biblical Tradition in English Literature* (Grand Rapids, Mich., 1992), xii.

175   "Where there is no vision": Proverbs 29.18.

175   "Every person must submit": Romans 13.1.

175   "Pay to Caesar": Matthew 22.21.

175   Emperor Constantine as "bishop in externals": Eusebius *Life of Constantine* 4.24.

175   polygamy practiced by the . . . patriarchs: Genesis 4.19; 16.3; 26.34; 28.9; 29.28.

175   community of property: Acts 4.34–5.11.

176   "to exercise all possible diligence": *First Helvetic Confession,* 26.

176   "The one definite thing": Maurice Powicke, *The Reformation in England* (London, 1941), 1.

177   "God is our refuge and stronghold": Psalm 46.1.

178   But in Protestant Switzerland: Lee Palmer Wandel , *Voracious Idols and Violent Hands* (New York, 1995).

179   "a fond . . . thing": *The Thirty-Nine Articles of the Church of England,* 22.

179   "warranty of Scripture" for prayers for the dead: 2 Maccabees 12.45.

TEN: The Canon and the Critics

Peter Gay, *The Enlightenment: An Interpretation* (2 vols.; New York, 1966–69) is fundamental. Emil Kraeling, *The Old Testament Since the Reformation* (New York, 1955) traces the vicissitudes of biblical criticism. Claude Welch's *Protestant Thought in the Nineteenth Century* (2 vols.; New Haven, Conn., 1972–85) is the standard work in English on the subject. Hans Frei, *The Eclipse of Biblical Narrative* (New Haven, Conn., 1974) is a keen analysis (or autopsy) of what happened in the eighteenth and nineteenth centuries. In my "Afterword" to *The Jefferson Bible* (Boston, 1989) I related Thomas Jefferson the biblical scholar to his Enlightenment contemporaries.

185   "There are four volumes": David Price in *The Reformation of the Bible / The Bible of the Reformation* (New Haven, Conn., 1996), 109–10.

186   "the antidogmatic, antienthusiastic": Welch, *Protestant Thought,* 1:31.

187   "They search": Gotthold Ephraim Lessing, *Nathan the Wise* (1779), Act III, Scene 7.

190   Leading statement of Reformation doctrine: *Westminster Confession,* 1.10.

193 "In the beginning": Genesis 1.1.

195 "Moses the servant": Deuteronomy 34.5.

195 "the book of Moses": Mark 12.26.

196 "the sun stood still": Joshua 10.12–13.

196 "God created man": Genesis 1.27; marriage instituted: Genesis 2.21–24.

196 "I the LORD am": Exodus 20.2.

196 "If Christ was not raised": 1 Corinthians 15.14.

197 "it was about the sixth hour": Luke 23.44 (King James).

197 "even this miraculous event": Edward Gibbon, *History of the Decline and Fall of the Roman Empire,* ch. 15.

197 "a decree issued by the emperor Augustus": Luke 2.1–2.

197 In spite of the detailed account: Exodus 5–14.

197 "in the history": Karl Barth, *Protestant Thought from Rousseau to Ritschl* (New York, 1959), 311.

198 "The Old Testament": Gay, *Enlightenment,* 1:93.

198 "Beyond the grandeur": Quoted in my essay in *The Jefferson Bible,* 164–65.

199 "'Eli, Eli'": Matthew 27.46.

200 "their sound is gone out": Handel, *Messiah;* Psalm 19.4; Romans 10.18.

200 "Heavenly Muse": Milton, *Paradise Lost,* book 1, lines 6–10, 24–26.

201 "My God, my God": Matthew 27.46.

201 "Every time I listen to it": *The Journals of Father Alexander Schmemann* (Crestwood, N.Y., 2000), 55.

202 "I know that my Redeemer liveth": Job 19.25–26; "For now is Christ risen": 1 Corinthians 15.20.

ELEVEN: A Message for the Whole Human Race

Just how vast this material is, both statistically and bibliographically, can be gauged by even skimming M. T. Hills, *The English Bible in America: A Bibliography* (New York, 1961), and E. North, ed., *The Book of a Thousand Tongues* (New York, 1938). John Wright, *Early Bibles of America* (New York, 1894) can still be consulted with profit. I have put my own views about interpreting Scripture into a comparative world perspective in *On Searching the Scriptures—Your Own or Someone Else's: A Reader's Guide to "Sacred Writings" and Methods of Studying Them* (New York, 1992).

205 "O Lord, my strength": Jeremiah 16.19–21; Zechariah 8.20; Malachi 1.11.

206 "all races and tribes": Revelation 7.9

206 "every part of the world": Mark 16.15.

206 "With psalms and hymns": Colossians 3.16.

207 "Good morning!": John 20.19, in *The Bible: An American Translation.*

208 "I am escaped with": Job 19.20.

208   "There is no new thing": Ecclesiastes 1.9.

208   "The powers that be": Romans 13.1.

208   "If a house be divided": Mark 3.25.

209   "awash in a sea of faith": Jon Butler, *Awash in a Sea of Faith: Christianizing the American People* (Cambridge, MA, 1990).

209   "It distributed nearly 100,000 Bibles": *The Encyclopedia of American Religious History* (New York, 1996), 1:69.

211   "no longer as a slave": Philemon 16.

212   "submitting to the authorities": Romans 13.1.

213   "fundamental assumptions": Alfred North Whitehead, *Science and the Modern World* (New York, 1948), 49–50.

214   polygamy of Abraham: Genesis 16.3

214   "the father of all who have faith": Romans 4.11.

214   "immorality such as even pagans": 1 Corinthians 5.1.

215   buried in a stone sepulcher: Matthew 27.66.

215   "all the world": Luke 2.1 (King James).

216   "the binding of Isaac": Genesis 22.1–19; Romans 8.32; Deuteronomy 12.31.

221   four horsemen of the Apocalypse: Revelation 6.2–7.

TWELVE: The Strange New World Within the Bible

The title of this chapter is also the title of an article originally published by Karl Barth in 1916 and reprinted in *The Word of God and the Word of Man* (New York, 1957). The history of controversy over New Testament expectations of the end of the world is the subject of Albert Schweitzer, *The Quest of the Historical Jesus* (New York, 1961). Modern debate about the subject of biblical "mythology" took on new life through Rudolf Bultmann in an essay that is reprinted in his *New Testament and Mythology* (Philadelphia, 1984). The Jewish-Christian-Muslim "obsession with sacred geography" is carefully examined by Robert L. Wilken, *The Land Called Holy* (New Haven, Conn., 1992).

225   "Paul, as a child": Karl Barth, *The Epistle to the Romans* (London, 1933), 1.

226   "Beauty ever ancient, ever new": Augustine *Confessions* 10.27.

226   "There is no speech nor language": Psalm 19.3–4 (King James).

227   "gnat can swim and an elephant can drown": Gregory the Great *Moralia on Job*.

227   Story of Joseph in the Torah: Genesis 37–50.

227   "the definitive modern rendering": *Dictionary of Biblical Tradition in English Literature*, 416.

228   "Source, Guide, and Goal": Romans 11.36 (New English Bible).

229   "the mystery that awes and fascinates": Rudolf Otto, *The Idea of the Holy* (New York, 1928).

229   "that he may run that readeth it": Habakkuk 2.2 (King James).

230   *Selah:* Psalm 3.2; *Raca:* Matthew 5.22.

230   "The LORD is my shepherd": Psalm 23.1.

230   "I am the good shepherd": John 10.11.

232   "our dear friend Luke": Colossians 4.14.

232   "the sky hung low": Shirley Jackson Case, *The Origins of Christian Supernaturalism* (Chicago, 1946), 1.

232   "that at the name of Jesus": Philippians 2.11.

233   "a chosen generation": 1 Peter 2.9 (King James).

234   "Sons are the provision": Psalm 127.3–5.

234   Paul's exposition of predestination: Romans 9.18, 22–24.

235   "that everyone who has faith": John 3.16.

235   "the body of Christ": 1 Corinthians 12.12–27; Ephesians 1.23; Colossians 1.18.

235   "*Ye are* the light of the world": Matthew 5.14 (King James).

235   "the feelings, acts, and experiences": William James, *The Varieties of Religious Experience* (New York, 1990), 36.

236   "the LORD your God brought": Exodus 20.2.

236   "May they all be one": John 17.21.

237   "assign this land": Genesis 15.1, 7, 18.

237   "God will surely": Genesis 50.24.

237   "Every spot on which your foot treads": Joshua 1.3–4.

237   "I brought you up": Judges 2.1.

237   "Be ever mindful": 1 Chronicles 16.15–18.

238   "I saw the Holy City": Revelation 21.2.

239   "Your word is a lamp": Psalm 119.105.

239   "The LORD your God": Deuteronomy 31.3–5.

239   "Now go, attack Amalek": 1 Samuel 15.3, 26.

239   "the LORD, valiant in battle": Psalm 24.8–10.

239   "angel of the LORD": 2 Kings 19.35.

240   "You have shed much blood": 1 Chronicles 22.8.

240   "the LORD of hosts": Psalm 46.8–10.

240   "Thus He will judge": Isaiah 2.4.

240   "on earth peace": Luke 2.14.

240   "the weapons we wield": 2 Corinthians 10.4; "full armor": Ephesians 6.12–17.

240   "those of us who are still alive": 1 Thessalonians 4.15–17.

240   "The end of all things is upon us": 1 Peter 4.7.

241   "He who gives this testimony": Revelation 22.20.

241   "I will not leave you": John 14.18.

241   "where two or three": Matthew 18.20.

241   "He who marries": 1 Corinthians 7.26, 31, 38.

241   "eunuchs who have made": Matthew 19.12 (King James).

242   "the hundred and forty-four thousand": Revelation 14.3–4.

242   mighty Samson: Judges 13.5; Numbers 6.1–21.

242   "Anyone who wishes": Matthew 16.24.

242   "prayer and fasting": Matthew 17.21.

242   "pray continually": 1 Thessalonians 5.17.

242   marriage as a "mystery": Ephesians 5.32.

243   "My plans are not your plans": Isaiah 55.8-9

243   "immeasurably more": Ephesians 3.20.

243   "When I come to the Israelites": Exodus 3.13.

243   "we of all people": 1 Corinthians 15.19.

243   "Immanuel, with us": Isaiah 7.14.

243   "I heard a loud voice": Revelation 21.3–4.

Afterword

247   "If ye continue in my word": John 8.31–32 (King James).

248   Because the purpose of the Tanakh: 2 Timothy 3.16.

248   "that you may believe": John 20.31.

248   "O LORD, You have examined me": Psalm 139.1.

248   "entire masters" . . . "temporary possessors": Edmund Burke, *Reflections on the Revolution in France* (Harmondsworth, England, 1986), 192.

250   "Since by man came death": 1 Corinthians 15.21.

250   covenants made with humanity: Genesis 9.9, 17.2; Exodus 6.4.

250   law through Moses, gospel through Christ: John 1.17.

250   "two distinct religious communities": see pp. x–xi.

251   "Is it nothing to you?": Lamentations 1.12 (King James).

251   "My God, my God": Psalm 22.1; Matthew 27.46.

251   "What therefore God hath joined together": Matthew 19.6 (King James).

FOR THE BEST IN PAPERBACKS, LOOK FOR THE 🐧

In every corner of the world, on every subject under the sun, Penguin represents quality and variety—the very best in publishing today.

For complete information about books available from Penguin—including Penguin Classics, Penguin Compass, and Puffins—and how to order them, write to us at the appropriate address below. Please note that for copyright reasons the selection of books varies from country to country.

In the United States: Please write to *Penguin Group (USA), P.O. Box 12289 Dept. B, Newark, New Jersey 07101-5289* or call 1-800-788-6262.

In the United Kingdom: Please write to *Dept. EP, Penguin Books Ltd, Bath Road, Harmondsworth, West Drayton, Middlesex UB7 0DA.*

In Canada: Please write to *Penguin Books Canada Ltd, 90 Eglinton Avenue East, Suite 700, Toronto, Ontario M4P 2Y3.*

In Australia: Please write to *Penguin Books Australia Ltd, P.O. Box 257, Ringwood, Victoria 3134.*

In New Zealand: Please write to *Penguin Books (NZ) Ltd, Private Bag 102902, North Shore Mail Centre, Auckland 10.*

In India: Please write to *Penguin Books India Pvt Ltd, 11 Panchsheel Shopping Centre, Panchsheel Park, New Delhi 110 017.*

In the Netherlands: Please write to *Penguin Books Netherlands bv, Postbus 3507, NL-1001 AH Amsterdam.*

In Germany: Please write to *Penguin Books Deutschland GmbH, Metzlerstrasse 26, 60594 Frankfurt am Main.*

In Spain: Please write to *Penguin Books S. A., Bravo Murillo 19, 1° B, 28015 Madrid.*

In Italy: Please write to *Penguin Italia s.r.l., Via Benedetto Croce 2, 20094 Corsico, Milano.*

In France: Please write to *Penguin France, Le Carré Wilson, 62 rue Benjamin Baillaud, 31500 Toulouse.*

In Japan: Please write to *Penguin Books Japan Ltd, Kaneko Building, 2-3-25 Koraku, Bunkyo-Ku, Tokyo 112.*

In South Africa: Please write to *Penguin Books South Africa (Pty) Ltd, Private Bag X14, Parkview, 2122 Johannesburg.*